Palgrave Modern Legal History

This series provides a forum for the publication of high-quality monographs that take innovative, contextual, and inter- or multi-disciplinary approaches to legal history. It brings legal history to a wider audience by exploring the history of law as part of a broader social, intellectual, cultural, literary, or economic context. Its focus is on modern British and Imperial legal history (post 1750), but within that time frame engages with the widest possible range of subject areas.

More information about this series at
http://www.palgrave.com/gp/series/14681

Ian Ward

Writing the Victorian Constitution

palgrave
macmillan

Ian Ward
Newcastle University
Newcastle upon Tyne, UK

Palgrave Modern Legal History
ISBN 978-3-030-07231-5 ISBN 978-3-319-96676-2 (eBook)
https://doi.org/10.1007/978-3-319-96676-2

Cover credit: Finnbarr Webster/Alamy Stock Photo

This Palgrave Macmillan imprint is published by the registered company Springer Nature Switzerland AG
The registered company address is: Gewerbestrasse 11, 6330 Cham, Switzerland

Contents

1 Introduction: The Written Constitution 1

2 The Revolution of Mr Burke 25

3 The Great Dramatist 63

4 The Greatest Victorian 99

5 Dicey's *Law* 147

Bibliography 195

Index 209

CHAPTER 1

Introduction: The Written Constitution

The morning of 28 June 1838 began well. Light showers gave way to bright sunshine. Awakened at four by a gunnery salute, the nineteen-year-old Princess Alexandrina Victoria was understandably excited. Eventually, at ten she clambered into the Gold State Coach for the short journey from Buckingham Palace to Westminster Abbey. The coach was pulled by six cream ponies especially brought over from Hannover, and escorted by a company of the Royal Huntsmen and the Yeoman Prickers. No expense was spared, on Prickers, ponies or anything else. Parliament had decided to make a bit of a splash on this coronation, the sum of £80,000 which it put aside being over twice that spent on the coronation of her predecessor William IV, though rather the less than the colossal £240,000 wasted on George IV. But hopes were up. In her diary, Victoria supposed that 'millions' had turned out to cheer. More sober chroniclers estimated nearer to 400,000 jostling around the Mall and adjoining streets; still enough, as the courtier diarist Charles Greville recorded, to be 'uncommonly tiresome' (Hibbert 2001, 70–1). Ten thousand waited inside Westminster Abbey.[1] Victoria, it was reported, looked awed. She certainly looked tiny, even tinier than usual in the

[1] Including the Duke of Wellington and, rather incongruously perhaps, his old adversary Marshal Soult, now French Ambassador Extraordinary to the Court of King James. Overcome by the warmth of the applause which greeted his entry to the Abbey, Soult recorded that 'C'est le plus beau jour de ma vie'. Wellington, it was reported, looked around 'with an air of vexation' (Hibbert 2001, 71–2).

I. Ward, *Writing the Victorian Constitution*, Palgrave Modern Legal History, https://doi.org/10.1007/978-3-319-96676-2_1

finery of her parliamentary robes, dressed 'like a girl on her birthday' according to one contemporary. The formalities of the coronation followed a strict precedence of medieval origin, refined most notably perhaps at the coronation of William III in 1689. Victoria first took an oath to maintain 'the Protestant reformed religion as it is established by law'. Having removed the parliamentary robes in a side-chapel, she then returned to take her seat on King Edward's Chair and be crowned by the Archbishop of Canterbury. After which the Queen descended from her throne, removed the crown and took the Sacrament. She was then invested with the Orb and Sceptre, before proceeding back down the nave. In her diary, Victoria recorded 'I shall ever remember this day as the proudest of my life'.

Or at least she did when she was able to write again. The evening of the 28 was passed with the royal hand dipped in a bucket of ice, the consequence of a short-sighted Archbishop trying to ram the ruby ring on the wrong figure. The Archbishop did not have a good coronation. Shortly after giving his Queen her Orb he tried to give it to her again and panicked when he could not find it. Eventually, he retired, very 'confused' as Victoria recorded, and visibly distressed. It had become evident, not least to Victoria, that far too many of those officiating were similarly lost. At one point, sensing that things were going awry, she had asked the sub-Dean 'Pray tell me what I am to do, for they don't know'. Unfortunately neither did the sub-Dean, nor the Bishop of Durham who was stood nearby. It transpired that the Litany had begun too soon, for which reason pretty much everything that followed was out of synch. Towards the end of the service a flustered Bishop of Bath and Wells had turned over two pages by mistake; for which reason Victoria had to be called back from St Edwards Chapel to do that bit of the service again. To the last man 'imperfect in their parts' a thoroughly unimpressed Greville concluded of the officiating clergy (Hibbert 2001, 73). The formidable Harriet Martineau was likewise appalled, observing that the very idea of investing a monarch with divine powers was anyway ridiculous. The behaviour of the attendant peerage was worse still. Lord Melbourne, entrusted with the sword of state, had clearly over-indulged and wobbled around alarmingly. When the ninety-year-old Lord Rolle fell over during the homage and tumbled down the steps the Abbey erupted in cheers; a foreign visitor was informed that it was part of the *droit de seigneur* for the most aged peer to roll down the stairs before his newly enthroned monarch. Shortly after, assorted generals and peers wrestled gamely on the floor to collect the medals which the Treasurer of the Household had, as custom demanded, tossed in their direction. Everyone cheered again. Victoria, it was reported, just kept smiling amidst the chaos.

It had all, as Lytton Strachey later recorded, resembled a very 'curious dream' (Strachey 1971, 64). Sat in the congregation was the new Member for Shrewsbury, Benjamin Disraeli. His chronicle of events, written it can be imagined with a distinctively wry grin, acknowledged that whilst Lord Melbourne had indeed held 'the great sword of state like a butcher' and the appearance of inebriated peers staggering about was hardly edifying, it had all the same been a 'splendid' day out (Hibbert 2004, 118–9; Kuhn 2006, 207–8).[2] Walter Bagehot was only twelve in June 1838. But as we shall see in due course it was exactly the kind of event, part 'dignified' part the precise opposite, about which he wrote with such delicious irony in his celebrated *English Constitution*. It was fun and it was ridiculous. But it was also, and for much the same reason, of huge significance. The coronation was more than just a day out. It said something about the Victorians, and in its writing, it became a part of their history. Bagehot knew this because he wrote this kind of history.

Writing History

It is only relatively recently that historians have started to think more seriously about how history is written. The practice has even assumed a generic identity. Historiographers write 'histories of history'. This is especially pertinent for historians of nineteenth-century England because there is here, to adopt terminology familiar to Jungian psychologists, a series of 'meaningful coincidences'. First, the Victorians evinced a peculiar fascination with the past. Walter Scott's historical novels sold in their thousands, as did Tennyson's *Idylls* and Ruskin's books on medieval art and architecture. 'Gothick' churches sprung up all across the country. The Public Record Office opened in 1838. The Historical Manuscripts Commission began publishing its first volumes in 1869. And more and more historians started writing histories. Second, and this was certainly

[2] He took a similarly sanguine view on the occasion of the Prince of Wales's equally under-rehearsed and chaotic marriage to Princess Alexander in 1863. Such was the shortage of seats on the train that was specially arranged to transport dignitaries back from Windsor to London that Disraeli was obliged to sit on his wife's knee.

no real coincidence, the historiographer and the 'professional' historian arrived more or less together in the second part of the century. Disciplinary awareness led in turn to an increasingly urgent debate as to the nature of historical writing. How much might history still be considered a 'literary art'? At the beginning of the century, there was little doubt; by the end there was plenty. Third at much the same moment the more particular historian of the English constitution began to think more closely about how that was being written too. Victorian historians and jurists recognised that there was a 'special responsibility' which attached to writing about the constitution; not simply chronicling events, but accounting for the building of a nation and an Empire. An intellectual storm was brewing over the practice of historical scholarship, and the writing of the Victorian constitution would lie at its heart (Tosh 1984, 7, 95–7; Howsam 2004, 525).

Whigs and Sceptics

Back at the beginning of the century, the storm was still in its depressive stage, a more familiar squall of Whig and Tory historians venting their intellectual spleens. The political nomenclatures were suggestive. Each wrote to a larger political prejudice. In essence, Whig historians made much of the consequences of the seventeenth-century revolutions, most especially the 'great and glorious' Revolution of 1688. The defining consequence was 'improvement'. As Lord Acton, one of the greatest of nineteenth-century Whig historians averred, 'We have no thread through the enormous intricacy and complexity of modern politics, except the idea of progress towards more perfect and assured freedom' (Burrow 2007, 405). Tory antagonists, commonly rather more sober in tone, preferred to laud the stability of Church and Crown and 'interests'. Whig historians tended to brush over 1649; a tragic but necessary prequel to the events of 1688. Tory historians lingered longer on regicide and its consequence and ensured that both were painted in shades of regret. We will revisit these alternative histories in the chapters which follow, and we will see that the delineation was never absolute. Back in 1984 Raphael Samuel suggested why; despite their evident differences both traditions 'shared' the essential 'Burkean notion of an organic constitution and a living continuity between past and present' (Mettam 1984, 7). Samuel was right. Both sides admitted merit in the Revolution of 1688, and to an extent in the place of Church and Crown too. The differences were of degree and tone. In simple terms, they wrote about it differently. There was an 'eternal breeziness' about the Whig version of English history which Tory historians found hard to emulate (Bentley 1999, 68).

To a considerable extent then much of the rest of the book will move around shifting perceptions of what has become known as the 'Whig constitution'. There are not supposed to be any Whigs now. Identifying the 'last' of the Whigs is a popular pass-time amongst historians of the nineteenth century. A recent biography of Lord Hartington is precisely entitled *The Last of the Whigs* (Jackson 1994). Other commonly presented candidates include Lord Palmerston, Walter Bagehot and the novelist Antony Trollope; a triumvirate whose peculiar relationship we will revisit in due course. Historiographers have invested just as much energy in trying to identify the 'last' of the Whig historians. David Cannadine suggests George Macaulay Trevelyan, whose various histories of all things English dominated college curricula for much of the first half the twentieth century (Cannadine 1992, 54; Carr 2001, 17).[3] It is a reasonable suggestion. Trevelyan had only just begun publishing when Victoria died in 1901, but he was shaped by a tradition of writing that was as Victorian as it was Whig. An entire generation of historians was shaped in much the same way, and as a consequence wrote much the same kind of history.

Edward Hallett Carr was born into this generation. Commonly esteemed as one of the most influential of modern historiographers, Carr famously held that history should be seen as an 'unending dialogue' between past and present (Carr 2001, 24). Here he followed Collingwood's insight, that the 'past which a historian studies is not a dead past, but a past which in some sense is still living in the present' (Carr 2001, 16). Carr was thus a relativist. He was also a historian who had, in his own words, grown up 'in the afterglow of the great Victorian age of faith and optimism'. It is for this reason that he retained a firm

[3] According to Cannadine, 'during the first half of the twentieth century Trevelyan was the most famous, the most honoured, the most influential and the most widely read historian of his generation'. In 1927, Trevelyan accepted the Regius Chair in Modern History at Cambridge (Cannadine 1992, xii, 26–9, 126). According to Blair Worden, Trevelyan was the 'twentieth century's most influential inheritor of the moderate Whig tradition' (Worden 2001, 18). Amongst his most influential and commercially successful works can be included his 1922 *British History in the Nineteenth Century*, his 1926 *History of England* and the rather later 1944 *English Social History*. Respective sales figures for these three texts, during his lifetime, were in the order of 70,000, 200,000 and 500,000.

conviction as to the 'proper' purpose of history, which is to discover meaning in this past (Carr 2001, lii). It is also why, as John Burrow has more recently concluded, it is impossible to read his history as anything other than 'emphatically whiggish' (Burrow 2007, 502). Macaulay's monumental *History of England* may have fallen out of fashion by the time that Carr wrote the lectures which would comprise his celebrated *What is History?*, but it comes as little surprise to learn that he remained a keen admirer of both the text and the author (Carr 2001, lix–x, 2). Macaulay's *History* is the focal point of our second chapter.

Someone who was rather less an admirer was Winston Churchill. Churchill never forgave Macaulay for his caustic assessment of his ancestor the Duke of Marlborough. But whilst he may not have liked Macaulay, Churchill did like writing Whiggish history. Churchill might have been a distinguished Tory Prime Minister but when it came to writing history he did so to the 'assumptions of his class', as Jack Plumb shrewdly noted, and the Spencer-Churchills had been Whiggish for centuries (Lukacs 2002, 124; Jenkins 2001, 899; Rose 2014, 411–24). Plumb was an admirer. So was Trevelyan, appraising Churchill as one of the few historians who wrote 'sense about history that gets read' (Adams 2011, 2–4; Cannadine 1992, 131, 139). Whig historians have always been better at getting read. The composition of Churchill's vast four volume *History of the English Speaking Peoples* is instructive. When he returned to the draft after the war Churchill was in his eighties and needed help. So he issued invitations to a range of prominent contemporary historians, along with some instructions. There should be lots of patriotism, and lots of great kings and queens and generals, lots of victories and most importantly lots of 'happy endings'.

And contributions must be 'dramatic', a series of 'lively histories' written, as the late Victorian constitutionalist William Stubbs advised, with 'charm' (Burrow 2007, 410). Trevelyan put it simply, the best history is written as 'poetry' (Evans 2000, 250). It was why he liked Churchill's *History* so much. Plumb did his best, contributing a potted history of the eighteenth century which was as 'lively' as might be reasonably expected. Others disappointed. Alan Bullock was invited to contribute a couple of thousand words on the 'life of ordinary people'. But it was a duff brief, the end product deemed to be far too 'drab' (Rose 2014, 149–50, 420). Maurice Ashley, given the more enviable task of drafting a chapter on Cromwell, was further reminded of the larger purpose; to craft an narrative that was 'entertaining' of course, but which also affirmed the 'growth of freedom and law, of the rights of the individual, of the subordination of State to the fundamental and moral conceptions of an ever-comprehending community' (Rose 2014, 157). Churchill's *History* was written for a readership which has been brought up on the canon of earlier Whig historians, most of them Victorian; Acton, Lecky, Stubbs, Froude, and of course Macaulay. It is worth taking closer note of the precise title of Churchill's *History* too. It was not just a history of England. It was a history of the English 'speaking' peoples, the history of a conversation written conversationally.

Whig history has then proven to be resilient. We still prefer happy endings, we still crave the reassurance. Take, for example, the close of Robert Tombs's recent *The English and Their History*. 'By the standards of humanity as a whole', Tombs ventures, 'England over the centuries has been among the richest, safest and best governed places on earth', for which reason the English, especially those who have lived during the later twentieth century can count themselves 'among the luckiest people in the existence of *Homo sapiens*, rich, peaceful and healthy' (Tombs 2014). Andrew Marr reaches exactly the same conclusion at the close of his *History of Modern Britain*. The future may be uncertain but history confirms that to have been 'born British remains a wonderful stroke of luck' (Marr 2007, 602). Niall Ferguson might seem an unlikely Whig, characterising the Revolution of 1688 as little more than an 'Anglo-Dutch business merger'. But he is not that unlikely, for reasons we will contemplate in due course, and there is much else in his history of how Britain 'made the modern world' which an old-fashioned Whig would have readily approved; not least being its love of 'free markets, the rule of law, investor protection' and its 'relatively incorrupt government' (Ferguson 2003, xx, 24). Whiggish history is not just something written by 'classical' Whigs like Macaulay or indeed Churchill; as Michael Bentley has surmised in his identification of a resurgent 'Carlylean vision of narrative' history. It is written by any historian who has a 'story' to tell (Bentley 1999, 158; Burrow 2007, 474).

At the same time, it would be a mistake to deny the determinedly sceptical turn in twentieth-century historical writing. By the end of the nineteenth century, the critique of classical Whig history was no longer simply a matter of countervailing political prejudice. It has acquired an intellectual dimension. Most importantly perhaps a new breed of 'professional' historian had begun to contemplate the possibility of writing history as a scientist writes science (Howsam 2004, 526–7). They were not alone in falling prey to the thought. Marxist historians were tempted by the same, and in time Marxist history would come to matter more. But in late nineteenth-century England, the historians who mattered were those who sat in their college studies commonly writing very big histories that were not supposed to be too obviously Whiggish. Henry Buckle was such a historian, his 1857 *History of Civilization in England* such a history. So too were Froude and Seeley, and the legal historian William Searle Holdsworth. Holdsworth's *History of English Law* ran to seventeen volumes. Samuel Rawson Gardiner's collected *History of England*, the *Civil War* and *Commonwealth and Protectorate* was a volume longer still. Gardiner was another historian seduced by science. 'We have had historians a plenty', he observed at the opening of his *History*, 'but they have been Whig historians or Tory historians', and such history is 'altogether destructive of real historical knowledge' (Lang 1995, 163, 167). There must be a better way. In a fulsome obituary for the German positivist historian Ranke, he wondered if 'it is not possible to do for history what Darwin did for science?' (Lang 1995, 165)

It was not. The allure of scientific determinism waned. Scepticism however simply mutated and quickened. In 1931, Herbert Butterfield published an essay entitled *The Whig Interpretation of History*. It was not a long essay; but its consequence reached far (Bentley 1999, 63–4). Butterfield focussed his critique on a pervasive 'habit of mind'. It was 'astonishing to what extent the historian has been Protestant, progressive and Whig, and the very model of the 19th century gentleman' (Butterfield 1931, 3–4, 7–8). He had spotted the 'meaningful coincidences'. The Whig 'interpretation' was dependent on a peculiar veneration for certain constitutional 'principles' and it had reached its intellectual high-water mark in the middle decades of the nineteenth century. There were, he further argued, three consequences of this 'interpretation'. First it was simple. All the 'vicissitudes' were written out. Butterfield wanted them written back in. Instead 'of seeing the modern world emerge as the victory of the children of light over the children of darkness', he countered, 'it is at least better to see it emerge as the result of a clash of wills', as often as not the product of tension and compromise and chance (Butterfield 1931, 28, 50, 64). Second it was biased, written to justify a particular political creed. Third it was made up, history as might have been imagined by 'strolling minstrels and pedlars of stories' (Butterfield 1931, 11–13, 39–41, 64). Butterfield did not dispute that the writing of history is an 'imaginative' and 'creative act'.

The historian should never succumb to the complacencies of 'indifference'. An effective historian seeks to engage the 'imaginative sympathy' of the reader (Butterfield 1931, 91–3). The problem was that Whig historians had been far too concerned with generating sympathies and far too little concerned with notions of historical veracity (Butterfield 1931, 109–18). And they had been far too successful.

The publication of Butterfield's *Interpretation* remains an iconic moment in the writing of a sceptical revisionist history of England. He would later repent the 'misguided austerity of youth' and 'rejoice in an interpretation of the past that has grown up with us', before concluding wistfully that 'in every Englishman there is a hidden something of a Whig tugging at the heartstrings'. He did so because it was 1944 and Britain was at war again. He also warned of the 'devils' that a mutating scepticism might let loose (Butterfield 1944, 1–4, 73). But it was already too late. Led by arch-revisionists such as Lewis Namier and Geoffrey Elton, successive generations of sceptical historians would continue their assault against an 'interpretation' which was so 'fiercely partisan and righteously judgemental' written, as a caustic David Cannadine concluded, by 'men wise after the event but foolish in every other way' (Cannadine 1992, 197). And there would indeed be further devils loosed, as Butterfield prophesied. By the end of the century, scepticism had mutated still more dramatically with the advance of post-structural and postmodern theories of historical writing; both of which made claims to historical 'truth' seem ever more fanciful (Evans 2000, 94–9). The relation of text and context becomes everything; the most that the sensible historicist might venture being the possibility of particular truths imagined by particular writers and readers in particular moments.

The Ironists

Not only has this recent mutation changed our perceptions of how history is written, but also who writes it. As Carr famously suggested, 'Before you study the history, study the historian' (Carr 2001, 38). In his recent study of modern historians and historiography, Keith Jenkins has placed Carr and Elton alongside Richard Rorty and Hayden White. The former two are categorised as 'certaintist' and 'mystifying', wedded in their different ways to the idea that historical truths might be extricated from uncovered 'facts' (Jenkins 1995, 10, 44–6). Carr's relativism did not, as we have already noted, preclude him from clinging to the thought that meaning might be recovered from the past. Elton clung even more firmly to the same. The 'proper' study of history was to 'discover' the 'truth of the past' (Elton 2002; Jenkins 1995, 72, 78). It comes as no surprise to discover that Elton had little time for the 'fads' of relativism; or indeed postmodernism, for which reason he would have been appalled to discover himself place alongside the likes of Rorty and White in any pantheon of modern historians (Evans 2000, 6–7).

Rorty's presence is certainly provocative. Truth, Rorty famously argued, is created not found, the product of nothing more than 'possible conversations' (Rorty 1980, 315–8). In a renowned passage in *Contingency, Irony, and Solidarity*, he affirmed:

> To say that truth is not out there is simply to say that where there are no sentences there is no truth… Truth cannot be out there – cannot exist independently of the human mind – because sentences cannot so exist, or be out there. The world is out there, but descriptions of the world are not. Only descriptions of the world can be true or false… The world does not speak. Only we do. (Rorty 1989, 5–6).

Truth is thus 'contingent' on the nature of the 'conversation'. Dominic LaCapra employs precisely the same metaphor; of history as 'conversational' practice (LaCapra 2000, 34–6, 40). This is more than mere relativism, and whilst Rorty's critique may not be levelled directly against the practice of 'proper' history its implications are considerable. First it denies the possibility of unmediated access to the past through documentary materials. It does not deny their existence, but it does demand their interpretation. Second, any meaning which is gleaned from the interpretive process is not only 'discursive' and 'fabricated', as Jenkins provocatively puts it, but also indeterminate; for 'you can always get another picture, you can always get another context'. Third, 'fabricated' history is prejudiced. History is 'always history for someone' (Jenkins 1995, 15, 21–4). These are the insights of the 'private ironist' (Rorty 1989, 50–4). And there is a fourth consequence too, no less unsettling.

It makes the writing of history different; or at least it refines our appreciation of how 'ironic' history is written. Ironic history seeks to uncover the 'fissures' which lie beneath the scripted surface (Jenkins 1995, 111). Accepting discontinuity and incongruity, it is reconciled to the reality that any historical narrative is prejudiced and partial, woven together from myriad incidental moments and scattered anecdotes.

Charles Darwin envisaged coral reefs constructed by 'myriads of tiny architects'; ironic history can be conceived similarly (Burrow 2007, 410). These anecdotes are not only illustrative, but also constitutive. History becomes a story of stories, the 'reflexive' coherence of which is dependent on the residual strength of the 'edifying' metaphors deployed (Rorty 1980, 320, 356–70). It is a style more familiar perhaps in the writing of cultural and 'micro' history; though not exclusively so (Burrow 2007, 510–17). Richard Evans suggests the histories written by contemporaries such as Orlando Figes and Simon Schama (Evans 2000, 244–5). Other examples might include James Chandler's *England in 1819*, an age written in a moment, and Michael Wood's *Story of England*, the history of a nation written in a village, conversational in tone, but so obviously Whiggish in its greater ambition.

Much of what Rorty suggests finds a resonance in Hayden White's essays on the practice of historical writing; not the least of which is the appreciation that any such writing is not only 'discursive' but 'ironic' in 'respect of its own adequacy' (White 1978, 3–6, 48–9). White too sees the writing of history as an act of creation rather than discovery, that its 'traces' are fragmentary, commonly 'accidental' as well as anecdotal; to borrow from the existential historian Burkhardt, a 'medley' of incidental happenings. And if there is any coherence it can only be fashioned 'fraudulently' through the judicious use of rhetoric and metaphor; the creation of what Auerbach terms 'atmospheric historicism' (White 1978, 29, 55–7, 62–3, 91). Here White seeks recourse to the work of Northrop Frye and the idea of authorial 'emplotment'. It supposes that the historian, like indeed the writer of fiction, deploys one of four compositional strategies; romantic, comedic, tragic and satirical or ironic (White 1978, 58–61, 73–4). The romantic and the satirical represent the extremes; the former describing heroic transcendence over adversity, the latter apprehensive recognition. There is, for us, an especial pertinence here; as we shall see the writing of the Victorian constitution evolves along precisely this continuum, from the romantically heroic to the anxiously ironic. But whilst 'emplotment' might help us to better appreciate how historians write their histories, it does not otherwise stabilise, precisely because history is messy and the practice of writing itself unstable; in both regards 'discontinuity and chaos are our lot' (White 1978, 50).

And it is prejudiced too. Here again White provides an example which, for us at least, is especially pertinent. Edmund Burke could have described the French Revolution as the great French historian Michelet; as something to be celebrated (White 1978, 61). But he did not. After a brief moment of celebration, Burke changed his mind. His *Reflections on the Revolution* became a vehement condemnation of the events of 1789, bolstered by a comparatively glowing account of the 'glorious' English Revolution of 1688 and its consequence. We will see why Burke changed his mind shortly and contemplate the consequence at rather greater length in subsequent chapters. Generations would come to think differently of the revolution because Burke thought that they should. There is a lot of romance in *Reflections*. Late eighteenth-century historians appreciated that theirs was a 'literary art'. But there is also a glimpse of the darker 'irony' which would in time overcome the writing of the English constitution (White 1978, 96, 123). Burke created his history, and in so doing imposed his order on the chaos of France in 1789. It is what historians do. And it is no different from what novelists do.

The Victorians and Their Constitution

Or it might be ventured the writers of 'nonsense' poems. In 1876, Lewis Carroll published *The Hunting of the Snark*. To this day, no one is entirely sure why. It might be an expression of existential angst, a commentary on Carroll's own crisis of faith, a common enough experience in mid-Victorian England as we shall see. It might be a satire of the notorious *Tichborne* case, or maybe just a gentle poke at some of Carroll's Oxford chums. Or maybe there is no meaning. It was after all a 'nonsense' poem. Thirty-six years earlier, the French writer and political scientist Alexis de Tocqueville had published his *Democracy in America*, in chapter six of which he had famously cast an aspersion. In England, 'Parliament has the right to modify the Constitution', for which reason it can 'change constantly, or rather it does not exist at all' (Tocqueville 1994, 101). It was meant ironically, and it did not preclude Tocqueville's admiration for what passed as the English constitution. But it did infer that there was something odd about it. It might seem a peculiar juxtaposition; a 'nonsense' poem about a mythic beast and a serious book about comparative constitutionalism. And it is. But there is an anecdotal affinity and a shared insinuation. Both gave existence to something which did not otherwise exist, and they did so by writing about it.

The purpose of this book is to investigate the writing of the 'Victorian' constitution in the 'long' nineteenth century. It will suppose that the English did indeed have a constitution, as Tocqueville in fact well knew. But it existed only in the form of an evolving narrative, the shape and the tone of which changed from one writer to another. In the following chapters, we will take a closer look at four particular writers and four particular texts; Edmund Burke's *Reflections on the Revolution in France*, Lord Macaulay's *History of England*, Walter Bagehot's *The English Constitution* and Albert Venn Dicey's *An Introduction to the Study of the Law of the Constitution*. It will not be argued that these four texts alone 'wrote' the Victorian constitution. But it will be argued that they are representative; of the way the constitution was written, and the way in which that writing changed. But they are not only representative. Because all constitutions are ultimately matters of perception, and reception, these texts are also constitutive. In Rortian parlance they 'edify', allowing us to fashion a narrative from the 'myriads of tiny architects' and anecdotes which history bequeaths. Before we engage these four texts however, and the immediate contexts within which they were written, we must spend a little more time contemplating what it meant to be Victorian and what it means to write constitutions.

Writing the Victorians

As we noted earlier, the coronation of Queen Victoria in June 1838 mattered because it was both representative and constitutive. Historians commonly alight on such moments for this precise reason. Particular deaths matter similarly. Victoria died in 1901. We can still see grainy images of the procession on a dreary February morning, replete with four reigning monarchs riding in attendance, streets full of mourning subjects and lots of damp artillerymen struggling to get the gun-carriage cortege to move in the mud.[4] The funeral was barely less chaotic than the coronation had been sixty-four years earlier. And the pathetic fallacy is prescient. Subsequent generations would be invited to recall a dumpy, rather grim-faced old lady, dressed in mourning weeds, as often as not pictured staring wistfully at a bust of her long-departed Albert. But if

[4] The four monarchs riding in attendance were Edward VII, George I of the Hellenes, Carlos of Portugal and Kaiser Wilhelm who, needless to say, shamelessly upstaged his fellow kings by riding a conspicuously overdressed white stallion. By tradition, the cortege was to be carried by the Royal Horse Artillery. But someone had misjudged the effect of recent rainstorms and miscalculated the necessary wheel gauge.

the tiny princess who walked up the nave of Westminster Abbey in June 1837 was forgotten, the Queen who succeeded her was not, and neither was the 'age' that would be named in her honour. All monarchs tend to get a place in history. But only few are bestowed with ages. It was, as Arthur Balfour observed in the Commons in the days following the announcement of Victoria's death, 'the end of a great epoch' (Arnstein 2003, 197).

And in a sense it was. Coronations and funerals present themselves as obvious demarcations in the histories of 'ages', especially those named after monarchs. But history, epochal or otherwise, is rarely quite so tidy. Centuries get to be termed 'long', or occasionally short, ages rarely map to monarchs or anything else. The Victorian 'age' is no exception, its cultural and political margins 'constantly shifting' and contestable (Kaplan 2007, 11). Victoria provides a focal point. But neither her coronation nor her funeral sets the boundaries. Here again an ironic historian might be more easily reconciled to the implication. The Victorians had a life of their own. And they certainly arrived before their Queen. Asa Briggs suggested that the 1790s should be comprehended as a Victorian 'prelude'.[5] We will work with this inference. Rather more recently Gertrude Himmelfarb has suggested that the 'early' Victorians were already beginning to depart the scene by the time Victoria had settled into her chambers at Windsor; a schemata that sees the mid-Victorians arriving by 1850, and the later Victorians looming by 1870 (Himmelfarb 2007, 6–10). It helps with the maths certainly. Otherwise the notion, enjoined by Geoffrey Best, that the 'mid' Victorians arrived with the Great Exhibition in 1851 does not add up (Best 1979, 250–1). It was from about then that the Victorians first began identifying themselves as such; for which reason writing in 1831 John Stuart Mill could not have anticipated a prospective Victorian age. But in redeploying Hazlitt's noted 'spirit of the age' in his eponymous essay published in the *Examiner* that year, Mill established an intellectual as well as social and political tone which would define both the early and mid-Victorian eras (Newsome 1998, 1–2). Of course the same might be just as readily supposed of Thomas Carlyle's *The Sign of the Times* which had appeared

[5] In his seminal *The Age of Improvement*, Briggs further noted the danger of trying to make 'ages' too neatly, confirming that in terms of social and political morality at least 'Victorianism' arrived long 'before Victoria', and lasted long after (Briggs 1959, 1, 72). The same argument is made by John Gardiner (2002, 5–6).

in the *Edinburgh Review* two years earlier in 1829. Prophecies were announced in tones of both light and dark; as we shall again see.

If the Victorians had arrived early so too did they depart early, or perhaps late. Roy Jenkins suggests Ascension Day 1898 marked the end of the Victorian era. Gladstone died on Ascension Day 1898 (Jenkins 1995, 630–1). EF Benson, author of the Mapp and Lucia novels, later reflected that 'Victorianism was already dead and buried' by the early 1890 s (Newsome 1998, 245). Some could not bring the Victorian age to an end quickly enough. Others could not live outside it. Just a few months before he died in 1922, Albert Venn Dicey confessed that 'I seem to have lived on into another age with new criterion of belief though what they are I know not' (Cosgrove 1980, 296). Victorians lingered much like Whig historians. Nearly half a century later the funeral cortege of Winston Churchill ended its very long journey from St Pauls to the chapel of St Martin's at Bladon on the Blenheim estate, ancestral resting place of the Spencer-Churchills. Churchill loved Victoria, and particularly her Empire; as any cursory glance at the fourth volume of his *History* eloquently confirms. And in neither was he alone. Seven months after Victoria's funeral, Edward Elgar's Pomp and Circumstance March No. 1 in D Major was given its first public performance at the Liverpool Orchestral Society. Edwardian just, but in spirit and everything else composed as a paean to Victoria and her Empire. It is still a centrepiece of the annual Proms, a surrogate national anthem in all but name.

Not everyone has welcomed the lingering. In his *Eminent Victorians*, published in 1918, Lytton Strachey famously derided the 'prim solidity' of the Victorian 'age' (Strachey 1971, 141–2). Evelyn Waugh likewise confirmed his generation's 'detestation' of Victorian 'quaintness'. In his essay *The Lion and the Unicorn*, published in 1940, George Orwell would depict a nation that resembled a 'rather stuffy Victorian family' (Orwell 1984, 155). But the tone can mislead. Orwell was not altogether disparaging. Writing in 1941, the relative calm of Victorian England had its attractions. Writing a few years later in 1948, as his compatriots were coming to terms with the consequences of fascism and war, Basil Willey, King Edward VII Professor of English Literature at Cambridge, reflected on a shared tendency to seek refuge in the imagined 'promised land' of Victorian England, an age of seeming 'peace, prosperity, plenty and freedom' as well as 'faith, purpose and buoyancy' (Heffer 2013, 815). Half a century on another Tory Prime Minister would endeavour to rally his party around the reinvestment of certain 'values' which, in the lexicon of imagined moral certainties, are most commonly assumed to be somehow Victorian. As Simon Heffer has recently affirmed whilst it can be said that a 'climate of prejudice about the Victorians still lingers', the assorted intellectual and cultural myths of 'Victoriana' retain their hold (Heffer 2013, 1; Kaplan 2007, 2–11). It is not just Elgar and the Proms. Victorian novels dominate our bookshops, alongside biographies of 'eminent' Victorian writers and politicians, and writers who write about Victorians, or perhaps as Victorians.[6] Strachey also surmised that the 'history of the Victorian age will never be written', because 'we know too much about it' (Strachey 1971, vii). It was meant ironically. Strachey knew historians would write histories about the Victorians. And he knew they would be big. And because they would be big they would, more commonly than not, be Whiggish too. And the reason is simple. We like to read about the Victorians because they are, as the author of one very big book on them has recently confirmed, still 'with us' (Wilson 2002, 1). And so is the constitution that they wrote.

Writing the Constitution

When they wrote their constitution is of course a matter of familiar contention. Gertrude Himmelfarb suggests that its writing began in 1832, the year of the 'Great' Reform Act (2007, 8). It is a perfectly sensible suggestion. Another possibility, earlier still, is 1790; a chronology which fits Asa Briggs's suggestion that the first Victorians had arrived before the nineteenth century had even begun, as well as the supposition that the publication of Burke's *Reflections* in that same year represented the birth of modern historicism. Both suppositions depend on a willingness to scramble chronology and to write our history around different 'moments'. The idea that different moments write different histories is more familiar perhaps to cultural and intellectual historians. Great kings and great battles do not matter quite so much to historians of gender or race or music or food (Evans 2000, 164–5). And the same, to an extent, can be said of constitutional thought. The French Revolution is again instructive. It matters to different historians differently. It matters to us less because of its impact on French society, or even world history, but because it changed the way in which nineteenth-century historians

[6]An intriguing example of the latter is Frank Prochaska's recent *The Memoirs of Walter Bagehot* (2013).

and jurists contemplated the English constitution. It will be suggested that the writing of the 'Victorian constitution' began in the early months of 1790, half a century before Victoria ascended to the throne.

And just as it can be argued that this writing had begun long before June 1838, so too can it again be supposed that the same continued long after February 1901. As Vernon Bogdanor has recently inferred, there is much about our 'new' constitution today which would seem very familiar to Bagehot and his contemporaries (2009, xii–xiii). At the opening of his *English Constitution*, Bagehot suggested that 'an ancient and ever-altering constitution is like an old man who still wears with attached fondness clothes in the fashion of his youth: what you see of him is the same, what you do not see is wholly altered' (Bagehot 2001, 3). Much might have changed since 1865, when Bagehot composed the first of the essays which would comprise his *Constitution*, but there is more that has not. And the same is every bit as true of the constitution described by Dicey in his *Law of the Constitution* published two decades later. It is why generations of law students continue to follow public law syllabuses sketched out in the definitive 1915 edition of Dicey's *Law*, their attention focussed on the same apparently distinguishing conceptual features, parliamentary sovereignty, the rule of law, the role of conventions. As we shall see, the Diceyan perspective, like the Bagehottian, is not received uncritically. But Dicey's *Law* continues to shape the way in which lawyers think about the English constitution, just as its various editions continue to fill our Law School Library shelves. It is beyond the remit of this book, but if we wanted to continue the narrative and trace the evolution of English constitutional law during the twentieth century, we could do worse than plot our path through successive editorial introductions to Dicey's *Law of the Constitution*.

Disrupting chronology is a common way of disturbing 'grand' historical narratives. Another, as we have already noted, is to insinuate prejudice and its consequence. Any historical text, as Michel Foucault affirmed, is the 'ideological product' of the controlling 'discourse' (Evans 2000, 195–6). The writing of constitutional history is no less the consequence of prejudice than the writing of any other kind of history. In chapter fifty-one of their delightful parody of Whig history *1066 and All That*, published in 1930, Justin Yeatman and Walter Sellar made account of the Great Reform Bill 'invented' by Lord Grey in order to end the 'confusion' which was 'caused by these rotten burrows'. The Act 'laid down clearly who had votes and who hadn't', so that 'When this unforgettable Law was made known there was great rejoicing and bonfires were lit all over the country' (Sellar and Yeatman 1993, 108–9). It was of course written tongue-in-cheek and intended to be read tongue-in-cheek. But save for the confusion of boroughs and burrows, there was not otherwise much with which Whig historians such as Froude or Macaulay or even Churchill might have take serious issue.

Or, assuming he spotted the irony, Herbert Butterfield whose *Whig Interpretation* was published just a year later. It too was intent on demolishing what his contemporary Namier referred to as the 'cant' of Whig constitutional 'principles'. And he had spotted the same 'meaningful coincidence'; that the Whig 'interpretation' of English history was founded on a particular 'myth' of constitution-making. Of the Whig historian, Butterfield observed:

> He is apt to imagine the British constitution as coming down to us by virtue of the work of long generations of Whigs and in spite of the obstructions of a long line of tyrants and Tories. In reality it is the result of a continual interplay and perpetual collision of the two. It is the very embodiment of all the balances and compromises and adjustments that were necessitated by this interplay. The Whig historian is apt to imagine the British constitution as coming down to us safely at last, in spite of so many vicissitudes; when in reality it is the result of those very vicissitudes of which he seems to complain. If there had never been a danger to our constitution there never would have been a constitution in danger. In the most concrete sense of the words our constitution is not merely the work of men and parties; it is the product of history. (Butterfield 1931, 41)

Here is the ironic appreciation; that the Whig constitution ultimately was the 'product' of its own writing. 'Every man in England understands what Revolution Principles are for', Lord Justice Holt opined in 1705, for which reason there was no need of further explanation. Lord Braxfield took the same approach. There were 'two things' which 'must be attended which require no proof'. The first is 'that the British Constitution is the best that ever was since the creation of the world'. The second is that 'it is not possible to make it better'. And there was, as a consequence, a third thing. Under no circumstance, his Lordship averred, should the 'rabble' be led to believe that they had a 'right to be represented' (Briggs 1959, 136, 176). The history of constitutional reform in the nineteenth century is a history of ameliorating this complacency and its consequence.

Sir William Blackstone endeavoured to provide some greater clarity in his celebrated *Commentaries on the Laws of England* published between 1766 and 1768. Alluding to its 'balanced' nature, Blackstone confirmed, 'Herein indeed consists the true excellence of the English government, that all the parts of it form a mutual check upon each other' (Blackstone 1828, 154–5; Briggs 1959, 90). And this was because of what had occurred in 1688. Macaulay, as we shall see, would assert exactly the same. So, in a rather different way, would Bagehot. The fact that Blackstone adhered to the Tory party merely confirms the extent to which the essential constitutional tenets of the 'glorious' revolution had become pervasively in-scripted. The *Commentaries* might have said a little more than Holt had felt was necessary; but not that much more. It did not famously satisfy a young Jeremy Bentham, in whose opinion the 'glorious' settlement of 1689 was a 'chimera'. 'Talk of balance will never do', he derided, 'leave that to Mother Goose and Mother Blackstone'. It was time to 'pluck the mask of Mystery from the face' of English constitutional jurisprudence (Bentham 1998, 4–7, 17–21, 30–2).

There was to be no plucking just yet however. Through into the nineteenth century Whig historians and jurists continued to write a narrative that placed the 'Great' Reform Act at the culmination of a long and 'glorious' history stretching back through the 'Great and Glorious' Revolution of 1688 to the 'Great Charter' of 1215. A series of 'great' things accounted for the past of English constitutional history, and the same past assured the future. 'No people', the Vice-Provost of Eton, CHK Marten, confirmed in 1906, 'has a nobler or more inspiring story' and it all started with the 'practical wisdom' of Magna Carta (Mettam 1984, 7). It was a 'story' which, as Michael Bentley confirms, was invariably 'approached' as if there was 'Good News to relate' (Bentley 1999, 65). The English were blessed with a 'temperate and balanced Constitution', Lord Chancellor Cairns confirmed in 1884, as the third Reform bill staggered its way through Parliament (Le May 1979, 3). And they should just be grateful. This was certainly the approach taken by Trevelyan in his various histories. The 'great and glorious' revolution had established the 'sure foundation' upon which the 'great' Act of 1832 had been built, the consequence of which had been 'peace' in England 'ever since' (Trevelyan 1939, 4–5). Gardiner confirmed the same. The 'great' statute of 1832 heralded a 'great age of legislation', lending jurisprudential certainty to a constitution which had hitherto been a 'mass of custom and opinion' (Gardiner [History] 6.83, 324–5). It comes as no surprise to learn that Gardiner was Dicey's favourite historian; of all contemporary historians the one who 'most nearly meets the wants of lawyers' (Dicey 1959, 17).[7] He met the wants of Dicey because he shared the same faith in the fallacies of scientific methodology, and the organising capacity of the statute book.

Butterfield had little time for either Trevelyan or Gardiner. In his opinion, the constitution after 1832 was as much a mess as it had been before. If there was order to be discerned in Gardiner's writing of it, it was the 'product' of the history that Gardiner preferred to write. The ironic inference is again resonant. We can only surmise what the older Butterfield might have thought of Rorty or Hayden White, or indeed a newer generation of 'critical' legal historians. He might have espied 'devils'. But he might also have espied something of his younger self in the endeavours of historically minded 'crits' such as Robert Gordon and Duncan Kennedy. According to Gordon, the purpose of critical legal history is to 'scramble' dominant narratives, to show that law only 'exists' in 'reference to particular contexts' and particular ideologies (Gordon 1981, 1017, 1023–4, 1054; Gordon 1996, 1024). And he would surely have appreciated that Kennedy's totemic deconstruction of Blackstone's *Commentaries* was written to the same purpose as his own *Whig Interpretation* (Kennedy 1979). It is perhaps the linguistic turn in later 'critical' legal history which would have unnerved Butterfield. He would very probably have sensed something demonic in Allan Hutchinson's reductive conjunction of law, history and Rortian irony. According to Hutchinson, the responsibility of critical legal scholarship is inherently historical because it is about recovering past 'conversations' which are 'themselves located and scripted in deeper stories' (Hutchinson 1988, 13–14). Not every 'critical' lawyer would agree with the insinuation. But few would disagree with the thought that no lawyer is better placed to appreciate the textual and the contextual nature of law than the lawyer who plays proper 'attention' to history (Gordon 1984, 57; Horwitz 1981, 1057).

And there is of course nothing wrong with writing history which is prejudiced, any more than there is in writing history which is 'scrambled'. All history is prejudiced and ironic, to some extent. The history

[7] Lytton Strachey was less so, suggesting that Gardiner 'could absorb facts, and he could state them; but he had no point of view' for which reason his writings invariably resemble 'nothing so much as a very large heap of sawdust' (Strachey 1931, 169–70).

that is written over the chapters to come is prejudiced for this simple reason. This does not mean that it is entirely anecdotal or 'fabricated'. But it is a bit of both. In chapter five, we will encounter the novelist Anthony Trollope's famously jaundiced account of standing for Parliament in 1867. It comprises an entire chapter of his *Autobiography*. Elsewhere in the *Autobiography*, which was published in 1883, can be found a chapter entitled 'On Novels and the Art of Writing Them', within which he discussed the relative merits and demerits of 'realist' and 'sensation' novels; a matter of considerable critical anxiety during the 1860s and early 1870s. The former were exemplified by writers such as George Eliot and, he liked to suppose, himself. The latter, comprised of early day crime thrillers and bodice-rippers, were meanwhile making the respective fortunes of writers such as Mary Elizabeth Braddon and his 'friend' Wilkie Collins. Trollope did not deny the distinction between the genres, but nor was he inclined to make too much of it. At the end of the day, a 'good novel should be both' and 'both in the highest degree' (Trollope 1996, 146).

The same might be said of writing history. Richard Evans finds himself recommending a 'middle course' on similar terms (Evans 2000, 182–9, 254). There will always be 'facts' and narrative, and there should always be irony (Burrow 2007, 474; Tosh 1984, 23–4). To write ironically is simply to be aware of the consequence of writing about the past. Lewis Namier compared the historian to the 'painter' who gets to 'stress that which is the nature of the thing' (Tosh 1984, 113). Evans varies the metaphor only slightly; likening the historian to a sculptor. The materials might be limited, but it is the writer who gets to choose finish, who determines the kind of history which is written (Evans 2000, 147; Carr 2001, 6). This book militates towards the ironic precisely because it is about the writing of something, and because it 'sanctions the ambiguous', embracing anecdote and incongruity, recovering 'traces' and imagining narratives which might be written round them (White 1978, 73, 127; Gordon 1996, 1028; Carr 2001, 7–8). Its attention is caught just as readily by the 'animals and plants' which are to 'be found in the verges and ditches by the roadside', to deploy another of Evans's neat metaphors, as it is those found 'on the highway itself' (Evans 2000, 244).

The highway is though still familiar. As noted before, we will chart a path through the successive writings of four of the most influential constitutional writers of the long Victorian 'age'; Burke, Macaulay, Bagehot and Dicey. It is the surroundings that begin to change, and the mood.

Victorian England evolves and so does the writing of its constitution. The constitutions written by Burke and Macaulay are classically Whig, romantic, nostalgic, defiantly celebratory and above all historical. The constitutions written by Bagehot and Dicey are not. In the place of history comes institutional pragmatics, a respective concern with the functioning of political and legal institutions. And doubt too. By the time that Bagehot came to write the first of the essays, only half a decade after the publication of the final volume of Macaulay's *History*, the collective mood has certainly begun to darken. The later Victorians came to doubt a lot of things, including God and capitalism. They even began to wonder the wisdom of monarchy. Accordingly, when readers turned the pages of Bagehot's *Constitution*, they encountered a very different kind of irony. Gone is the romance, the cloying reassurance and the happy endings. In its place come doubt and disdain. And if the more jurisprudentially inclined then turned to Dicey for an alternative reassurance, they would find more of the same, and then something else. Where there once was God, now there was science and the 'fetishism of fact' (Carr 2001, 10). Dealing with doubt and its consequence came to define the later Victorian, and it would radically change how they wrote about their constitution. First however we must reach back a century at least, to London in the late autumn of 1789.

References

Adams, E. (2011). *Liberal Epic: The Victorian Practice of History from Gibbon to Churchill.* Charlottesville: University of Virginia Press.

Arnstein, W. (2003). *Queen Victoria.* Basingstoke: Palgrave.

Bagehot, W. (2001). *The English Constitution.* Cambridge: Cambridge University Press.

Bentham, J. (1998). *A Fragment on Government.* Cambridge: Cambridge University Press.

Bentley, M. (1999). *Modern Historiography: An Introduction.* London: Routledge.

Best, G. (1979). *Mid-Victorian Britain 1851–75.* London: Fontana.

Blackstone, W. (1828). *Commentaries on the Laws of England.* London: William Walker.

Bogdanor, V. (2009). *The New British Constitution.* Oxford: Hart.

Briggs, A. (1959). *The Age of Improvement.* London: Longmans.

Burrow, J. (2007). *A History of Histories.* London: Penguin.

Butterfield, H. (1931). *The Whig Interpretation of History.* London: Bell & Sons.

Butterfield, H. (1944). *The Englishman and His History*. Cambridge: Cambridge University Press.

Cannadine, D. (1992). *GM Trevelyan: A Life in History*. London: HarperCollins.

Carr, E. (2001). *What Is History?* Basingstoke: Palgrave.

Cosgrove, R. (1980). *The Rule of Law: Albert Venn Dicey, Victorian Jurist*. Chapel Hill: University of North Carolina Press.

De Tocqueville, A. (1994). *Democracy in America*. London: Fontana.

Dicey, A. (1959). *An Introduction to the Study of the Law of the Constitution*. London: Macmillan.

Elton, G. (2002). *The Practice of History*. London: Wiley-Blackwell.

Evans, R. (2000). *In Defence of History*. London: Granta.

Ferguson, N. (2003). *Empire: How Britain Made the Modern World*. London: Penguin.

Gardiner, J. (2002). *The Victorians: An Age in Retrospect*. London: Hambledon.

Gordon, R. (1981). Historicism in Legal Scholarship. *Yale Law Journal, 90*, 1017–1056.

Gordon, R. (1984). Critical Legal Histories. *Stanford Law Review, 36*, 57–125.

Gordon, R. (1996). The Arrival of Critical Historicism. *Stanford Law Review, 49*, 1023–1029.

Heffer, S. (2013). *High Minds: The Victorians and the Making of Modern Britain*. London: Random House.

Hibbert, C. (2001). *Queen Victoria: A Personal History*. London: HarperCollins.

Hibbert, C. (2004). *Disraeli: A Personal History*. London: HarperCollins.

Himmelfarb, G. (2007). *The Spirit of the Age: Victorian Essays*. New Haven: Yale University Press.

Horwitz, M. (1981). The Historical Contingency of the Role of Law. *Yale Law Journal, 90*, 1057–.

Howsam, L. (2004). Academic Discipline or Literary Genre? The Establishment of Boundaries in Historical Writing. *Victorian Literature and Culture, 32*, 525–545.

Hutchinson, A. (1988). *Dwelling on the Threshold: Critical Essays in Modern Legal Thought*. London: Sweet and Maxwell.

Jackson, P. (1994). *The Last of the Whigs: A Political Biography of Lord Hartington*. Cranbury, NJ: Associated Presses.

Jenkins, K. (1995). *On 'What Is History?' From Carr and Elton to Rorty and White*. London: Routledge.

Jenkins, R. (2001). *Churchill*. London: Macmillan.

Kaplan, C. (2007). *Victoriana: Histories, Fictions, Criticism*. Edinburgh: Edinburgh University Press.

Kennedy, D. (1979). The Structure of Blackstone's *Commentaries*. *Buffalo Law Review, 28*, 205–382.

Kuhn, W. (2006). *The Politics of Pleasure: A Portrait of Benjamin Disraeli*. London: Simon & Schuster.

LaCapra, D. (2000). *Rethinking Intellectual History: Texts, Contexts, Language*. Ithaca: Cornell University Press.
Lang, T. (1995). *The Victorians and the Stuart Age*. Cambridge: Cambridge University Press.
Le May, G. (1979). *The Victorian Constitution: Conventions, Usages and Contingencies*. London: Duckworth.
Lukacs, J. (2002). *Churchill: Visionary, Statesman, Historian*. New Haven: Yale University Press.
Marr, A. (2007). *A History of Modern Britain*. London: Macmillan.
Mettam, R., et al. (1984). What Is History? The Great Debate. *History Today, 34*(May), 5–16.
Newsome, D. (1998). *The Victorian World Picture*. London: Fontana.
Orwell, G. (1984). *The Penguin Essays of George Orwell*. London: Penguin.
Prochaska, F. (2013). *The Memoirs of Walter Bagehot*. New Haven: Yale University Press.
Rorty, R. (1980). *Philosophy and the Mirror of Nature*. Princeton: Princeton University Press.
Rorty, R. (1989). *Contingency, Irony, and Solidarity*. Cambridge: Cambridge University Press.
Rose, K. (2014). *The Literary Churchill: Author, Reader, Actor*. New Haven: Yale University Press.
Sellars, W., & Yeatman, R. (1993). *1066 and All That: A Memorable History of England*. Stroud: Sutton.
Strachey, L. (1931). *Portraits in Miniature and Other Essays*. London: Chatto and Windus.
Strachey, L. (1971). *Queen Victoria*. London: Penguin.
Tombs, R. (2014). *The English and Their History*. New York: Alfred Knopf.
Tosh, J. (1984). *The Pursuit of History: Aims, Methods and New Directions in the Study of Modern History*. London: Longman.
Trevelyan, G. (1939). *The English Revolution 1688–1689*. London: Henry Holt.
Trollope, A. (1996). *An Autobiography*. London: Penguin.
White, H. (1978). *Tropics of Discourse: Essays in Cultural Criticism*. Baltimore: Johns Hopkins University Press.
Wilson, A. (2002). *The Victorians*. London: Hutchinson.
Worden, B. (2001). *Roundhead Reputations: The English Civil Wars and the Passions of Posterity*. London: Penguin.

CHAPTER 2

The Revolution of Mr Burke

In summer 1798, a collection of poems was published entitled *Lyrical Ballads*. The authors were Samuel Taylor Coleridge and William Wordsworth. It contained a number of poems which have since entered the canon of English romantic poetry. The first in the collection was Coleridge's *The Rime of the Ancient Mariner*. The rest were in the main written by Wordsworth, as was the Preface to the second edition of the collection which appeared two years later in 1800.[1] The Preface was remarkable. In it, Wordsworth expressed an intention to write poems that 'speak a plainer and more emphatic language', the 'language really used by men' (Wordsworth 1935, 734–5). The very title *Lyrical Ballads* was intended to evoke ideas of expressive voice. In an immediate sense, Wordsworth wanted to justify writing in verse rather than metre. But there was, at the same time, a rather deeper revolutionary impulse.[2] Many of the poems had been written and revised, whilst Wordsworth stayed at Alfoxden in Somerset in the spring and summer of 1797. Locals had informed the authorities that there was something odd going on at Alfoxden. There were lots of concerned locals and agitated authorities in England in 1797. Radicalism had emerged emboldened by

[1] Coleridge contributed just four poems to the collection.

[2] Wordsworth deployed the very term, referring to 'revolutions' of taste which were not merely aesthetic matters, but also social and political (1935, 734). Quite what made the *Ballads* revolutionary has remained a matter of intense critical debate (Mayo 1972, 79, 85; Swann 1977, 62; Danby 1960, 36–8).

I. Ward, *Writing the Victorian Constitution*, Palgrave Modern Legal History, https://doi.org/10.1007/978-3-319-96676-2_2

the chaotic collapse of the Treason Trials a couple of years earlier. The Corresponding Societies were still corresponding, in terms which many viewed as seditious. The Seditious Meetings Act which Parliament had rushed through in 1795 did not seem to be stopping either the sedition or the meetings. A hundred and fifty thousand turned up at Copenhagen Fields later in the year to hear one of the 'heroes' of the Trials, John Thelwall, demand an end to the war with France or else. Stones were thrown at the carriage taking George III to open Parliament; 1796 was no more settled: a series of violent disturbances in Ireland, rumours of a French invasion fleet gathering across the Channel, and then in early 1797 naval mutinies at Nore and Spithead.

Given events in London, Ireland, the Medway and elsewhere, rural Somerset might have seemed a rather odd place to start a revolution. But the Home Secretary Lord Portland was not inclined to take any chances. An agent was despatched to take a look at what was going in the rectory at Alfoxden. A week later, he sent his report back to London. There was indeed a self-styled 'phylosopher' in residence, and some 'French people', and whilst he was not entirely sure what they talked about, a certain 'Spy Nozy' kept coming into the conversation, and overall it was clear that they were 'doing no good there'. It was quite possible that Alfoxden had become a meeting place for a 'Sett of violent Democrats'.[3] He was in a sense right, for Wordsworth was indeed fashioning a revolution. But not in the sense which Portland's agent imagined. Wordsworth was fashioning a revolutionary poetic. By raising the voices of 'ordinary men', by reinvesting a politics of passion and emotion, of 'regular feeling', the *Lyrical Ballads* strove to make poetry democratic, at least a bit. Wordsworth's poet was a 'man speaking to men' (Wordsworth 1935, 737).

The revolution that Wordsworth was writing at Alfoxden in the summer of 1797 was the product of a longer imagining. Only a few years earlier, he had famously expressed an equivalent enthusiasm for a more familiar kind of revolution. In his *Prelude*, he confessed that he had embraced the 'Dances of Liberty' in the 'guise/ of an enthusiast' (Wordsworth 1935, 532, 556). 'Bliss' indeed had it been 'that dawn to be alive/ But to be young was very heaven' (Wordsworth 1935, 570). Coleridge too had been much taken by the events of 1790: 'Liberty the soul of life shall reign/ Shall throb in every pulse, shall flow thro; every vein!/ Shall France alone a Despot spurn?' Both would later

[3] Spy Nozy was, of course, Spinoza.

abjure their 'deep delusion' (Coleridge 1969, 261). By then, reports of the 'great terror' had filtered across the Channel. Versailles had been stormed. The 'Murder of the Queen of France', *The Times* reported, had 'been attempted in the dead of night' (Fennessy 1963, 5). Many, however, had shared the initial excitement. 'How much the greatest event it is that ever happened in the world and how much the best', Charles James Fox had enthused to his fellow Parliamentarians. The notorious dissenting preacher Richard Price was equally excited. On the morning of 4 November 1789, Price treated his congregation at the Old Jewry Meeting House in the City of London to a sermon entitled *A Discourse on the Love of Our Country*.[4] Patriotism, as the title suggested, was the driving theme; the 'love of our country has at all times been a subject of warm recommendation and is certainly a noble passion' (Price 1991, 178). It was because Price loved England so much that he was so keen to commend the need to contemplate, once again, the virtues of revolution. Lightly touching on events first in America and now in France, he arrived at the revered memory of 'that event in this country to which the name of the Revolution has been given' (Price 1991, 188–9). It was, he confirmed, an event blessed by God. But it was also an event wanting completion, for 'though the Revolution was a great work, it was by no means a perfect work, and that all was not then gained which was necessary to put the kingdom in the secure and complete blessings of liberty' (Price 1991, 191).

Particularly pressing was the need to broaden religious toleration, most obviously by means of repealing the Test Acts. But it was not the only need. There was also the need to sweep away the 'adulation and servility' and 'idolatry' that attended the office of the King (Price 1991, 184–5). And there was the need, too, to address the 'inequality of our representation', as well as the 'vice and venality' which pervaded government of church and nation (Price 1991, 191–2, 194). Above all, however, there was the need to embrace Enlightenment, to reverence the

[4] Price had been educated at one of the more notorious Dissenting Academies, Coward's near Tenter Alley in London. He first took up a position as an assistant at the Old Jewry Meeting House most probably around 1744. The *Discourse* was his final significant contribution to Dissenting literature, in some ways representing an intellectual epitome. Amongst close friends of Price could be counted the fellow Dissenter and prominent scientist Joseph Priestley. Whilst he claimed that the strongest intellectual influence was that of John Locke, critics have commonly identified the equally evident influence of Rousseauian idealism in many of Price's writings and sermons.

'illumination' of its progenitors, men such as Milton, Sidney and Locke, men who had in their writings 'sowed the seed which has since taken root and is now growing up to a glorious harvest' (Price 1991, 162). Price closed his *Discourse* thus:

> What an eventful period is this! … I have lived to see a diffusion of knowledge which has undermined superstition and error. I have lived to see the rights of men better understood than ever, and nations panting for liberty, which seemed to have lost the idea of it. I have lived to see thirty millions of people, indignant and resolute, spurning at slavery, and demanding liberty with an irresistible voice, their king led in triumph, and an arbitrary monarch surrendering himself to his subjects. After sharing in the benefits of one Revolution, I have been spared to be a witness to two other Revolutions, both glorious. And now, methinks, I see the ardour for liberty catching and spreading, a general amendment beginning in human affairs, the dominion of kings changed for the dominion of laws, and the dominion of priests giving way to the dominion of reason and conscience.
>
> Be encouraged all ye friends of freedom and writers in its defence! The times are auspicious. Your labours have not been in vain. Behold kingdoms admonished by you, starting from sleep, breaking their fetters, and claiming justice from their oppressors! Behold, the light you have struck out, after setting America free, reflected to France and there kindled into a blaze that lays despotism in ashes and warms and illuminates Europe! (Price 1991, 195–6)

The name of Richard Price might have been largely forgotten by 1837. In the history of English constitutional thought, however, the sermon he gave that November morning assumes considerable import; not simply because of what Price said, but because of the incendiary effect it had on one of those who had, if only for a moment, counted himself amongst the most ardent celebrants of revolution. What a 'wonderful spectacle', the great Whig Parliamentarian Edmund Burke had declared to Lord Charlemont, and 'what actors' (De Bruyn 2004, 722). But he too quickly abjured, composing his *Reflections on the Revolution in France* during the final months of that year, in part as a testament to this abjuration, and in the greater part as a pointed and venomous rebuttal of Price and his sermon. Thomas Jefferson noted the remarkable 'revolution of Mr Burke' (McCalman 1996, 343). Its consequence would stretch long into the coming century.

The title of Burke's essay on the events of 1789 and early 1790 was of course disingenuous. He certainly wanted to terrify the imagination, which is why there had to be lots of demonic Jacobins. But when he set about writing the *Reflections* in early 1790, Burke was not concerned only with what had happened in France. His greater concern was England and what might happen there; for the 'triumph of the victorious party' in France, as Burke pointedly advised, is 'over the principles of a British constitution' (Burke 1986, 241). Burke's reflections may have been stimulated by what had happened across the Channel, but the constitution upon which he wished to reflect the deepest was his own, and the revolution in which he had the greater interest had occurred a century before (Burke 1986, 275, 376). It was this revolution, the 'Great and Glorious' Revolution of 1688, which had acquired a mythic status in the writing of a distinctive Whig constitutionalism. Burke's *Reflections* remains one of the defining, and most influential, contributions to this writing. Of course, there is also a defining tension in this writing; for alongside the celebration of 1688, there is a distinctive and instinctive Tory veneration of Church and Crown. It was in a sense Burke's intellectual bequest. Subsequent generations of constitutional historians and jurists would be left to conjure Whig principles with Tory institutions and interests. Burke's solution was to transcend politics with poetry, to present a constitutional history comprised of revolution and reform, of kings murdered and queens harassed, of civil wars and constitutional settlements, of churches defiled and nations rebuilt.[5] Burke's *Reflections* was indeed epic. It was also, quite literally, fantastic.

The Furies of Hell

And at centre-stage of *Reflections* could be found the imagined 'rape' and prophetic martyrdom of the French Queen, Marie Antoinette.[6]

[5] As was his *Letters on a Regicide Peace*, written three years later, in which Burke premised his reprise with the observation 'I shall not live to behold the unravelling of the intricate plot which saddens and perplexes the awful drama of Providence now acting on the moral theatre of the world' (Burke 1999, 62).

[6] Marie Antoinette was already a figure of contestation in English political debate. Lord George Gordon notoriously likened her to the 'whore of Babylon'. He was not alone. For the very same reason, of course, it was incumbent upon counter-revolutionaries to present an altogether different picture of female, and queenly, decorum (McCalman 1996, 364–6; De Bruyn 2004, 724; Furniss 1993, 155–6).

> History will record that on the morning of 6th of October 1789, the king and queen of France, after a day of confusion, alarm, dismay, and slaughter, lay down, under the pledged security of public faith, to indulge nature in a few hours of respite and troubled melancholy repose. From this sleep the queen was first startled by the voice of the sentinel at her door, who cried out to her, to save herself by flight – that this was the last proof of fidelity he could give – that they were upon him, and he was dead, instantly he was cut down. A band of cruel ruffians and assassins, reeking with his blood, rushed into the chamber of the queen and pierced with an hundred strokes of bayonets and poniards the bed, from whence this persecuted woman had but just time to fly almost naked and through ways unknown to the murderers had escaped to seek refuge at the feet of a king and husband, not secure in his own life for a moment. (Burke 1986, 164)

The passage, compositionally placed at the fulcrum of the essay, has retained its notoriety. The following paragraphs, similarly suffused with images of sanguinary and sexual violence, recount the ensuing sacking of the palace of Versailles 'left swimming in blood, polluted by massacre, and strewed with scattered limbs and mutilated carcases', and the final transportation of Marie Antoinette and her husband, to Paris, accompanied by 'shrilling screams, and frantic dances, and infamous contumelies; and all the unutterable abominations of the furies of hell' (Burke 1986, 164–5).

To a certain degree, historical record accords with Burke's narrative. The storming of Versailles on 6 October was, it seems, high drama indeed, replete with mobs of drunken *poissardes* roaming the corridors, of beheaded guards and cowering ministers, of a queen running from chamber to chamber looking for her children. Of course, later historians have also expressed some doubt with regard to the precise veracity of Burke's account (Furniss 1993, 27, 138–9; Paulson 1983, 60). Much in simple terms was made up. But to make this complaint is to miss the point. Burke was not interested in cold chronicle, in whether the Queen's bed was really pierced by poniards, or whether she had run nearly naked, or as contemporaries suggested, merely barefoot. Burke was certainly interested in history. In terms of writing about politics and constitutions, history was the defining discipline. But he was not in thrall to the miasma of historical 'truth'. The writing of history, for Burke, was an aesthetic exercise, a matter of composing narratives and conjuring imaginations. Burke was, in this sense, an edifying historian. And it was not merely a function of peculiar political prejudice. He wrote in the same way that David Hume had written his *History of England* and Adam Ferguson his *Essay on the History of Civil Society*. Tory historians, as Adam Smith confirmed, wrote the same, 'for exciting in the heart' (Goode 2007, 832–3, 839–40). As Burke later admitted, he did not want his audience to read his account of the events of 6 October so that they could muse soberly on the merits and demerits of revolutionary ideology. He wanted them to read, to shed 'tears' as if 'such a spectacle were exhibited on state' and to be terrified that the same might one day happen to the Queen of England (Burke 1986, 175). Burke certainly did, his friend Philip Francis confirming that its author dissolved into floods of tears 'almost as often' as he read the famed passage (Lock 2000, 33).

And in case anyone doubted the possibility Burke insinuated a very particular affinity, between Price and Hugh Peter, the notorious puritan divine who justified the execution of Charles I as God's 'great work'. Price's *Sermon*, Burke alleged, 'is in a strain which I believe has not been heard in this kingdom, in any of the pulpits which are tolerated or encouraged in it, since the year 1648, when a predecessor of Dr Price, the Reverend Hugh Peter' invoked a perverse scripture to urge his countrymen to 'bind their king with chains, and their nobles with fetters of iron' (Burke 1986, 94).[7] Regicide, he added, was undoubtedly the aspiration of the Revolution Society, the irreducible logic of republicanism.[8] The road from a pulpit in Old Jewry to a Whitehall scaffold was marked and short. Every Englishman, and Englishwoman, should beware. In the Preface to the fourth edition of his *Discourse*, Price vigorously denied Burke's insinuation that, like Peters, he was a 'barbarian delighted with blood' (Price 1991, 177). But the damage was done, the allusion cast.

From the very start of *Reflections*, Burke confirms that 'late proceedings' in France warrant attention because the same could so easily happen in England (Burke 1986, 265). There is 'continual talk of resistance and revolution' and whilst the 'beginnings of confusion' might be 'at present feeble', they can in 'moments' grow 'into a strength to heap mountains upon mountains and to wage war with Heaven itself'

[7]The association of late eighteenth-century Dissenters with Puritan radicals such as Peters was commonly made. Writing of the Gordon riots in 1780, Gibbon supposed that 'forty thousand Puritans such as there might have been at the time of Cromwell have started out of their graves' (McCalman 1996, 354; De Bruyn 2004, 47–50).

[8]Price's *Sermon* was published under the auspices of the Revolution Society.

(Burke 1986, 92, 154). The threat of insurrection, in Burke's eyes, was very real, resting, he feared, on nothing more tangible than the susceptibility of excitable minds sat in 'giddy coffee-houses' (Burke 1986, 160, 238). He recognised the rhetorical strength of Price's *Sermon*. And he also knew that if it was to be countered, it must be done in like terms, for 'Writers have great influence on the public mind' (Burke 1986, 213). They have, above all, a responsibility to husband 'the wardrobe of a moral imagination, which the heart owns, and the understanding ratifies, as necessary to cover the defects of our naked shivering nature', a responsibility which can, where necessary, include a duty to conjure judicious images of 'salutary terrors' (Burke 1986, 171). Burke acknowledged the inevitable paradox which this responsibility imports. If politics is a poetic or dramatic art, the possibility of dissimulation is ever-present; the risk that those who populate the 'giddy coffee-houses' might be persuaded by 'perverted history' (Burke 1986, 250). To play with the political imagination, past or prospective, is to flirt with perversity, and ultimately, the trust of the reader can only be placed in the integrity of the chronicler and the dramatist.

The appreciation of politics as art form can be detected in Burke's earlier *Philosophical Enquiry*, published in 1757. Here, Burke had employed a utilitarian premise for a theory of aesthetics, recognising that the 'imagination' is a reflective quality, something that varies the 'disposition' of received ideas (Burke 1990, 16–17). The 'disposition' of the mind, in turn, is governed by 'impressions' of 'pain and pleasure', impressions that can be aesthetically and dramatically shaped (Burke 1990, 31). Words do not create new ideas, but they do create 'pictures', and in doing so can excite 'passions'. As to the passions, Burke distinguished between those of the 'sublime', which were depicted as being masculine, and those which attached to feelings of 'beauty', which were female. Amongst the former were feelings of 'terror', amongst the latter feelings of 'delight' and 'sympathy' (Burke 1990, 36, 41–2, 53–6). The necessary gender pejoratives assume an obvious consonance in *Reflections* and more particularly in his depiction of the 'rape' of Marie Antoinette. In the very final part of his *Enquiry*, Burke concluded:

> Now, as words affect, not by any original power, but by representation, it might be supposed, that their influence over the passions should be but light; yet is it quite otherwise; for we find by experience that eloquence and poetry are as capable, nay indeed much more capable of making deep

> and lively impressions than any other arts, and even than nature itself in very many cases. (Burke 1990, 158)

The reasons for this, he continued, are threefold. First, 'we take an extraordinary part in the passions of others'. Second, the writings and 'opinions' of others can make a 'deep impression' in the 'mind'. Third, the writer, by his choice of words, can choose to 'give new life and force' to events and objects which might otherwise seem plain. The writer, in short, has the ability to conjure the sympathetic, and indeed terrified, imagination through 'enlivening touches' and, like the politician and the priest, has the power, and the responsibility, to fashion and constrain the 'contagion of our passions' (Burke 1990, 158, 160).

Here, again the supposition that the 'strongest' expression of the sublime was 'terror' assumed a considerable and obvious import in *Reflections*. We are, as he there confirmed, 'alarmed into reflexion; our minds... are purified by terror and pity; our weak unthinking pride is humbled, under the dispensations of a mysterious wisdom' (Burke 1986, 175). Thus, discussing his depiction of the storming of Versailles in *Reflections*, Burke confirms that the writer of political essays should emulate the skills of the dramatist, for 'theatre' is very often 'a better school of moral sentiment'. The public must be entranced by the 'marvellous'; it craves to be so (Burke 1986, 285). It is 'natural' that an audience should:

> be affected by such spectacles with melancholy sentiments upon the unstable condition of moral prosperity, and the tremulous uncertainty of human greatness; because in those natural feelings we learn great lessons; because in events like these our passions instruct our reason; because when kings are hurl'd from their thrones by the Supreme Director of this great drama, and become the objects of insult to the base, and of pity to the good, we behold such disasters in the moral, as we should behold a miracle in the physical order of things. (Burke 1986, 175)

Politics is a dramatic art, monarchs and revolutionaries dramatic players. The medieval notion of a king's 'two bodies' endured in French, as in English, constitutional thought. The imagined rape of a French Queen thus assumed an immediate metaphorical resonance. Later parts of *Reflections* would be immersed in pejorative analysis of the new system of regional and central government in France. But the need to horrify was a vital precursor. The spectre of prospective regicide could thus be found raised alongside the fictive rape of Marie Antoinette and the imputed rape of France itself. Dramatic allusion recurs, the revolution itself as a 'monstrous tragic-comic scene', the storming of Versailles and the rape of Marie Antoinette resonant of the Theban orgies depicted by Euripides; all intended to confirm in the mind of the reader that the 'late proceedings' in France presented a 'false sublime' (Burke 1986, 92, 165).

It is often suggested that the French Revolution represented a critical break with history, ushering in a 'modern' age of ideology, totalitarianism and state terror. Blessed with hindsight, it is a debate which presumes much. But Burke's desire to terrorise is unarguable, and terror, as he also knew, is a subjective sentiment. Regicide might terrify some, so too images of blood-soaked revolutionaries rampaging round palaces. For others, the greater terror might lie in images of moral dissipation, reports of simple unkindness even. On hearing that Louis and Marie Antoinette had been executed, the Duchess of Sutherland wrote to her daughter, the Duchess of Devonshire, confirming that worse still during their confinement they had not been 'suffered to have servants' (Foreman 1998, 278–9). Burke understood this mind, and he wrote for it. It is for this same reason that so many paragraphs in *Reflections* were devoted to the dissolution of the church in France as well as the attendant and 'terrible revolution in property' (Burke 1986, 216, 270, 309–10).[9] Terror can be raised in myriad forms and felt in just as many ways.

And so, accordingly, alongside the destruction of political institutions, the dissolution of estates and the execution of kings can be seen the equally terrifying prospect of a world with debased 'manners', where the natural rankings of society are swept away and where the age of 'chivalry' has been replaced by that of the 'sophister' and the speculator (Burke 1986, 170). And this, Burke confirmed, is what has happened in France. Apologising for having 'dwelt too long on the atrocious spectacle of the sixth October', he emphasises that these particular events are worthy of

[9] The sanctity of property as the foundation of a stable and well-ordered constitution was, of course, a centrepiece of the Whig constitutional tradition, finding famous expression in Locke's second *Treatise*. In a speech given in the House of Commons in 1794, Burke confirmed that the first principle of any government must be the security of property 'because for the protection of property all governments were instituted' (Dinwiddy 1974, 116).

especial 'reflection' insofar as they confirm the horrors that attend to the 'most important of all revolutions… I mean a revolution in sentiments, manners and moral opinions'. For:

> As things now stand, with everything respectable destroyed without us, and an attempt to destroy within us every principle of respect, one is almost forced to apologize for harbouring the common feelings of men. (Burke 1986, 175)

The revolution in France was more than a mere insurrection. It represented an assault on a way of life, on civilisation itself, the 'inversion of all natural sentiment'. It is here that the sexual insinuation in written into the 'rape' of Marie Antoinette assumes such significance. Stripping the Queen, forcing her to flee unkempt through the corridors of Versailles, was not only terrifying; it was un-gentlemanly. Following his fervid account of the 6 October with a 'more delightful vision' of a younger and rather happier Queen at the same palace 'glittering like the morning star', Burke left his audience to wonder why the swords of the 'gallant men' of France have not 'leaped from their scabbards' (Burke 1986, 169–70).

The reason was simple. The 'age of chivalry is gone', something which matters for reasons altogether more serious than nostalgic whimsy. For Burke, chivalry was the glue which held a commonwealth and a constitution together obliging sovereigns to 'submit to the soft collar of esteem' (Burke 1986, 170). Appearances matter. The right to govern must be earned. The 'affections' of the Commonwealth must be engaged. The prescience is again sharp and will find more famous articulation in Bagehot's identification of a 'dignified' aspect of the English constitution half a century later. It is chivalry which impels a gentleman to draw his sword in defence of his Queen, and it is the same chivalry which makes the same gentleman defer to the propriety of the myriad conventions which likewise hold commonwealth and constitution together. We shall see Burke, like Bagehot, is keen to impress the importance of Englishmen and women holding their constitution in 'dignified' reflection; if they are to do so, it is first necessary that they continue to 'look up with awe to kings; with affection to Parliaments; with duty to magistrates; with reverence to priests; and with respect to nobility' (Burke 1986, 182). For this reason, he concludes, 'There ought to be a system of manners in every nation which a well-formed mind would be disposed to relish', for

'To make us love our country, our country ought to be lovely' (Burke 1986, 130–2).

And with the destruction of manners, critically, comes the 'fall of language'. 'Everything', the revolutionary Defarge famously declared, 'even the language must be regenerated according to the Republic system' (Blakemore 1988, 88). Burke, it has been argued, identified this 'revolution in language' as the greatest threat presented by the events of 1789 (Blakemore 1988, 13). A new 'jargon' of 'liberty, equality, fraternity', a '*patois* of fraud' as he termed it, sought to erase the received 'traditionary language' of reverence and majesty (Burke 1986, 369). And not just in France. The collapse of chivalry was a European crisis, the 'late proceedings' a threat to an entire civilisation. It was for his reason that he would later confirm that manners 'are more important than laws' (Bourke 2000, 632–9, 654; Stanlis 1992, 98–105; Hampsher-Monk 2005, 94–8). But it was the prospective impact of this collapse in England which pressed most urgently; for the complementary, 'fall' of 'manners' and 'traditionary language' could only lead, inevitably, to the fall of the English constitution.

Glory and Emulation

And it was this which really mattered. As we have already noted, the account of the 'late proceedings' in France, presented in terms not just of assaulted French Queens but of executed English Kings, was intended to serve an altogether greater purpose. For where the 'gentlemen of Old Jewry' have the revolutions of 1789 and indeed 1649 'so much before their eyes', Burke wants to redirect his audience towards a rather more estimable alternative, the 'glorious' Revolution of 1688 (Burke 1986, 99). Here, Burke shared a common 'reverence', joining the likes of Blackstone and Braxfield in concluding that the 'situation' of the English, by virtue of their constitution, was indeed a 'happy' one (Burke 1986, 86, 375). But that did not mean that the question of constitutional settlement was beyond debate. All constitutions must have a means of their reform. Burke was very obviously keen to distinguish his interpretation from the 'unheard-of bill of rights' which, he suggested, was to be found in Price's *Sermon* (Burke 1986, 99). But he did not expect to preclude interpretive debate. Such debates had continued throughout much of the intervening century since 1688, their ferocity invariably heightened during moments of perceived social or political unrest; 1790 was precisely such a moment.

Reflections on the Revolution in France really urges its readers to reflect upon the constitutive revolutions of seventeenth-century England, a process which culminated in the 'glorious' events of 1688 and 1689 which, in comparison with the anarchy which currently 'presides' in France, should be cherished for its 'cautious and deliberate spirit', as indeed an expression of 'practical resistance' (Burke 1986, 86, 154; White 1984, 192–5). The constitutional settlement articulated in the Declaration of Right is a 'most wise, sober, and considerate document, drawn up by great lawyers and great statesmen, and not by warm and inexperienced enthusiasts' (Burke 1986, 100). The rights which are found within are moreover 'real' rather than 'abstract'. They include the 'right to justice', to property and to 'good government' (Burke 1986, 150–1). At the heart of this irreducibly narrative jurisprudence, of course, could be found the associated mythology of the 'ancient constitution' (Burke 1986, 117; Pocock 1960, 125–43). Burke had long affirmed the rule of a distinctively 'common' law as the defining characteristic of the English constitution. In a 1782 speech in the House of Commons, he declared that 'Our constitution is a prescriptive constitution', one whose 'authority is that it has existed time out of mind' (Hill 1974, 5–7; Kilcup 1977, 400–2). In *Reflections*, Burke contrasts the 'spirit' of a constitution, expressed in the myriad cases and commentaries described by generations of common lawyers, against the alternative 'fabrication' of law in revolutionary France. The spirit of this constitutional jurisprudence is, thus, raised by language. Burke did not want his audience to reflect calmly upon the jurisprudential integrity of the English constitution, its statutes and principles, or at least not only. He wanted them to praise it, to be awed by it, and to love it; to hold it in a just measure of 'glory and emulation' and to appreciate the 'dispensation of stupendous wisdom' it represented (Burke 1986, 120, 137, 181).

In this way, the 'ancient constitution' is a written constitution, an epic historical narrative, one that must be read as a constitutive chronicle of the history of an entire people. It acquires the authority of testamentary experience, the 'collected reason of ages', an 'inheritance from our forefathers' (Burke 1986, 116–8). And it is an 'entailed inheritance', the expression of a 'partnership not only between those who are living, but between those who are living, those who are dead, and those who are to be born' (Burke 1986, 119, 194–5). It is for this reason that the English constitution has not changed 'materially' since the days of Bracton, and it is for the same reason that the prospects of its change are necessarily constrained (Burke 1986, 181). The 1689 settlement, read as part of this history, is to be understood as an expression of organic growth, again a very different kind of revolution from that which can be seen across the Channel. The enduring strength of a constitution, Burke repeatedly avers, lies in its ability but to promote measured change, precisely so that there is no need for a more violent alternative. 'A state without the means of some change', he affirms, 'is without the means of its conservation' (Burke 1986, 106–7). In a rather different context, half a century later, John Henry Newman would reconcile himself to Church reform in like tones. To 'live is to change, and to be perfect is to have changed often' (Gilmour 1993, 84). Newman was not obviously a Whig. But in his pragmatic rationalisation of institutional reform, he was, very obviously, a Burkean.

It is this adoration of the 'glorious' revolution, and the reason of history, which defined Burke's Whiggism. Along with it came collateral expressions of classical Whig constitutionalism. There is praise for the convention of separate powers, the principle means with which the English constitution preserves its 'balance' (Burke 1986, 320–1). There is also applause for the 'fundamental excellence' of an independent judiciary, and for the principle of the rule of law, without which there can be 'nothing stable' in social or political life (Burke 1986, 193, 325–9). The same is true of the institutional arrangements which Burke so urgently recommends, especially those which attach to the integral functions of the established Church and the Crown (Burke 1986, 100–2). It is here, of course, that Burke the Whig begins to sound like Burke the closet Tory. The Church is a place of 'high and worthy notions', a place where only the 'healing voice of Christian charity' can be heard (Burke 1986, 94–6, 189). There is indeed a kind of democracy in membership of the Church, one which, to Burke, has far greater reality than the notional forms of representation presently being instituted in France (Burke 1986, 190–1, 202). The monarchy, meanwhile, sets the 'frame to the commonwealth', binding all together in common cause, regardless of the 'inevitable tendency to party tyranny' which representative democracy, no matter how limited, nurtures (Burke 1986, 111, 229, 319). This relation finds expression in the idea of the 'original compact', which itself serves as a metaphorical confirmation of the greatest of all virtues of the 1689 settlement, the system of 'balances' (Burke 1986, 105, 194). It is this system of checks and balances which allows Burke to prefer a 'manly, moral, regulated liberty' that is 'combined with government' (Burke 1986, 89–91, 303–4). It is also what confirms the strength of Burke's underlying Whiggism, an ultimate scepticism of power, wherever it might be accreted.

The Church and the monarchy, however, have a further and still greater virtue; for the vitality of a 'glorious' constitution, such as the English, needs a deeper root. Englishmen and women must be persuaded to revere their institutions of government, just as they do their God. It is, again, a matter of esteem, of constitutional 'manners'. The English 'mind' is given to reverence, but this reverence must be earned. It is for this reason that Burke rails against the idea that Parliament should be peopled by 'professional' men, men who actually want political power. It is the abiding shame of France that it now has an Assembly populated by 'country curates' and 'stock-jobbers' (Burke 1986, 132–4, 142, 146). Critically, despite the many 'massacres' of the seventeenth century the English constitutional 'mind' was 'not slain'. On 'the contrary, it was kindled and inflamed'. It is for this reason that the English, when contemplating their constitution, continue to regard it with a 'conscious dignity, a noble pride, a generous sense of glory and emulation' (Burke 1986, 137, 181). A 'moral, regulated liberty' is one that is 'governed' by 'civil and social manners', as well as by Parliaments and ministers (Burke 1986, 91). As we have seen, it is for this reason that Burke littered *Reflections* with accounts of insensibility, of stormed palaces, terrified Queens, desecrated churches and dislocated families. Revolution flourishes where the culture of 'manners' is dissipated.

Church and Crown together describe the 'foundation' of the English constitutional sensibility, along with a 'reverence' for the common law (Burke 1986, 198, 372). Here, again Burke the Whig flirts with Burke the Tory. The principal role of the King was to serve as the 'affectionate father' of the nation: an exemplar of cohesion and chivalry, and calmness against the tumult of ideology and the libertine egoism. King George III was certainly keen for his subjects to perceive him to be the constitutional head of the myriad constituent families of his people. Each Sunday George dragooned his wife and as many of his fifteen children as could be found in residence to stroll along the terrace at Windsor Castle in full public view. At the height of republican fervour in 1792, Dorothy Wordsworth observed the ritual and confessed herself to be entranced. 'I fancied myself treading on Fairy Ground', she recorded, 'and that the gay company around me was brought there by

Enchantment', concluding that it was 'impossible to see the King and his Family at Windsor without loving them, even if you eye them with impartiality and consider them really as man and woman' (Byatt 1997, 107; Hibbert 1998, 300–1, 390–3). Burke wrote for women such as Dorothy Wordsworth. And the Victorians, as we shall see, came to revere the same fetish. In 1874, Cooke Taylor would affirm that the family was 'the unit upon which a constitutional government has been raised which is the admiration and envy of mankind' (Briggs 1959, 447). The idea of patriarchy, however, had a rather ambivalent place in Whig constitutional thought. It was against Sir Robert Filmer's notorious articulation of patriarchy as a justification for 'divine right' monarchy that both Algernon Sidney and John Locke had written a century before. Even so, whilst the rebuttal of Filmer had entered the canon of Whig constitutionalism, there was much in the same reverence for family which recommended itself to Whigs of a more conservative temper.

The associated iconography of 'natural subordination', of monarch, Church and family, finds repeated lyrical, and 'sacramental', expression too in *Reflections* (Burke 1986, 372; McLamore 1993, 180–2; Blakemore 1988, 17–18; White 1984, 213–4). The 'constitution of our country' is inextricably bound to 'our dearest domestic ties' and described accordingly in the shared semiotics of the English Commonwealth, 'our state, our hearths, our sepulchres, and our altars'. The 'liberties' of the 'ancient constitution', Burke confirms, are 'locked fast as in a sort of family settlement; grasped as in a kind of mortmain for ever' (Burke 1986, 120). History confirms the surety of a natural harmony, not the 'unadulterated metaphysics' of the 'intriguing' philosopher and the 'stock-jobbing' speculator (Burke 1986, 93, 187; Pocock 1982, 336–8, 343; McNally 2000, 433–5). The delusions of 'abstract perfection' are invariably unmasked by the reality of 'practical defect' (Burke 1986, 150–1). Constitutions are human constructs, 'states of being' as Samuel Johnson had famously declared, the products not of idle 'speculation' but of received experience (Burke 1986, 151, 299–300; Blakemore 1988, 6–7; White 1984, 227–9). What, Burke muses, is the 'use of discussing a man's abstract right to food or to medicine?' (Burke 1986, 151)[10] Government is a 'practical

[10] In his *Letter* to his Bristol constituents, Burke had famously affirmed 'I do not pretend to be an antiquary, a lawyer, or qualified for the chair of professor of metaphysics. I never ventured to put your solid interests on speculative grounds' (Herzog 1991, 336).

science', one which must engage all 'the gross and complicated mass of human passions and concerns' that everyday life throws up (Burke 1986, 152). Human nature, Burke continues, in a pointed rejoinder to philosophers of 'perfectibility' such as William Godwin, is defined by its 'prejudices', just as life is lived through its contingencies (Burke 1986, 183, 238–9). Englishmen and women are not perfectible. They cannot be shaped in accordance with 'specious goods' and neither can their constitution (Burke 1986, 248).

A constitution can, however, be 'harmonious'. Concluding his discussion of the 'entailed' and 'harmonious' nature of the English constitution, Burke wrote:

> By a constitutional policy, working after the pattern of nature, we receive, we hold, we transmit our government, our privileges, in the same manner in which we enjoy and transmit our property and our lives. The institutions of policy, the goods of fortune, the gifts of Providence, are handed down, to us and from us, in the same course and order. Our political system is placed in a just correspondence and symmetry with the order of the world, and with the mode of existence decreed to a permanent body composed of transitory parts; wherein, by the dispensation of a stupendous wisdom, moulding together the great mysterious incorporation of the human race, the whole, at one time, is never old, or middle-aged, or young, but in a condition of unchangeable constancy, moves on through the varied tenor of perpetual, decay, fall, renovation, and progression... In this choice of inheritance we have given to our frame of polity the image of blood; binding up the constitution of the country with our dear domestic ties; adopting our fundamental laws into the bosom of our family affections. (Burke 1986, 120)

It might seem to be rather less spectacular than the images of rampaging revolutionaries and fleeing Queens, but the metaphor of the entailed patriarchal constitution was for Burke definitive.[11]

[11] It was to assume a central position in Burke's later *Letters on a Regicide Peace*. The consistency of its place in Burke's thinking is attested by its equal importance in his earlier essay on the *Present Discontents*, published in 1770, wherein he affirmed that 'Commonwealths are made of families' (Ritchie 1989, 134; Wood 1964, 50–7).

A Wilderness of Rhapsodies

Reflections was an immediate publishing sensation, selling seven thousand copies in the first week, and nearly twenty thousand by the end of the year. 'Without our remembrance', wrote the *London Chronicle* a few weeks later, 'no publication has excited more anxious curiosity' (Fennessy 1963, 1; Claeys 2000, 41–2). Amongst the admirers of Burke's essay could be found, apparently, Catherine of Russia and the Emperor of Germany, as well as King George III himself, who famously recommended 'a good book, a very good book; every gentlemen ought to read it'. It was reported that the King took the opportunity to whisper his thanks to Burke in person, for supporting the 'cause of gentlemen'.[12] Gibbon, who 'adored his chivalry', thought Burke's essay was a 'most admirable medicine against the French disease' (Kramnick 1977, 39). Fanny Burney confessed that she found it 'the noblest, deepest, most animated and exalted work that I think I have ever read' (Claeys 2000, 42). Approval also came from close political allies, such as Lords Fitzwilliam and Loughborough, as well as the Tory Home Secretary, Grenville.

There were of course critics. Tone worried some, even friends. Francis regretted the 'pure foppery' to which Burke had sought recourse, most obviously in his depiction of the fleeing Marie Antoinette (Claeys 2000, 43). The *Monthly Review* articulated its distaste for history written like a 'popular harangue'. The *Critical Review* likewise wondered why Burke had been led to 'substitute invective for enquiry, and the deepest lamentations instead of more sober disapprobation', whilst the reviewer for the *English Review* despaired of an essay which aspired to lead the reader 'from one region of fairy land to the next' (Hodson 2007, 48–5, 51). The most substantive critique to emerge from the Radical wing of the Whig 'party' was James Mackintosh's *Vindicae Gallicae*, which appeared in April 1791. Revolutions, Mackintosh countered with a pointed simplicity, are not supposed to be achieved with an air of 'tranquillity'. The English revolutions of the seventeenth century were not tranquil, and

[12]The comments were originally recorded by William Hazlitt in his essay *On Court Influence*, published in the 1819 edition of his *Political Essays*. Hazlitt was in fact deeply ambivalent in regard to Burke, troubled by his politics, admiring of his aesthetics. The extent and nature of the King's discernment were open to question. He was also reported as being an interested reader of Paine's *Rights of Man* (Gilmartin 2000, 96–8; Kramnick 1977, 4, 39).

so it is hardly to be surprised if the revolution in France was not either. Alongside doubts as to Burke's aesthetic strategy, there were also darker insinuations, of betrayal and corruption and mendacity even, a species of wilful naivety. Most famously, publication of *Reflections* led to a schism with Burke's hitherto ally Charles James Fox, along with other leading Foxites such as the Richard Brinsley Sheridan, a schism which necessarily delighted the Tory presses. In parliamentary debate in early 1791, Fox proudly reiterated his support for the new French constitution, 'the most stupendous and glorious edifice of liberty which has been erected on the foundation of human integrity in any time or country'. When he tried to reassure Burke that public difference should not be allowed to diminish personal respect, Fox was curtly told 'Our friendship is at an end', at which point it was recorded that he burst into tears. Accusations of betrayal were fuelled by rumours that Burke had angled for a pension from Pitt's Tory government.

The first substantive published rebuttal was Mary Wollstonecraft's *Vindication of the Rights of Women*, which appeared in 1892. Wollstonecraft took particular exception to the sexual pejoratives written into *Reflections*, and more closely still the insinuation, found in the pivotal description of the storming of Versailles, that the presence of female revolutionaries represented a peculiarly demonic kind of perversion. Burke had a 'debauched imagination' (Fairer 1997, 18; Bromwich 1995, 617, 631–3). If so, it was hardly preclusive. The supposed coincidence of sexuality and revolution was a pervasive cultural misogyny (Goode 2007, 829–30, 840–3). Dickens would reinvest it half a century later in his *Tale of Two Cities* in the person of Madame Defarge, as well as the images of 'delicate' female feet dancing the Carmagnole in the 'slough of blood and dirt' (Hutter 1978, 456–7; Kucich 1980, 126–8). There was, Wollstonecraft continued, a peculiar perversion in Burke's seeming distress at the fate of Marie Antoinette but apparent indifference at 'the distress of many industrious mothers, whose helpmates have been torn from them, and the hungry cry of helpless babes' (Bromwich 1995, 620–2; Fennessy 1963, 203–6; Blakemore 1988, 52–5). Sharing the same broad distrust of Burke's historical 'perversions', Wollstonecraft's future husband, William Godwin, enjoined the radical repost, identifying Burke as an apologist for 'political imposture' in his *Enquiry Concerning Political Justice* and revisiting the same criticism albeit more allusively in his novel *Caleb Williams* (Godwin 1985, 788–9; Ward 2005, 33–5).

Another who immediately recognised the need to unmask Burke's strategy, as much as counter his politics, was Tom Paine. It appears that even Paine was startled by the venom he found when he first read *Reflections*.[13] The first part of *Rights of Man* was written as a direct repost to Burke's *Reflections*, a book which is nothing but a piece of rhetorical 'fancy', a 'pathless wilderness of rhapsodies' (Paine 1985, 64). Burke, he pointed observed, 'should recollect that he is writing History, and not Plays', and as to his 'rhapsody' of Marie Antoinette, the 'mob' which descended on Versailles, Paine countered, was an expression of the 'ill construction of all old governments in Europe' (Paine 1985, 58–9). In fantasising about barefoot princesses running along palatial corridors, Burke 'pities the plumage, but forgets the dying the bird' (Paine 1985, 51). 'Accustomed as he is to kiss the aristocratical hand that hath purloined him from himself' the author of *Reflections* 'degenerates into a composition of art, and the genuine soul of nature forsakes him' (Paine 1985, 51). The events of 1789 can be taken as an expression of a determination to rid politics of such rhetorical and poetic fancy. The people of France, Paine advised, have 'brought their' specious constitutional mythologies 'to the altar, and made of them a burnt-offering to reason' (Paine 1985, 81). In their place can be discerned an emergent universal jurisprudence of individual rights, one that will be written in a plainer 'common-sensical' language for the benefit of the 'living, not for the dead' (Paine 1985, 45).

The same, Paine added, should be anticipated, and welcomed, in England: a stripping away of its constitutional 'mythologies', the 'idol' of divine right and hereditary monarchy and the delusion of 'common' laws, above all the attendant mythologies of the so-called Revolution of 1688 and the Bill of Rights 'more properly called a bill of wrongs' (Paine 1985, 192–3). The idea that those who designed this Declaration should presume to prescribe for future generations is an 'absurdity', the aspiration to govern 'beyond the grave', one of the 'most ridiculous and insolent of all tyrannies' (Paine 1985, 41–2). The 'ancient constitution' as recast and recommended by Burke is a chimera, a 'burlesque'

[13] Paine had anticipated the publication of *Reflections* as early as the April and had stayed on reasonably friendly terms with Burke through the summer of 1790. Whilst recognising Burke's growing doubts as to certain aspects of the French Revolution, it seems that Paine still anticipated a broadly approving, if slightly more measured, series of 'reflections'.

the obscenity of which is barely shrouded by 'the fog and time of antiquity' (Paine 1985, 78, 174). But the enchantment is passed, the 'ragged relic and the antiquated precedent, the monk and the monarch, will moulder together' (Paine 1985, 196). The 'morning of reason', as Price had announced, has arrived enlightened by the 'luminous revolutions of America and France' (Paine 1985, 78, 91, 208). There may be much talk about the 'great and glorious' constitutional settlement. But that is all there is, talk. The 'continual use of the word Constitution in the English Parliament, shows there is none; and that the whole is merely a form of Government without a Constitution' (Paine 1985, 131). It was of course the conclusion which Alexis de Tocqueville would famously reach half a century later. What England needed was a proper constitution, by which Paine meant a written constitution, composed in one document, comprised of a series of readily enumerated and comprehended rights; for a constitution is 'not an ideal, but a real existence', and one moreover which is not intended to simply reflect some kind of mystic presence, but to found government and to confirm its limitations (Paine 1985, 71). Two hundred thousand copies of Paine's *Rights of Man* were printed and sold. Burke was right to be worried.

In 1795, the *Annual Register* reviewed the impact of Paine's engagement with Burke. It managed to strike a tone that was both nostalgic and prophetic; for which reason, it was also accordingly both reassuring and unsettling:

> The publication of Mr Burke's sentiments on the French revolution and the subsequent answer to Mr Paine, in his celebrated performance, styled the Rights of Man, were the first signals to the ministerial and popular parties in this country, to engage in that violent and acrimonious contest, which is not yet terminated. These two famous performances revived, as it were, the royal and republican parties that had divided this nation in the last century, and had lain dormant since the Revolution in 1688. They now returned to the charge with a rage and animosity equal to that which characterized our ancestors during the civil wars in the reign of King Charles the First, and it remained a long time in suspense, whether this renewed contest would not be attended with the same calamities, so eager were the partisans of the respected tenets contained in those performances, to assert them with unbounded vehemence. (Royle 2000, 15–16)

There was not much upon which Burke and Paine agreed. But there was nothing here with which either would have disagreed. The French

Revolution was not just a French Revolution. And neither, despite the editorial protestation, was it over. It was certainly not over for Burke, who returned to the events and its consequence repeatedly right up until his death in 1797. In immediate response to his Whig critics, Burke penned his *Appeal to the New from the Old Whigs*, published in August 1791; in which he argued that whilst the 'new' Whigs have been blinded by events in France, he remained faithful to the principles of 1689. However, Burke's most concerted reprise could be found in his *Letters on a Regicide Peace*, much of which was written in the final months of his life. Here, aside from reiterating, more strongly than ever, his belief that the 'late proceedings' ushered in a new age of 'total' revolution by means of state-organised terror, Burke intensified his metaphorical concentration on the Jacobin destruction of the core of the Christian Commonwealth, the sanctity of 'family' and hearth. 'Let us not deceive ourselves', a dying Burke concluded in grimly prophetic terms in 1796, 'we are at the beginning of great troubles' (Mosher 1991, 414; Kramnick 1977, 37, 183–5).

As the nineteenth century rolled out, commentators began to fashion a distinctive Burkean critique, much of which tended to be shaped by his debate with Paine. In time, Burke the classical Whig would mutate into Burke the founder of modern conservatism and the arch-opponent of radicalism, and in so doing sustain a 'revived Whiggism' for another generation or more.[14] A pejorative variant depicted an anguished antiquarian railing against the age of reason and liberalism, the fated prophet living at the cusp of modernity and advising against its potential horrors. At the same time, however, events served to contribute a certain prophetic quality to *Reflections*. As early as 1799, Wordsworth acclaimed the 'Genius of Burke' in precisely these terms: 'But some – While he forewarns, denounces, launches forth./ Against all systems built on abstract rights,/ Keen ridicule' (Wordsworth 1936, 544). Coleridge, unsurprisingly, followed suit, admitting his admiration for Burke's style as much as his politics in his introduction to *A Lay Sermon* and again in *Biographia Literaria*. 'In Mr Burke's writings', Coleridge opined, 'indeed the germ of almost all political truths can be found' (Coleridge 1977, 129; Parker

[14]Much here can be attributed to the presence of Burke in Leo Strauss's pantheon of pre-Straussian conservatives, in *Natural Right and Natural History* (1953, 294–323). As was the case with all those similarly elevated, Strauss detected something wrong with Burke, in this case a residual tendency to sentimental liberalism.

1991, 696–8). Within a generation, George Canning was advising, with obvious admiration, that virtually all of *Reflections* 'has been justified by the course of subsequent events; and almost every prophecy has been strictly fulfilled' (Claeys 2000, 50).

Ghosts

Burke endured. Indeed, it might be argued that it was because of Burke that Whiggism lasted so long as it did. It comes as no surprise to learn that Churchill was a considerable admirer, studying Burke's oratory so as to replicate their cadence in his own great parliamentary addresses (Cannadine 2003, 90, 95, 107). And it is reasonable to suppose that Burke would have found much to like in Churchill's *History of the English Speaking Peoples.* At the end of the nineteenth century, a generation of 'newer', darker, more sceptical Whigs such as Bagehot and Dicey were still wrestling with Burke, his *Reflections* and its consequences. Conor Cruise O'Brien has intimated the presence of Burke in Dicey's later writings (O'Brien; Dicey 1959, 56–8). We will revisit this possibility in due course, as we will the intimation that Burke might, through Bagehot, retain a ghostly presence in the writing of the 'new' British constitution (Bogdanor 2009, 272). Burkean spectres can be found stalking a range of modern historical 'discourses'. His place in the history of revolutions is pivotal, the first it is commonly suggested to recognise the 'full weight' of the French Revolution 'as an event in the history of civilization' (Roberts 1978, 139). Historians of terror are likewise reverential. The twenty-first-century war 'against terror', as Jean Baudrillard has recently argued, is an 'imaginative' engagement, of precisely the same kind which Burke discerned in the 'giddy coffee-houses' of London in late 1789 and early 1790 (Baudrillard 2002, 4–5, 73–4; Eagleton 2005, 49–53).

But above all, as Steven Blakemore suggests, Burke changed the way that history was written, his engagement with Paine on the 'late proceedings in France' reconfiguring political discourse in distinctly Miltonic terms, as a debate about 'the fall of language' (Blakemore 1988). John Tosh dates the origins of modern historicism to 1790 for this very reason (Tosh 1999, 11). Tom Furniss likewise argues that in engaging Burke on the subject of the English 'constitution', Paine necessarily found himself trapped in a discourse about discourse (Furniss 1990, 26–9). Burke, as James Boyd White has appreciated, wrote ironically, casting his constitution as an 'active' organism in a state of 'perpetual reconstitution'

(White 1984, 206–8, 221, 227). Burke's constitution was both representative and constitutive, written in a distinctively Aristotelian tradition of the kind which had earlier found expression in the writings of sixteenth- and seventeenth-century English jurists such as Richard Hooker and Robert Filmer, and which was, as Burke wrote, animating a first generation of Republican Framers across the Atlantic (White 1984, 222–3). 'Sentimental' Burkeans do not simply recognise an affinity with an institution or a 'structure'. They feel like they belong to something which they are always creating and re-creating that 'comes to life' through 'actual' political and constitutional 'conversations' (White 1984, 195–7, 228–9). In other words, they edify.

And it was a conversation which remained virulent throughout the nineteenth century, as Wordsworth foretold. When challenged by Peel as to why he wished to stand for Parliament a young Palmerston invoked Burke and the 'honour and instincts of England' (Brown 2010, 139). Palmerston, as we shall see, is commonly cited as the last Whig Prime Minister. Similar sentiments can be found crossing narrower political boundaries across much of nineteenth-century England. We will contemplate the extent of Disraeli's debt shortly. According to his old adversary William Ewart Gladstone, England was quite simply 'steeped' in Burke (Gardiner 2002, 183, 186–9). Whilst he did not make much of *Reflections* in his *Constitution*, in Bagehot's opinion Burke was the greatest of Whig historians. Thomas Carlyle reached the same conclusion. Any subsequent history of revolutions must be written in deference to the 'great' Burke and his *Reflections* (Frye 1997, 100). John Gardiner has suggested that Burke's ghost was one of two particular spectres which continued to haunt the parliamentary corridors and university 'common rooms' of Victorian England and beyond (Gardiner 2002, 100; Collini et al. 1983, 20–21). The other was Macaulay. It has been said that Thomas Arnold, the renowned headmaster of Rugby school 'trained' the Victorian mind, even though, dying in 1842, he was barely a Victorian (Heffer 2013, 11, 25–6). The same can be just as credibly said of Burke.

But it was not just a matter of training the Victorian mind. Burke terrified it. Victorian England never forgot the events of 1790 because they were never allowed to. As late as 1917, Dicey, as we shall see, raised the same spectres of 'Jacobin tyranny' in his late essay on Wordsworth; the consequence of defeat in northern France would be the politics of revolutionary France on the streets of London. The French Revolution could never be simply consigned to history, not least because it was not finished. Writing in 1856, the Whig lawyer Cockburn concluded that mid-Victorian England was still, in terms of its political and cultural perspective, 'soaked in this one event', entranced by the 'Great Terror'; in much the same perhaps as later twentieth-century generations would remain in thrall to increasingly distant memories of successive world wars, not just unable to detach their memories, but unwilling (Briggs 1959, 129). The great 'terror' embedded itself in the cultural memory of nineteenth-century England. Whenever a group of Chartists were espied gathering in a market town somewhere in the 1830s or 1840s, anxious Tories would invariably conjure images of bloodthirsty Jacobins roaming the streets looking for throats to cut. Macaulay, as we shall see in the next chapter, sought to terrify recalcitrant Whig peers on precisely these terms during the 'heady days' of May 1832. And it clearly resonated still thirty-five years later, or at least it did with Queen Victoria. Asked to give her assent to the second Reform Act in 1867, she did so persuaded by Disraeli's insinuation that if she refused there might be a 'new French Revolution' (Longford 1998, 352). Amidst a long letter to Princess Vicky chronicling the excesses of her wayward brother Bertie, Victoria observed that his aristocratic cronies were 'so frivolous, pleasure-seeking, heartless, selfish, immoral', so 'ignorant, luxurious and self-indulgent' that 'it makes one think' of 'the days before the French revolution' (Arnstein 2003, 116). When a little later in the nineteenth century, Charles Kingsley was asked why his compatriots seemed to be so obsessed with the possibility of revolution, however distant, he replied simply: 'Look at France, and see!' (Craig 1983, 79)

This was certainly the supposition of Thomas Carlyle, whose 1837 three-volume *History of the French Revolution* proved to be the first publishing sensation of the Victorian era. 'These Chartisms, Radicalisms, Reform Bill, Tithe Bill, and infinite other discrepancy, and acrid argument and jargon that there is yet to be, are *our* French Revolution', he confirmed three years later in his essay on *Chartism* (Carlyle 1986, 161). In Carlyle's opinion, Victorian politics could only be understood in the context of the French Revolution and the demons it had let loose. There is ideology in Carlyle's chronicle, and occasionally moments of quieter reflection, the 'rumbling Calvinist authorial sermon' as John Burrow puts it. But there is more that is visceral and violent, that is written to evoke the Burkean 'sublime' (Burrow 2007, 379–80). Like Burke, he wrote to draw tears. The revolution, he advised John Stuart Mill, was simply the 'grand Poem of our time', a metaphor which Mill obligingly recycled in his warm review of the *French Revolution* (Heffer 1995, 139–40). The 'sage' of Ecclefechan was widely regarded, not least by himself, as the leading conservative mind of his generation. To Gladstone, he was simply a 'genius' (Heffer 2013, 813). George Eliot surmised that every book written by her generation would have 'been different if Carlyle had not lived' (Heffer 1996, 1). Carlyle too trained the Victorian mind, mainly by turning it against stuff, against reform and Whiggery, very definitely against the 'pig philosophy' of utilitarianism, against industrialisation and urbanisation, against the 'palaver' of Parliament and against the 'puddle of sentimentalities' that passed for organised religion. He 'seems', an admiring Froude observed, 'best contented if he can make the rest of us as discontented as himself' (Heffer 2013, 182, 233, 578, 817).

Like Burke, Carlyle used the French Revolution as a means with which to revisit the merits and demerits of the English Revolution a century before. The difference between the two historians and their histories was the consequence of 1832 which, as we shall see in the next chapter, was presented by its Whig advocates as a further and final stage in a process which had commenced in the seventeenth century. According to Carlyle, the Reform Act confirmed the extent to which the English Revolution had been misinterpreted. It had 'availed' nothing constructive, but merely reawakened a revolutionary 'spirit' which would have been far better left dormant (Carlyle 1986, 153–4; Brantlinger 1977, 66–7). What the English working man required was not the vote, but better governance and enough to eat. Any student of the French Revolution, particularly Carlyle's history of it, would have predicted the devastating consequences which might flow from listening to 'quacks' spouting abstract metaphysical notions of liberty, equality and fraternity. Whilst the English 'peasantry' was the 'finest' in the world, it was still a peasantry, and there was nothing to be gained from enfranchising a class of men characterised only by its 'blockheadedness, gullibility, bribeability, amenability to beer and balderdash'. The 1832 Act had not enfranchised the peasantry. But it had given them hope and the precedent was clear. The so-called 'Great' Reform Act was 'our French revolution' (Carlyle 1986, 182, 189–91; Frye 1997, 84; Brantlinger 1977, 67–8).

The *History* was one of two books which, aside from a series of essays and journal articles, made Carlyle's reputation. Thackeray thought it a mark of 'genius'. So did Mill, the 'truest of histories'. The formidable

Harriet Martineau informed Carlyle's wife Jane that she had bought up 'a houseful of copies' to pass on to friends who, for some reason, had not already acquired their own (Heffer 1995, 174). The other book was the *Letters and Speeches of Oliver Cromwell* which appeared eight years later in 1845. Having dealt with the French Revolution, Carlyle had become obsessed with rewriting the English. His larger ambition was in the end tempered. Even so, as Gardiner affirmed, his *Letters and Speeches* was 'more than a book'. Its publication was itself 'an historical event, changing our whole conception of English history in its most heroic period' (Lang 1995, 198). Victorian England, as we have already noted, became entranced by its past. And like Carlyle, it was especially fascinated by heroes and revolutions, and more especially still by what Dickens famously termed the 'great seventeenth century time' (Goldberg 1972, 65). Cromwell remained a contentious figure: God-fearing hero to some, murderous regicide to others. As late as 1895, a public subscription to fund a statue of Cromwell outside Westminster fell badly short. In the end, the Prime Minister Lord Rosebery paid for it himself.

There again if the English were looking for a hero, and Carlyle certainly was, they were not blessed with an abundance of choice. There was Alfred, popular amongst devotees of Tennyson, Nelson and Wellington. There might have been Prince Albert if he had lived long enough to become less obviously German. But otherwise prospective English heroes were oddly scarce. So Carlyle recast Cromwell. The 'frantic enthusiast' painted by Hume was replaced with a reactionary pragmatist who saved the 'chosen' people from their darker selves, whilst also ridding England once and for all from the tyrannies of 'idolatrous' kingship. Gardiner was persuaded, at the end of the century acclaiming the 'most typical Englishman of all time', the guardian of protestant liberties who made 1688 possible and with it the 'essence of the British constitution' (Lang 1995, 3, 139–41). But Carlyle's Cromwell was heroic in a different way too. Humble and industrious, he was a hero for all those aspiring mid-Victorians who spent their evenings, when not reading Carlyle, instead reading Samuel Smiles's *Self-Help*, with Illustrations of Character and Conduct. There was much about Middle England that was round-headed, just as there was about their favourite chronicler.

Carlyle is an invariable presence in histories of nineteenth-century conservative political. So too is Burke. A third presence is Benjamin Disraeli, Tory Prime Minister briefly in 1868 and then again between 1874 and 1880. In a more personal sense, there was of course much that distinguished Carlyle from Disraeli, the most cavalier of cavaliers. The most 'superlative Hebrew conjuror', in Carlyle's opinion, was nothing more than a 'charlatan and he knows it' (Weintraub 1993, 535; Speare 1924, 162; Hibbert 2004, 314). Politically and ideologically, however, there was much that they had in common, not least a shared loathing of the traitor Peel and the 'shallow voluptuary' politics of Whig aristocrats such as Lord Melbourne (Mitchell 1997, 157). The younger Disraeli had even flirted with the 'Radical interest' and liked to present himself as a radical conservative. Standing as an independent at Wycombe in the 1832 election, he had declared himself 'a Conservative to preserve all that is good in our constitution, a Radical to remove all that is bad' (Hibbert 2004, 69). As such, he identified himself with Burke, concerned above all with redressing the present 'condition' of England and its constitution. The 'phantom of Mr Burke still haunts our hills and woods', he confirmed to his friend Lord Stanley in correspondence on the subject of 'one-nation' conservatism (Bentley 2001, 24).

In his Maidstone manifesto in 1837, Disraeli had averted to the reinvestment of the 'conservative cause' in the same resonantly Burkean terms: 'I mean the splendour of the Crown, the lustre of the peerage, the privileges of the Commons, the right of the poor. I mean the harmonious union, that magnificent concord of all interests, of all classes on which our national greatness and prosperity depends' (Weeks 1989, 394). It was a sentiment which he had refined during the course of the 1830s, in a series of essays written to condemn the 'union of oligarchical wealth and mob poverty' which had given birth to the 1832 Reform Act (Hutcheon 1913, 329, 350). Disraeli's principal target was Whiggery, his greater purpose to detach Burke from the stigma of association. It was for this very reason that his essays focussed most closely on the constitution and more especially the mythologies spun by less scrupulous Whig historians. The 'spirit of Whiggism', he baldly asserted in an eponymous essay, 'is hostile to the English constitution'. The English 'people', conservative by inclination, should not be distracted by the 'fancy' of Whig mythology, the purpose of which is to hold monarchy and the Lords in a state of 'unconstitutional thraldom' and thereby insinuate a 'republic' behind the façade of Parliament and 'people' (Hutcheon 1913, 260, 337–40). We will encounter Bagehot making precisely the same insinuation in due course.

In the most substantive of these early essays, his *Vindication of the English Constitution*, Disraeli presented readers with an alternative history of the constitution, reaching back to Magna Carta, the 'memorable' Parliament of 1264 and the unexpectedly libertarian Plantagenets. By the time it gets to the seventeenth century, the root of the 'ancient constitution' is thus securely planted, the civil war recast as the Long Parliament's attempt to reinvest the 'Constitution of the Plantagenets'. The Revolution of 1688 conversely 'added' nothing constitutionally to the settlement of 1640. Here, Disraeli articulated a perspective common to Tory historians of the seventeenth century, including of course Carlyle. Moving on to the eighteenth century, Disraeli recasts the Hanoverian settlement as a supremely Tory achievement, one that dispelled the 'fancy' principles of Whig constitutional history and instead reinvested a proper appreciation of settled institutions and interests (Hutcheon 1913, 113–5, 175–8, 338). Three decades later, Disraeli would articulate precisely the same in a famous speech given at the Manchester Free Trade Hall in 1872. The 'creed' of responsible conservatism was nothing other than to 'maintain the monarchy limited by the co-ordinate authority of the Estates of the Realm' (Heffer 2013, 772).

Disraeli was not of course entirely averse to fancy. The *Vindication* just preferred a different fancy, the belief that the English constitution is 'founded not only on a profound knowledge of human nature, but of human nature in England' (Hutcheon 1913, 230). Later, opposing Russell's 1865 Reform bill, Disraeli reminded fellow parliamentarians that England was 'governed by a most singular series of traditionary influences, which generation after generation cherishes because it knows that they embalm custom and represent law' (Weintraub 1993, 378). If it all seemed a little elusive, this 'national spirit' found a more solid institutional expression. England had 'become great by her institutions' (Hutcheon 1913, 327). Peel articulated the same definitively Burkean faith in 'settled institutions', along with a necessary 'deference to prescriptive authority'. It was part of conservative creed, and it made the Tory party, in the words of *Blackwood's Magazine*, the 'constitutional party' (Gash 1965, 131–2, 139). And when Disraeli ousted Peel, he did so on the grounds that he would restore a proper reverence for 'these institutions which make us a nation', not just 'our Crown, our Church, our Universities' but sundry other expressions of aspiring mid-Victorian England, 'our great municipal and commercial corporations, and its dependent scheme of provincial polity' (Gaunt 2010, 91). And when, in turn, he sought to defend his second Reform

Act, the justification was the same. The 1867 Act would secure those 'institutions' which are the 'embodiment of the national requirements and security of the national rights', and which had been unsettled in 1832 (Aldous 2007, 186). Parliament was never intended to represent the 'people'. It represented interests and 'estates', for the 'essence of good government' is respect for property (Speare 1924, 57–8). Here, it might be supposed that Tory and Whig had something in common. Both calibrated their respective reform acts in terms of who had enough stuff to be trusted with a vote. And both very obviously were wrestling over who better comprehended Burke. We shall take a closer look at the Whig interpretation of Burkean 'principles' in the next chapter.

The ideas which Disraeli had advanced in his essays during the 1830s were recast a decade later in his two renowned 'condition of England' novels, *Coningsby* published in 1844, and *Sybil* a year later. Both were written to political purpose, intended to 'vindicate the just claims of the Tory party to be the popular confederation of the country' (Speare 1924, 50–1). They were also written to vindicate Disraeli and his ideological prejudice, the 'memoirs he never wrote' (Kuhn 2006, 5). Both moved around the prospective consequence of the 1832 Reform Act, the treachery of Peel and the demands of living in a 'progressive age'. It was in *Sybil* that Disraeli famously coined the term 'two Nations'. The idea that England was populated by some very rich people and a lot of very poor people was hardly new. And neither was the insinuation; that unless something was done to bring the two 'nations' sooner or later, the poorer masses would rise up and destroy the richer. England in 1845 was a lot like France in 1789, the same familiar referent. Fortunately, there was Disraeli, and his 'Young England' chums, willing to spend their medieval-themed dinners chewing over how best to chart a way to England's future through its past. The solution, Disraeli concluded, was a reinvestment of the 'feudal principle', the 'noblest principle, the grandest, the most magnificent that was ever conceived by sage or ever produced by patriot' (Newsome 1998, 181). The chief sage of 'Young England' was of course the great chronicler of old England, Edmund Burke (Kuhn 2006, 48–9, 75–6; Speare 1924, 61; Aldous 2007, 17–20).

Disraeli's essays, and perhaps even more so his novels, confirm the extent to which the vicarious experience of 1790 helped to shape the writing of conservative history (Evans 2000, 16–17). The same can of course be said of Burke and Carlyle, and perhaps a fourth rather different kind of historian, Charles Dickens. Here, again it might be thought that Dickens and Disraeli would have had much in common, not least their admiration for Carlyle. But they evinced nothing but contempt for one another, whilst Carlyle evinced little but contempt for both.[15] 'Fiction', Carlyle famously declaimed, 'partakes' of 'the nature of lying', and there was altogether too much Whiggery in the 'waterest of twaddle' that characterised so much of Dickens's writing (Brantlinger 1977, 29). He did, however, make an exception in regard to one novel. *A Tale of Two Cities* was 'wonderful' (Pratt 1983, 235–6). *Two Cities*, published in 1859, was of course Dickens's history of the French Revolution. It was also his testament to Carlyle and his 'wonderful' history of the same. 'I am always reading you faithfully and trying to go your way', Dickens drooled in the Preface to his novel. He had paid similar obeisance in the dedication to his earlier *Hard Times*. His biographer John Forster would later record that there was no one Dickens 'honoured so much' as the 'sage' of Ecclefechan (Forster 1966, 1.204). The consonance of imagery between Carlyle's *History* and Dickens's novel is evident and striking, the 'rages uncontrollable', the blood running through the gutters of Paris and the cavorting of the demented 'sansculottes'. And so is the same difficulty with endings. Whig historians were much better at happy endings. Carlyle famously struggled to bring his chronicle to a resolution. So did Dickens. The final scene of *Two Cities*, as Carton assumes Darnay's place, might seem uplifting, the invocation of New Testament imagery redeeming humanity from the Old Testament savagery of Madame Defarge and 'the Vengeance'. But it is also evasive, insinuating only what Carton might have wished to say on the scaffold as he awaits his death alongside the innocent young seamstress whose imminent sacrifice to the idols of the Carmagnole is quite literally inexplicable.

Dickens's novel, like Carlyle's *History*, was intended to reinvest Victorian perceptions of the 'Terror', making it more visceral and more immediate too. Their Jacobins were not figures from history, but the kind of revolutionaries who could still be found lurking in the smog-ridden alleyways of east London. It was not moreover the first time that Dickens had addressed the darker side of radicalism. As he drafted the riot scenes in *Barnaby Rudge* in 1841, the younger Dickens had written excitedly to Forster 'By Jove how radical I am getting! I wax stronger

[15] Dickens disapproved of Disraeli's parliamentary 'antics', whilst Disraeli famously, and loudly, confirmed that he had never bothered to read any of Dickens novels (Hibbert 2004, 157, 285).

and stronger in the true principles every day' (Fleishman 1971, 103). The plot of *Barnaby Rudge* moved around the Gordon riots of 1780. Both *Rudge* and the riots tend to be rather forgotten today, at least when compared with *Two Cities* and the events of 1790. According to Samuel Johnson though, the riots of 1780 were truly a 'time of terror', whilst critics such as Gissing would later proclaim *Rudge* to be amongst Dickens's 'best' (McCalman 1999, 458; Sanders 1978, 76). The young Dickens may have harboured radical pretensions, but he shared a common fear of revolutionary pathologies. The rioters who rampage through the pages of *Barnaby Rudge* bear a striking resemblance to the Jacobins who race around the streets of Carlyle's Paris; young, naïve, easily led by malevolent intelligence. The leader of Dickens's rioters is the 'savage prophet' Hugh, but the real malevolence is Gordon's fawning secretary Gashford. And the riots they lead are terrifying, moments when the fragile bonds of society are ripped asunder, when the 'scum and refuse' rise to the surface and demonic anarchy is let loose. Initial cries of 'No Popery' give way to a more manic 'Down with everything'. 'I have let all the prisoners out of Newgate, burnt down Lord Mansfield's and played the very devil', Dickens reported to Forster (Fleishman 1971, 102–3; Marcus 1985, 174–5; Rice 1983, 59–62; Michasiw 1989, 571, 577–81).

But if the mob is terrifying it is not beyond comprehension. As Carlyle likewise argued revolutions happen for a reason, most commonly when institutions of law and government fail. The Lord Mayor is a coward, the subsequent vengeance of the courts in *Rudge* no less contemptible than that of the rioters. The law is rarely recommended in Dickens. It does little good in *Two Cities.* Both Darnay trials are travesties, whilst Carton's legal partner Stryver is an archetype of unappealing Dickensian lawyers. But it is never as unremittingly condemned as it is in *Barnaby Rudge*. Barbarity is met with barbarity, rioters strung up indiscriminately following perfunctory trials. Hugh goes to his execution with peculiar nobility unveiling all the hypocrisies of those who would condemn him, whilst the self-serving rhetoric of Ned the hangman darkens the irony still further. His profession, the hanging of 'man, woman or child' is 'sound, Protestant, constitutional, English work' (Dickens 2003, 310). There again, in the opinion of Lord Gordon at least, so is revolution. His supporters have taken to the streets to defend the 'constitution' enacted in 1689. The 'history' of *Barnaby Rudge* is confused because the histories of England are so contestable.

Critics have commonly identified *Rudge* as part of a sub-genre of Chartist novels, many of which evince the same critical tension, between a visceral sympathy for the 'condition' of the poor and a countervailing, if no less visceral, terror of them rising up and rioting. It is the tension which again makes the ending so difficult, in *Rudge* as in *Two Cities*. There is in fact no ending to *Rudge*. The forces of good do not triumph over the forces of evil. There is no reconciliation, no restoration of order. The novel just stops, whilst revolution takes a breather. The Preface to *Rudge* reminded readers that history 'teaches us'. But what it teaches more than anything is that we tend not to heed its lessons. History fascinated Dickens. He only wrote to historical novels, *Barnaby Rudge* and *A Tale of Two Cities*, and he found both peculiarly difficult to write, still more difficult to resolve. And ultimately, it is this difficulty which distinguished the sceptical mind. As we will see dealing with doubt came to define the later Victorian. But it was already seeding by the 1840s. There were still happy endings to be written, as we shall see in the next chapter. But they were becoming increasingly difficult to write convincingly.

It is interesting to note that Burke was just as fascinated by the behaviour of 'Mad Lord George' and the 'diabolic incendiaries' of 1780, as Horace Walpole termed them. It has even been suggested that the memory of the Gordon riots provided a further stimulus to the *Reflections*. Burke had been popularly associated with the riots at the time, in large part because Gordon presented himself as something of a protégé. But Burke was appalled by the violence of 1780, as he would be the violence of 1790. It would require similar abjuration. In his 1796 *Letter to a Noble Lord*, he would iterate his belief that 'had the portentous comet of the Rights of Man… crossed upon us in that infernal state of England' in 1780 'nothing human could have prevented our being irresistibly hurried out of the highway of heaven into all the vices, crimes, horrors and miseries of the French Revolution'.[16] Raising the same images in order to terrify the same imaginations, Burke set the scene for Dickens's tortured tale of Gordon and Gashford and Hugh of the Maypole. For:

> There was indeed much intestine heat; there was dreadful fermentation. Wild and savage insurrection quitted the woods, and prowled around our streets in the name of Reform. Such was the distemper in the public mind, that there was no madman, in his maddest ideas and maddest projects,

[16] According to Ian McCalman, Gordon is the 'archetypal revolutionary figure who stalks through the pages of the *Reflections*' (McCalman 1996, 346).

> who might not count upon numbers to support his principles and execute his designs. (McCalman 1996, 357)

Reform in 1780 meant something rather different from reform half a century on, but not, to mid-Victorians of Burke's temper, that much different. Judicious reform was one thing, the 'direct application of a remedy to the grievance complained of', as Carlyle would later put it (Frye 1997, 90). The politics of Reform, however, was a potentially violent and terrifying something else. It betokened the poniard and carmagnole. As we shall now see, it would fall to the coming generation of Whig prophets to somehow detach the cause of Reform from the castigations of Burke and his *Reflections*.

References

Aldous, R. (2007). *The Lion and the Unicorn: Gladstone v Disraeli*. London: Pimlico.

Arnstein, W. (2003). *Queen Victoria*. Basingstoke: Palgrave.

Baudrillard, J. (2002). *The Spirit of Terrorism*. London: Verso.

Bentley, M. (2001). *Lord Salisbury's World: Conservative Environments in Late-Victorian Britain*. Cambridge: Cambridge University Press.

Blakemore, S. (1988). *Burke and the Fall of Language*. Lebanon, NH: University Press of New England.

Bogdanor, V. (2009). *The New British Constitution*. Oxford: Hart.

Bourke, R. (2000). Edmund Burke and Enlightenment Sociability: Justice, Honour and the Principles of Government. *History of Political Thought, 21*, 632–656.

Brantlinger, P. (1977). *The Spirit of Reform: British Literature and Politics 1832–1867*. Cambridge, MA: Harvard University Press.

Briggs, A. (1959). *The Age of Improvement*. London: Longmans.

Bromwich, D. (1995). Wollstonecraft as a Critic of Burke. *Political Theory, 23*, 617–634.

Brown, D. (2010). *Palmerston: A Biography*. New Haven: Yale University Press.

Burke, E. (1986). *Reflections on the Revolution in France*. London: Penguin.

Burke, E. (1990). *A Philosophical Enquiry into the Origins Our Ideas of the Sublime and the Beautiful*. Oxford: Oxford University Press.

Burke, E. (1999). *Letters on a Regicide Peace*. Indianapolis: Liberty Fund.

Burrow, J. (2007). *A History of Histories*. London: Penguin.

Byatt, A. (1997). *Unruly Times*. London: Vintage.

Cannadine, D. (2003). *In Churchill's Shadow: Confronting the Past in Modern Britain*. Oxford: Oxford University Press.

Carlyle, T. (1986). *Selected Writings*. Harmondsworth: Penguin.

Claeys, G. (2000). The *Reflections* Refracted: The Critical Reception of Burke's *Reflections on the Revolution in France* During the Early 1790s. In J. Whale (Ed.), *Edmund Burke's Reflections on the Revolution in France: New Interdisciplinary Essays'*. Manchester: Manchester University Press.

Coleridge, S. (1969). *Complete Poetical Works.* Oxford: Oxford University Press.

Coleridge, S. (1977). *Biographia Literaria.* London: Dent.

Collini, S., Winch, D., & Burrow, J. (1983). The Governing Science: Things Political and the Intellectual Historian. In S. Collini, D. Winch, & J. Burrow (Eds.), *That Noble Science of Politics: A Study in Nineteenth Century Intellectual History.* Cambridge: Cambridge University Press.

Craig, D. (1983). The Crowd in Dickens. In R. Giddings (Ed.), *The Changing World of Charles Dickens.* New York: Barnes and Noble.

Danby, J. (1960). *The Simple Wordsworth: Studies in His Poems 1797–1807.* London: Routledge.

De Bruyn, F. (2004). Edmund Burke, the Political Quixote: Romance, Chivalry, and the Political Imagination. *Eighteenth Century Fiction, 16,* 695–753.

Dicey, A. (1959). *An Introduction to the Study of the Law of the Constitution.* London: Macmillan.

Dickens, C. (2003). *Barnaby Rudge.* London: Penguin.

Dinwiddy, J. (1974). Utility and Natural Law in Burke's Thought: A Reconsideration. *Studies in Burke and His Time, 16,* 105–128.

Eagleton, T. (2005). *Holy Terror.* Oxford: Oxford University Press.

Evans, R. (2000). *In Defence of History.* London: Granta.

Fairer, D. (1997). Organizing Verse: Burke's *Reflections* and Eighteenth Century Poetry. *Romanticism, 3,* 1–19.

Fennessy, R. (1963). *Burke, Paine and the Rights of Man.* Dordrecht: Martinus Nihoff.

Fleishman, A. (1971). *The English Historical Novel: Walter Scott to Virginia Woolf.* Baltimore: Johns Hopkins University Press.

Foreman, A. (1998). *Georgiana Duchess of Devonshire.* London: HarperCollins.

Forster, J. (1966). *The Life of Charles Dickens.* London: Chapman & Hall.

Frye, L. (1997). "Great Burke", Thomas Carlyle, and the French Revolution. In L. Crafton (Ed.), *The French Revolution Debate in English Literature and Culture.* London: Greenwood Press.

Furniss, T. (1990). Rhetoric in Revolution: The Role of Language in Paine's Critique of Burke. In K. Hanley & R. Selden (Eds.), *Revolution and English Romanticism.* London: Harvester Wheatsheaf.

Furniss, T. (1993). *Edmund Burke's Aesthetic Ideology: Language, Gender and Political Economy in Revolution.* Cambridge: Cambridge University Press.

Gardiner, J. (2002). *The Victorians: An Age in Retrospect.* London: Hambledon.

Gash, N. (1965). *Reaction and Reconstruction in English Politics 1832–1852.* Oxford: Oxford University Press.

Gaunt, R. (2010). *Sir Robert Peel: The Life and Legacy.* London: I.B. Tauris.

Gilmartin, K. (2000). Burke, Popular Opinion, and the Problem of a Counter-Revolutionary Sphere. In J. Whale (Ed.), *Edmund Burke's Reflections on the Revolution in France: New Interdisciplinary Essays*. Manchester: Manchester University Press.

Gilmour, R. (1993). *The Victorian Period: The Intellectual and Cultural Context of English Literature 1830–1890*. London: Longman.

Godwin, W. (1985). *An Enquiry Concerning Political Justice*. Harmondsworth: Penguin.

Goldberg, M. (1972). From Bentham to Carlyle: Dickens' Political Development. *Journal of the History of Ideas, 33*, 61–76.

Goode, M. (2007). The Man of Feeling: The Erotics of Historicism in *Reflections on the Revolution in France*. *ELH, 74*, 829–857.

Hampsher-Monk, I. (2005). Edmund Burke's Changing Justification for Intervention. *Historical Journal, 48*, 65–100.

Heffer, S. (1995). *Moral Desperado: A Life of Thomas Carlyle*. Weidenfeld and Nicolson.

Heffer, S. (1996). *Moral Desperado: A Life of Thomas Carlyle*. London: Phoenix.

Heffer, S. (2013). *High Minds: The Victorians and the Making of Modern Britain*. London: Random House.

Herzog, D. (1991). Puzzling Through Burke. *Political Theory, 19*, 336–363.

Hibbert, C. (1998). *George III*. London: Viking.

Hibbert, C. (2004). *Disraeli: A Personal History*. London: HarperCollins.

Hill, B. (1974). Fox and Burke: The Whig Party and the Question of Principles 1784–1789. *English Historical Review, 89*, 1–24.

Hodson, J. (2007). *Language and Revolution in Burke, Wollstonecraft, Paine and Godwin*. Aldershot: Ashgate.

Hutcheon, W. (Ed.). (1913). *Whigs and Whiggism: Political Writings by Benjamin Disraeli*. London: John Murray.

Hutter, A. (1978). Nation and Generation in *A Tale of Two Cities*. *Proceedings of the Modern Language Association, 93*, 448–462.

Kilcup, R. (1977). Burke's Historicism. *Journal of Modern History, 49*, 394–410.

Kramnick, I. (1977). *The Rage of Edmund Burke: Portrait of an Ambivalent Conservative*. New York: Basic Books.

Kucich, J. (1980). The Purity of Violence: *A Tale of Two Cities*. *Dickens Studies Annual, 8*, 119–137.

Kuhn, W. (2006). *The Politics of Pleasure: A Portrait of Benjamin Disraeli*. London: Simon & Schuster.

Lang, T. (1995). *The Victorians and the Stuart Age*. Cambridge: Cambridge University Press.

Lock, F. (2000). Rhetoric and Representation in Burke's *Reflections*. In J. Whale (Ed.), *Edmund Burke's Reflections on the Revolution in France: New Interdisciplinary Essays*. Manchester: Manchester University Press.

Longford, E. (1998). *Victoria RI*. London: Weidenfield & Nicolson.

Marcus, S. (1985). *Dickens from Pickwick to Dombey*. London: Penguin.

Mayo, R. (1972). The Contemporaneity of the *Lyrical Ballads*. In A. Jones & W. Tydeman (Eds.), *Wordsworth's Lyrical Ballads*. London: Macmillan.

McCalman, I. (1996). Mad Lord George and Madame La Motte: Riot and Sexuality in the Genesis of Burke's *Reflections on the Revolution in France*. *Journal of British Studies, 35*, 343–367.

McCalman, I. (1999). Controlling the Riots: Dickens, Barnaby Rudge and Romantic Revolution. *History, 84*, 458–476.

McLamore, R. (1993). To Forge a New Language: Burke and Paine. *Prose Studies, 16*, 179–192.

McNally, D. (2000). Political Economy to the Fore: Burke, Malthus and the Whig Response to Popular Radicalism in the Age of the French Revolution. *History of Political Thought, 21*, 427–447.

Michasiw, K. (1989). *Barnaby Rudge*: The Since of the Fathers. *English Literary History, 56*, 571–592.

Mitchell, L. (1997). *Lord Melbourne 1779–1848*. Oxford: Oxford University Press.

Mosher, M. (1991). The Skeptic's Burke. *Political Theory, 19*, 391–418.

Newsome, D. (1998). *The Victorian World Picture*. London: Fontana.

Paine, T. (1985). *The Rights of Man*. Harmondsworth: Penguin.

Parker, M. (1991). The Institutionalization of a Burkean-Coleridgean Literary Culture. *Studies in English Literature, 31*, 693–713.

Paulson, S. (1983). *Representations of Revolution*. New Haven: Yale University Press.

Pocock, J. (1960). Burke and the Ancient Constitution—A Problem in the History of Ideas. *Historical Journal, 3*, 125–143.

Pocock, J. (1982). The Political Economy of Burke's Analysis of the French Revolution. *Historical Journal, 25*, 331–349.

Pratt, B. (1983). Carlyle and Dickens: Heroes and Hero-Worshippers. *Dickens Studies Annual, 12*, 233–246.

Price, R. (1991). *Political Writings*. Cambridge: Cambridge University Press.

Rice, T. (1983). The Politics of *Barnaby Rudge*. In R. Giddings (Ed.), *The Changing World of Charles Dickens*. New York: Barnes & Noble.

Ritchie, D. (1989). Burke's Influence on the Imagination of Walter Bagehot. *The Modern Age, 32*, 324–328.

Roberts, J. (1978). *The French Revolution*. Oxford: Oxford University Press.

Royle, E. (2000). *Revolutionary Britannia? Reflections on the Threat of Revolution in Britain 1789–1848*. Manchester: Manchester University Press.

Sanders, A. (1978). *The Victorian Historical Novel 1840–1880*. London: Macmillan.

Speare, M. (1924). *The Political Novel: Its Development in England and in America*. Oxford: Oxford University Press.

Stanlis, P. (1992). Burke, Rousseau and the French Revolution. In S. Blakemore (Ed.), *Burke and the French Revolution: Bicentennial Essays*. Athens: University of Georgia Press.

Strauss, L. (1953). *Natural Right and Natural History*. Chicago: Chicago University Press.

Swann, K. (1977). Martha's Name or the Scandal of "The Thorn". In Y. Prins & M. Schreiber (Eds.), *Dwelling in Possibility: Women Poets and Critics of Poetry.* Ithaca: Cornell University Press.
Tosh, J. (1999). *A Man's Place: Masculinity and the Middle-Class Home in Victorian England.* Yale University Press
Ward, I. (2005). A Man of Feelings: William Godwin's Romantic Embrace. *Law and Literature, 17,* 21–46.
Weeks, R. (1989). Disraeli as Political Egoist: A Literary and Historical Investigation. *Journal of British Studies, 28,* 387–410.
Weintraub, S. (1993). *Disraeli: A Biography.* London: Hamish Hamilton.
White, J. (1984). *When Words Lose Their Meaning: Constitutions and Reconstitutions of Language, Character and Community.* Chicago: Chicago University Press.
Wood, N. (1964). The Aesthetic Dimension of Burke's Political Thought. *Journal of British Studies, 4,* 41–64.
Wordsworth, W. (1935). *The Complete Poetical Works.* Oxford: Oxford University Press.
Wordsworth, W. (1936). *Complete Poetical Works.* Oxford University Press.

CHAPTER 3

The Great Dramatist

On 4 April 1848, the Chartist Convention announced an intention to present a new petition to Parliament. Agitation was not new in early nineteenth century; Luddites, Swing-rioters, various species of machine-breakers. But the 1840s seemed different, angrier, hungrier, and for reasons of organisation and scale, and to a degree articulation too, it was evident that the Chartists were different. Their immediate genesis could be discerned in the kind of people who rampaged through the pages of *Barnaby Rudge* and cheered Richard Price at Old Jewry in 1790; 'slaves of the most degraded sort' in the perception of Dr. Arnold (Heffer 2013, 17). Predictably enough Arnold recommended a classical solution, the 'Roman way'; flog the rank and file, and fling the ringleaders from the Tarpeian Rock (Brantlinger 1977, 83). Chartism preferred a different history, rather more Anglo-Saxon and a lot less Roman. Its very name was evocative. Back in 1832, as it urged every Englishman to consider 'Revolution or Reform', the *Despatch* had wondered aloud why the people had 'so long submitted to the delay of their new Magna Carta' (Royle 2000, 74). Late eighteenth- and early nineteenth-century radical rhetoric was studiously jurisprudential. The petition of the London Corresponding Society written by John Thelwall in 1795 had appealed to the Commons as the 'constitutional guardian of the people's liberties' (Royle 2000, 146). The Commons had not been particularly impressed. It did not like reform petitions. It did not much like newspapers either, particularly newspapers that agitated for petitions. On the eve of 'Peterloo', the *Manchester Mercury* had identified the 'root' of

I. Ward, *Writing the Victorian Constitution*, Palgrave Modern Legal History, https://doi.org/10.1007/978-3-319-96676-2_3

present 'evil' in a Constitution that had 'become rotten to the core', and reminded its readers that petitioning was an ancient constitutional right enjoyed by all Englishmen (Briggs 1959, 210).

Chartism adopted precisely the same strategy. Invocations of Norman yokes, Witenagemots and 'ancient' constitutions were invariably present in Chartists petitions, alongside the customary 'Six Points' extracted, with a certain interpretive license, from the original 'great' Charter of 1215; universal suffrage, a ballot, the removal of property qualifications, the payment of MPs, equal constituencies and annual parliaments. 'Here's that we may live to see the restoration of old English times, old English fare, old English holidays, and old English justice', declared the Chartist leader Feargus O'Connor (Thompson 1991, 255). Petitions would invariably identify more recent statutes, most commonly successive Poor Laws, which it deemed to be 'unconstitutional'. Like its predecessors, the 1848 Chartist petition would proclaim, first and foremost, an adherence to the 'laws and customs of our ancestors under which', apparently, 'property was secure and the working people happy and contented', and employed. Alongside the more distant mythologies of the 'ancient' constitution, there was the rather more contemporary mythology of the great Whig 'betrayal' (Royle 2000, 97–9, 146). Chartist petitions were written in this bifocal context, and read in it too. Some were taken in. Charles Kingsley, invited to attend a meeting of incipient Christian socialists at a Soho tavern, proclaimed himself to be 'a Christian parson, and a Chartist' (Brantlinger 1977, 139).

Parliament, however, was most certainly not taken in. And it no more welcomed Chartist petitions than it the Corresponding petitions of the 1790s. It had disliked the 1839 petition, which arrived alongside news of rioting in South Wales and it had disliked the petitions of 1841 and 1842 just as much. Few Members had much in common with the young Friedrich Engels. But they did share a common historical referent. Invoking an immediate comparison with the 'rage of 1793', Engels suggested that the six points of the Charter would be 'sufficient to overthrow the whole English Constitution, Queen and Lords included' (Brantlinger 1977, 82). On the arrival of the 1841 petition, the Radical MP Thomas Attwood adopted the same tone, reminding the House, if it needed much reminding, that the times were resonant of the 'situation of Louis XVI in 1787 and 1798'. 'When Louis was asleep ruin was stalking through the land', Attwood continued, before concluding 'What is the position of the Queen of England in this hour?' Russell agreed.

The petition, he confirmed, had been presented in 'language not exceeded in violence and atrocity in the worst times of the French Revolution' and was intended to 'subvert' by 'force of arms' nothing less than the constitution itself (Heffer 2013, 118, 124).[1] The 1841 petition had been accompanied by equally discomforting news of strikes across Lancashire, Yorkshire and Staffordshire. The petition of April 1848 was therefore most unwelcome. Parliament was even less enamoured by the idea of thousands of sympathisers wandering the streets of London. The 1842 petition had been presented to Parliament with a two-mile procession behind it. This time Chartist organisers had announced plans to hold a mass rally on the tenth of the month.

In a gesture loaded with symbolic import, the decrepit Duke of Wellington, long ago victor of Waterloo, was tasked with organising the London militia, to be reinforced by however many regiments of Guards and hussars were to be deemed necessary as events unfolded. Wellington assumed a characteristically brusque attitude to the Chartist cause: 'Plunder is the object. Plunder is likewise the means' (Mather 1959, 372). Thousands of cavalrymen, and their horses, were piled onto railway carriages to be transported, if rather slowly, to the northern cities, whilst the Prime Minister Lord Russell authorised the seizure of 'the electric telegraph to prevent false reports spreading in the country' (Heffer 2013, 127). Meanwhile in London, 85,000 special constables were enlisted, including a young Gladstone and the soon to be Emperor Napoleon III of France. There were reasons to be fearful. The French had just had yet another revolution and now had a Republic again, whilst there were rumours of rebellions across the continent, from Schleswig to Sicily to the distant reaches of the western Ukraine. The *Northern Star* excitedly announced the 'springtime of the peoples' (Royle 1996, 42). The Queen blamed her Foreign Secretary, Lord Palmerston. He had as ever been behaving 'like a naughty child' over-exciting all the revolutionaries in Rome, Lisbon and Paris (Brown 2010, 289, 309–10). Disraeli was inclined to agree. It all went to show what might happen when the 'sentimental principle' was allowed to run to excess (Brown 2010, 313).

[1]The 1839 petition famously had 1.2 million signatures appended. Disraeli spoke in favour of receiving it. But the vote against was passed by 235 to 46. It was understandable if Parliament was a little distracted. The petition arrived at Westminster Hall on precisely the same day as Lord Melbourne's administration resigned.

On the afternoon of the 9th, the day before the intended presentation of the petition, it was reported that soldiers had been heard chatting pleasantly to gathering marchers, promising to shoot over their heads if ordered to fire. The Royal family was sent to Osborne House on the Isle of Wight, though the Duke expressed misgivings in the event of the Chartists managing to commandeer a warship. The royal gardeners were armed with sticks and told to stay near the house just in case. By late morning on the 10th an estimated 15,000 had gathered at Kennington Common to listen to the famed, and feared, Feargus O'Connor. Another rather smaller gathering of around 2000 was apparently enjoying a sing-a-long and a picnic in the drizzle at Stepney Green. Even if it was not the half million confidently projected by O'Connor, 15,000 were still enough to start a riot, except that no one, least of all O'Connor, seemed keen on rioting. After a brief and amicable chat with the local authorities, it was agreed that a handful of petitioners, as many as could be crammed into three cabs, would be allowed across the Thames to present their petition. After which they would go quietly home. Those who remained on the Common meanwhile could finish their snacks in peace on the understanding that they too would then quietly disperse. Everyone agreed, according to Greville with 'apparent alacrity and good humour' (Hibbert 2001, 202). At 2 pm, the Prime Minister Lord Russell was able to inform the Queen that the crisis, insofar as there had been one, was 'passed' (Royle 1996, 44–5; Longford 1998, 198). Gladstone expressed his thanks in prayer, 'our hearts feel profoundly the mercies of this very remarkable day' (Bentley 1996, 137). Victoria wrote to Uncle Leopold, sympathising with the rather greater travails that he and other crowned heads were having to endure, compared with which 'our little riots are a mere nothing' (Newsome 1998, 46).

Making ironic reference to the unseasonal climactic conditions, which had brought the communal picnicking to a quicker end, *Punch* proclaimed the 'rain of terror' to be over (Brantlinger 1977, 131). The English, a disdainful Hector Berlioz observed from across the Channel, seemed to 'know as much about starting a riot as the Italians do about writing a symphony'. Rumblings continued over the summer, a handful of leaders including O'Connor and Ernest Jones, were arrested and put on trial; the prejudicial handling of which attracted the ire of Charles Dickens. But the revolutionary moment was passed; if indeed it had ever been that much present. The argument of 'moral' as opposed to 'physical force' appeared to have triumphed.[2] Later historians have tended to presume the failure of Chartism, ascribing it variously to a failure of leadership, the lack of a clear manifesto, the indifference of the ever-burgeoning 'middling sort', the simple fact that the English working class was in fact rather conservative in temper and disinclined to violence (Thompson 1991, 176; Mather 1959, 394). Hindsight supposes that there was in truth little for middle England to worry about in the spring of 1848. But that did not stop it worrying. Those who could read German might have had particular cause for concern if they had alighted upon the first published editions of *The Communist Manifesto* which had appeared in the summer of 1848. But not many Londoners read German, fewer still read Marx.

They did, however, read lots of Carlyle, for which reason they would have known first that revolution was never more than a casual riot away and second that there were particular reasons why the Chartists kept presenting petitions. Some of these reasons were prosaic. Not enough food was perhaps the most obvious. 'I defy you to agitate a fellow with a full stomach', William Cobbett had famously observed; a sentiment shared a little later by Sir Charles Napier, who was tasked in 1839 with suppressing Chartist agitation in the north. The 'doctrine of slowly reforming when men are starving', Napier had observed, 'is of all things the most silly; famishing men cannot wait' (Royle 1996, 3; Briggs 1959, 309). Napier, like Cobbett, had probably read Thomas Malthus's *An Essay on the Principles of Population*, published in 1798, for which reason the events of 1839 would have come as little surprise. Malthus had predicted a rapidly rising population for which there would be inadequate provision. As a result, there would be either mass starvation or revolution, or both. Events suggested he might be right. So did statistics. The 1811 census revealed a national population of 12 million. Forty years later that figure was 21 million. More significantly, the bulk of this population explosion was urban. Liverpool, Leeds, Sheffield, Birmingham, Manchester; all doubled in size between 1801 and 1831. The 1861 census report concluded that the 'English nation' had 'assumed the

[2]The tension between 'moral' and 'physical' force Chartism was first identified by the contemporary historian RC Gammage. By 1848 O'Connor was a firm advocate of 'moral force' and indeed the rule of law; a reflection perhaps of his own enhanced sense of propriety as Chartist MP for Nottingham (Royle 1996, 53–56, 89, 92–93; Woodward 1962, 144–6).

character of a preponderating city population'. By 1871 62% of the population resided in cities, most living in the kind of grim tenements depicted in Engels *Working Class* and Mayhew's *London Labour*, as well as Dickens's *Oliver Twist* and Gaskell's *North and South*, and which so appalled Henry James when he first arrived in London. Half a century earlier, Robert Owen had coined the phrase 'working-class'. In 1868, the Trades Union Congress was founded.

Carlyle had certainly read Malthus, as the sombre tones of his 1829 essay *The Sign of the Times* confirmed. In the absence of good governance, he predicted, the 'condition' of England during the coming 'Mechanical Age' must prove to be an unhappy one (Carlyle 1986, 64–5, 70–2, 77). Those who read his history of the *French Revolution* closely enough would have detected the same insinuation. Edwin Paxton Hood was minded to agree and preferred the same all too familiar imagery. There was nothing to be gained by 'dreaming of Eden in the very midst of a reign of terror indeed'. 'Already', he concluded, 'we have a revolution, slumbering, but gathering power in our cities' (Briggs 1959, 449). The tone with which Carlyle duly opened his 1840 essay on *Chartism* would not, accordingly, have come as much of a surprise to Paxton Hood:

> A feeling very generally exists that the condition and disposition of the Working Classes is a rather ominous matter at present: that something ought to be said, something ought to be done, in regard to it... Chartism means the bitter discontent grown fierce and mad, the wrong condition or the wrong disposition of the Working Classes of England. (Carlyle 1986, 151)

And it was 'no answer', Carlyle confirmed, to ascribe such 'discontent' to natural circumstances, to some notion of innate brutality (Carlyle 1986, 152). Revolutions, as he had inferred time and again, not least in his *History of the French Revolution*, happen for a reason; when those who have the responsibility to govern the 'Swammery', and to feed it, neglect to do so. Arnold reached the same conclusion. The 'strong' had failed the 'weak' (Heffer 1996, 169–70, 185–6, 194–5; 2013, 18). 'Surely', Carlyle observed, 'of all "rights of man", this right of the ignorant man to be guided by the wiser, to be, gently or forcibly, held in the true course by him, is the indisputablest' (Carlyle 1986, 177, 180–1). Carlyle's rhetoric, like Atwood's in 1842, and Russell's, was intended to raise the ghosts of 1790, but not only those of 1790.

The question of Reform would not go away. The 'Great' Reform Act of 1832 was supposed to have brought 'finality'. But it had not, as we shall shortly see. Meanwhile, the likes of Dickens and Carlyle were busy scribbling away, invoking memories of the Gordon riots and the Jacobin terror. Between the pages of their various novels and essays, and so many others, there was, as Henry Crabbe Robinson averred, an irreducible 'poetical truth'; that revolution does not have an end (Dransfield 1998, 89). After all, they were still living in the same revolutionary 'age', with the same threat of insurrection, of blood running through the gutters, and men like Hugh of the Maypole charging about streets of London intent on banging heads and butchering babies. The politics of reform and the literature of revolution proved to be a potent mix in the England of the 1840s. For some it was thoroughly unsettling, for others it was a way of making a fortune.

And no one made a bigger fortune from this conjunction than Thomas Babington, later Lord, Macaulay, the first two volumes of whose epic *History of England* began to roll off the presses later that same febrile summer of 1848 when, as its author put it, the 'world' was 'convulsed by the agonies of great nations' (Hamburger 1976, 33). Except, as we shall see, that it was not really a history of England, or if it was it was only a history of a relatively small bit of it. Macaulay's vast *History* was really a history, or more accurately a hagiography, of just one event, the 'great and glorious' Revolution of 1688. Macaulay had originally conceived a history that would chronicle a century and a half. In the end, the fourteen hundred printed pages covered just sixteen years. Macaulay simply could not get past the 'glorious' revolution and its consequence. Queen Victoria once remarked of Lord Russell that he was in clear need of a 'third subject: because he was interested in nothing except the Constitution of 1688 and himself' (Hibbert 2001, 204). The same might just as easily have been said of Macaulay.

The Great Act and the Great Betrayal

Macaulay's *History* must be read as a history of three years. 1688 is the first, and perhaps most obvious. The other two are to be inferred. 1832 is the second, the year of 'finality'. The third is 1848, the year when the entire Whig narrative threatened to unravel. In due course, we will take a closer look at England in 1688, or at least Macaulay's preferred account of England in 1688. First, however, we need to revisit England in 1832, and in order to do that we need to go back a further two years. Macaulay, as we shall see, was an edifying historian, liking to spin larger his narratives around picturesque, sometimes dramatic 'moments'. He might then have approved the idea that a history of his *History* should commence in the Royal Chambers at Windsor in June 1830, where King George IV was entering his final days. Quite how Swellfoot the Tyrant, as Percy Shelley famously ridiculed the grotesque former Prince Regent, had survived so long was something of a mystery. A few weeks before the end, the Duchess of Gloucester reported that the King had 'become enormous, like a feather bed', his legs 'also swollen, are as hard as stone: his face is drawn and his features pinched, and he has attacks of choking' (Smith 1999, 269–70). The decline had been evident for some time. Agonising gout swelled the royal foot. Draining it was not much fun. Neither was getting dressed. Lacing the royal torso took three hours, most of which had to be endured standing. Breathing had become ever more difficult. A lifetime of over-indulgence had its price. The Duke of Wellington further mused on the wisdom of taking 250 drops of laudanum a day. George's long-suffering mistress, Maria Fitzherbert, suspected that much was in the mind. The King, she observed, 'always liked to make himself out worse than he was to excite compassion' (Smith 1999, 269). Laudanum, hypochondria and too much cake and port; all it seemed had played their part. George, however, blamed something else, the associated stresses which accompanied the passage, a year earlier, of the Roman Catholic Relief Act.

The end, when it finally came in the early hours of the 26th, was a pivotal moment in English constitutional history; although it did not immediately seem that way. Wellington said a few bland words in Parliament. Sir Walter Scott attested to George's 'kindness' and 'good breeding'. The editor of *The Times*, conversely, took the opportunity for a final castigation of the late King's 'most reckless, unceasing and unbounded prodigality' (Smith 1999, 272–3). But no one seemed to compass any larger implications. As was customary on the death of a monarch, a general election was held, at which a Tory majority was returned to the Commons. The new king, William IV, invited Wellington to form a government. The Duke accepted and set about drawing up his defensive lines. For much of the summer, England had been agitated by the prospect of reform. Political Unions had sprung up in the rapidly growing urban conurbations, the most famous and most agitated of which was Thomas Attwood's Birmingham Union.

Petitions flooded into Westminster, not from starving peasants, but from those such as the 'bankers, merchants, manufacturers and others' of the city of Leeds (Cannon 1973, 189). They wanted the vote. Wellington was sensitive to the occasion. But he was not sympathetic to the cause. 'Beginning Reform is beginning Revolution', he informed Mrs Arbuthnot; a view he was happy to reiterate in the House. Reform 'will date the downfall of the Constitution'. 'I am fully convinced that the country possesses at the present moment a Legislature which answers all the good purposes of legislation, and this to a greater degree than any Legislature ever has answered in any country whatever', the Duke concluded in tones that might have earned the approval of many a wavering Whig (Hibbert 1997, 289).

The Duke's lines were not however as resilient in 1830 as they had been fifteen years earlier on the fields of Waterloo. Days later a vote of confidence was lost, and the Duke tendered his resignation; too many 'commanders', not enough 'troops' (Hibbert 1997, 296). With a marked reluctance, William called on the leader of the Whigs, Lord Grey, to form an administration. Grey accepted. He was not by temperament much of a radical. Reform was a matter of 'limitation' not 'extension', he sought to reassure the House. He had 'never urged the question of reform on the principle of abstract right', certainly not with 'a view to universal suffrage', something that was 'incompatible' with the 'right of the people' to have 'good government' (Smith 1990, 257). There was, however, a 'public expectation' to manage, and it was his responsibility to manage it (Briggs 1959, 239; Mandler 1990, 71–2, 125–6). Lord Russell introduced a Reform Bill on 22 March 1831. Tory opposition remained fierce. Sir Robert Peel was scathing. The role of Parliament was 'to consult the interests of the people'. It was 'not to obey the will of the people' (Hawkins 1989, 652). The bill, according to Sir Robert Inglis, betokened a 'revolution that will overturn all the natural influence of rank and property' (Briggs 1959, 241). Goulburn likewise recoiled from the prospect of 'unrestrained democracy' (Gash 1965, 153). Wellington trundled round the corridors of Westminster muttering darkly about levellers and Jacobins and the attendant horrors that must follow if dukes of the realm were obliged to listen to the opinions of 'the blacksmith, the carpenter, the mason' (Bentley 1996, 93).

A few days after its introduction Russell's Bill passed its second reading in the Commons by just one vote; 302 to 301. Macaulay recorded a 'shout that you might have heard to Charing Cross', gleefully observing that the faces of Peel and his colleagues on the opposition benches resembled those of the collective 'damned' (Cannon 1973, 218). Tory strategists had been confounded by the defection of one MP in the very final minutes of the division. Shortly after, as expected, Grey lost a procedural vote and consequently went to Buckingham Palace to demand the dissolution of Parliament. The Tory party was duly slaughtered at the ensuing election, left with a mere 187 Members. A revised second bill was presented to Parliament in July 1831, this time passing its second reading by a more comfortable majority of 367 votes to 231. It arrived at a patently hostile House of Lords just over a month later, at which point Macaulay, serving as Grey's chief propagandist, chose to raise a familiar, if chilling, spectre: 'have they ever seen the ruins of those castles whose terraces and gardens overhang the Loire?' (Cannon 1973, 224). If they had their Lordships were undaunted. Responding to the pleadings of the collected Lords Spiritual, the House rejected the bill by forty-one votes; an 'honourable and manly decision' a young Gladstone observed approvingly (Cannon 1973, 225). A placard was posted on Bond Street. It read '199 versus 22,000,000'. Russell loudly questioned whether the 'whisper of a faction should prevail against the voice of a nation' (Briggs 1959, 252). The Radical *Poor Man's Guardian* predicted the likely consequences if the 'peasantry of England' was allowed to remain in a state of 'sullen discontent' (Briggs 1959, 250). Riots broke out; 'something very like Jacobinism' the Whig Home Secretary Lord Melbourne observed (Mitchell 1997, 120). The Duke of Newcastle's residence at Nottingham Castle was set on fire. Peel stockpiled arms at his beloved Drayton Manor. The Birmingham Political Union resolved to withhold taxes until the Bill passed.

A third bill was introduced in the Commons in December 1831. By May it was back in the Lords.[3] On this occasion it was another of Grey's parliamentary henchman who twisted their Lordships' tail, wondering how many of those who shared Peel's apparently fragile sense of security were prepared to retreat indefinitely to 'your mansions fortified with canon' (Cannon 1973, 232). You cannot legislate against 'broken windows', Melbourne informed an evidently anxious Duke of Buckingham;

[3] The amendments relating largely to the selection of boroughs included in the second schedule, which were to have the number of MPs adjusted in line with demographic changes. Russell reprieved a number of Tory boroughs, which would now lose only one member, whilst also granting second seats to a number of others.

who had probably assumed, reasonably enough, that the common law was written precisely so as to preserve the integrity of ducal windows (Mitchell 1997, 129). 'Reform or Revolution is the cry of every man who deserves the name of Englishman', proclaimed *The Despatch*, 'The idea of twenty-four millions of free men submitting to a denial of their undoubted rights by less than two hundred beings called peers, is utterly out of the question' (Royle 2000, 74). The Duke of Wellington's card was certainly marked. To 'stop the Duke, go for gold' was the cry heard in the streets of Birmingham and Leeds and much of the rest of the country during the frenetic 'days of May' as the Lords contemplated the possible consequences of rejecting the bill for a third time. In the space of less than a week, the Bank of England was brought to its knees as investors withdrew £1.5 million in protest. If reform was a popular measure in 1832, it was, as Grey readily appreciated and Albert Venn Dicey rather later agreed, most popular amongst the 'middle classes' (Cannon 1973, 245; Dicey 1914, 185). The Reform Act was their act, intended as Lord Brougham confirmed, to admit the 'wealth and intelligence of the country, the glory of the British name' (Newsome 1998, 64). Lord Russell concurred. The Act was written for the benefit of 'men of property and intelligence', not those of 'low passions' (Cannon 1973, 208). So did Lord Melbourne who, in characteristically pithy terms, calculated that the franchise had been extended just far enough to encompass those who took the *Morning Chronicle* (Aldous 2007, 25).

Of course, rather more had been proposed, and lost; the idea of a secret ballot, vigorously supported by John Stuart Mill in the pages of the *Westminster Review*, was sacrificed, to the chagrin of relatively few others. It would have to wait until 1872. In the end, the 1832 Act introduced a complex franchise which saw an estimated increase in the electorate of around 70–80%, but which still left 95% of the population without a vote. There were of course no women voters, the Act exclusively directing itself to 'male persons'. The provisions of the Act extended the franchise to all £10 householders in the boroughs, together with 40 shilling freeholders in the counties, copyholders worth £10 and leaseholders worth either £50 or £10 depending on the length of tenure. The so-called Chandos clause also gave the vote to tenants-at-will paying £50. The number of MPs meanwhile was unchanged at 658. But four schedules contained details of various adjustments in constituency representation designed to address the most rotten of rotten boroughs and most blatant of electoral abuses. In all 143 boroughs were disenfranchised, including 56 of the most notorious nomination or 'rotten' boroughs. The 'Accursed Hill' of Old Sarum, which had attracted William Cobbett's ire in his *Rural Rides* was amongst those to go. And the sole elector of Higham Ferrer was obliged to contemplate a future in which he would be exercising his suffrage in the company of at least a few more. And in their place came 135 new constituencies carved out of cities such as Birmingham, Manchester and Leeds, as well as fast-growing textile towns such as Oldham and Stockport.

In a sense, however, it was not the provisions that really mattered. Rather, as Sidonia observed in Disraeli's *Coningsby*, it was 'the means by which that Bill was carried'. When push came to shove, the Prime Minister had made the King tell his Lords to do it. William IV was entirely opposed to the idea of reform, but his options were diminishing. He had not wanted to dissolve Parliament in April 1831 at Grey's behest. But he had. And he was appalled at Grey's subsequent suggestion, bolstered by his success in the ensuing election, that he should wield his prerogative to bully the recalcitrant upper House. Grey proposed that the King might elevate, or threaten to elevate, up to a hundred new Whig peers; a number which the King found 'very distressing'.[4] But he agreed all the same; the threat was made. And he was far from thrilled at having to give his royal assent on June 7th. But he did, not in tears as was the case when his predecessor George IV had signed the Catholic Emancipation Act, but rather pointedly *in absentia*. In matters of high politics monarchs still mattered. But they did not matter quite so much, or in quite the same way. We will take a closer look at the changing shape of monarchy, and its constitutional implications, in the next chapter.

The soubriquet which attaches to the 'great' Reform Act of 1832 is, of course, as much a testament to its symbolic as to its substantive importance. It 'set men athinking' as Disraeli observed (Aldous 2007, 25). Erskine May, writing in 1861, likened the 1832 Act to the Bill of Rights in these terms and suggested that it 'conferred immortal honour on the statesmen who had the wisdom to conceive it' (Erskine May 1861, 1.357). Coke of Holkham, whose family had been Whig for centuries, erected a bas-relief in his house depicting William IV in the guise of King John surrounded by an array of Whig nobles dressed up as the barons

[4] In a moment of panic, William asked Wellington to see if he could form an alternative Tory administration. He could not (Cannon 1973, 230–1, 234; Smith 1990, 268–77).

of Runnymede. Not that all Whig statesmen were especially enthused, or that many in truth. Lord Melbourne later informed his new Queen that the Act was regrettable but 'unavoidable'. In private he harboured greater doubts. 'If it was not absolutely necessary', he reflected, 'it was the foolishest thing ever done' (Parry 1993, 112; Cannon 1973, 251). Grey of course had deployed this same imperative defence. He barely convinced himself, later in his 1834 resignation speech wondering aloud if his administration may have 'done rather too much'. The essence of Whiggery, as he reminded his son, was to preclude anything that was 'sudden' or 'sweeping'. Whiggery was a 'gradual' politics, and an intensely conservative one. Whigs did not embrace change. Nor did they embrace the people, figuratively or physically. Lord Grey found the mere presence of ordinary people entirely 'odious' (Smith 1990, 141, 306, 326). The grandest of Whig matriarchs Lady Spencer likewise expressed a glorious disgust at the prospect of her sons 'clasping dirty palms' in order to recruit potential supporters, a general 'toadying to our Sovereign people' (Bentley 1996, 45, 147).

Tory horror was more predictable still; not least at the prospect that the 1832 Act might herald an 'age of reform'. As we have already noted the young Disraeli penned a series of highly personalised attacks directed towards the 'desperate and long-baffled oligarchy' which had proved itself 'ready to sacrifice' the 'laws, the empire and the religion of England' in order to retain 'possession of a power to which they are incompetent' (Hutcheon 1913, 323). 'No doubt', Peel had chastised his Whig opponents in the Commons, 'your' Act might gain some transient 'popularity', but 'these are vulgar arts of government; others will outbid you, not now, but at no remote period' (Cannon 1973, 215). It was of course Peel who reacted quickest to the demands of vulgarity, in his Tamworth Manifesto inviting conversation with the 'intelligent class' in a 'sprit' of good 'intentions' and 'friendly temper' (Gash 1965, 122–3, 139–40; Brantlinger 1977, 5). When it was all done, the Tory ultra JW Croker felt moved to apologise to an entire continent for the venality of his fellow Members. 'We are now become a fire-ship, which will spread the conflagration' he confessed (Cannon 1973, 240). Far away on the other side of this continent, Tsar Nicholas assumed that the fire which engulfed the Palace of Westminster in 1834 was evidence of God's displeasure. Carlyle assumed a tone that was only marginally less apocalyptic. What must follow reform, he mused, 'Revolution on the back of Revolution for a century yet?' (Frye 1997, 84).

The Act, as Carlyle well knew, was justified in precisely these terms; as an expression of those revolution 'principles' which Whig historians so dearly cherished. The 'great' Act of 1832 was preordained by the 'great and glorious' Revolution of 1688; or at least so Grey and his parliamentary propagandists managed to persuade enough of their wary colleagues. There were of course more prosaic considerations. Avoiding a more violent 'convulsion' was one, as Grey reminded one dithering colleague in the heady 'days of May'; for 'without some such concessions the change alluded to will lead rapidly to republicanism and the destruction of established institutions'. On a rather brighter note, he further insinuated, if done properly reform might secure Whig government for generations to come (Cannon 1973, 250–1; Mandler 1990, 38–9). Those who trundled however reluctantly through respective lobbies in support of successive draft bills in the spring and summer of 1831 and then again in spring 1832 did so in equal part because they were persuaded that it would vitiate the need for any subsequent reform. The Committee which Grey had established to explore the question of reform in the winter of 1830–1831 was specifically instructed 'to afford sure ground of resistance to further innovation' (Cannon 1973, 204). Macaulay, as we shall see, argued in these terms. So did Lord Russell. In 1819 mere talk of reform was dangerous as it filled 'the minds of the people with vague and indefinite alarms' (Woodward 1962, 27). By 1832, however, Russell was converted, consoling himself with the thought that the Reform Bill would bring the process began a century and a half before to 'finality'. Sceptical Tories clung to the same delusion. Peel's Tamworth Manifesto referred to a 'final and irrevocable settlement of a great constitutional question' (Briggs 1959, 273).

For a moment it seemed that they might be right. But it was a very brief moment. Four Whig administrations came and went in the five years that followed the passage of the 1832 Act. Parliament appeared so shattered that it was barely capable of functioning. Lord Beauvale wondered if the 'country's mad fit' was 'passed'. It was not. The 'public appetite for discussion and legislation', as Greville feared, had been 'whetted' (Mandler 1990, 151). Radical journals took to ridiculing 'little John' Russell and the 'Whiglings'. Patience began to run out. A less welcome myth was born, that of the 'great Whig betrayal' (Royle 2000, 97). There remained, as even Peel recognised, 'practical grievances' (Mather 1959, 402). In 1843 readers of the *Times* were regaled with accounts of radical and free traders holding rallies at the Drury Lane theatre, attended by 'maids and matrons' as well as the more familiar 'Cant and Cotton men' (Briggs 1959, 318). Three years later, following the passage of the statute which repealed the Corn Laws, and broke Peel's Tory Party, one of the leaders of the more notorious of the 'Cotton men', Richard Cobden, wrote a consoling letter to the outgoing Prime Minister. Politics, he observed, had changed irrevocably, the 'Reform bill decreed it; the passing of the Corn Bill has realized it' (Briggs 1959, 324–5). The Chartist *Northern Echo* agreed. Peel's 1846 Act 'enshrined the remains of Whiggery' (Gaunt 2010, 125). The allusion was not meant to flatter.

If a genetic line might be traced between the events of 1846 and 1832, so too might it be traced a little further back still. As his fellow peers nervously awaited the new bill in late 1831, Lord Falmouth wondered on 'what principle will you talk of preserving the tree of the constitution, when you have laid your axe to the root?' (Cannon 1973, 191–2) The allusion was to the Catholic Relief Act which had been placed before a distraught Swellfoot in 1829. Of course, Whig historians commonly preferred rather longer narratives. Macaulay went back to the late sixteenth century, to the later Elizabethan anti-monopolists. Others though went much further back. Edward Freeman supposed that Earl Godwin might have been the first Whig. Acton identified the origins of Whig constitutionalism in the writings of Aquinas. Tracing the origins of Whiggery was never easy, not least because there were so many variants, none of which were easily distinguishable; Ciceronian Whigs, Court Whigs and Country Whigs, Radical Whigs, sceptical Whig and 'vulgar' Whigs, to name but some. To an extent, the distinctions did not translate into any significant political disaggregation, at least not for most of the eighteenth century. The important thing was that the leading Whig families continued to dine together and marry each other. Having a 'party', Lady Palmerston once observed, was the surest way of securing a parliamentary majority (Halperin 1977, 218). And for much of the previous century, this was precisely how successive Whig administrations had governed; occasionally at Westminster, but more commonly at Brook's and Bowood and Holland House, the natural habitats of 'Grand Whiggery'.

The age of 'Grand Whiggery' was however passing, and deep down Macaulay knew it. 1832 had not brought 'finality', and Disraeli was busy sequestering Burke as the sage of his new Tory party. The days when England might be ruled by men Lord Melbourne, part-time and between mistresses, was passing. Being Prime Minister, Melbourne once opined, was nothing more than a 'damned bore', a constant struggle to ameliorate between men who seem to 'hate each other so damnably' (Mandler 1990, 105; Briggs 1959, 272; Gash 1965, 128). He would have preferred to retire to his estates, but his family was destined to rule, so he was stuck. Lord Grey felt much the same way, frequently having to be cajoled from his distant Northumbrian estates in order to pass Reform statutes and actually run the country. In 1847 Lord Normanby concluded that the Whig party was 'dying out rapidly' (Mandler 1990, 269). The Duke of Newcastle wondered if it would not be better if they renamed themselves the 'conservative liberal' party (Burrow 1988, 12). They would, but not just yet. There was, as we shall see, one last Whig administration to come and go. And in the meantime, there was history to be rewritten.

The Romance of History

It is said that only one publication in nineteenth-century England outsold Macaulay's *History of England*; the Bible (Sullivan 2009, 1; Knowles 1960, 4). The Victorians as we have already noted liked their history, and Macaulay wrote well. But there was a further reason why the *History* was such a success. 'All is quiet in appearance', a wary Macaulay observed in the spring of 1848, 'But yet, I feel, I fear' (Hamburger 1976, 47, 115–6, 123). So did his readers. They craved reassurance, and Macaulay wrote his *History* to precisely this aspiration. As its prefatory 'declaration' of 'purpose' confirmed, it was intended to 'excite' above all a sense of 'thankfulness' amongst its readers (Macaulay 1986, 52). Amongst the many things which his *History* would show was 'how, under the 'great' settlement' of 1688–1690, 'the authority of law and the security of property were found to be compatible with a liberty of discussion and of individual action never before known'. It was from this particular moment and this particular settlement that the progressive 'prosperity' of England 'sprang' (Macaulay 1986, 51).

And it was because England had already had such a 'glorious' revolution that it did not need another. This did not preclude change. As Charles James Fox had famously declared back in the heady days of 1792, 'the greatest innovation that could be introduced into the Constitution of England was to come to a vote that there shall be no innovation in it' (Briggs 1959, 110). Instead, there was reform. Macaulay, as we have already noted, spoke loudly in support of reform;

not because he favoured democracy, but because he dreaded it, 'the restless and turbid hopes of those who have everything to gain, the dimly-hinted forebodings of those who have everything to lose' (Macaulay 1828, 168). The purpose of a Reform Act, Macaulay had written in anticipation of 1832, was 'to soothe the public mind', to 'avert civil discord, and to uphold the authority of the law', for the 'healing of great distempers'; in short to 'reform that we may preserve' (Macaulay 1828, 168–9). The same was true of the *History*. Macaulay's rhetorical strategy was much the same as Burke's in its essentials, mounting its assault on two fronts; one emotional, the other intellectual and constitutional. On the one hand, there was fear:

> The danger is terrible. The time is short. If this bill is rejected, I pray to God, that none of those who concur in rejecting it may ever remember their votes with unavailing regret, amidst the wreck of laws, the confusions of ranks, the spoliation of property, and the dissolution of social order. (Cannon 1973, 216)

On the other hand was the countervailing reassurance of history. Macaulay revisited the familiar Whig argument; the 1832 Act would reform and thereby reinvest the 'glorious' Revolution of 1688. 'To the Whigs of the seventeenth century we owe it that we have a House of Commons', the electors of Edinburgh were informed in 1839, 'To the Whigs of the nineteenth century we owe it that the House of Commons has been purified' (Firth 1938, 260). The *History* would confirm the same. The Act 'brought Parliament into harmony with the nation' in much the same way as the 1688 Revolution had 'brought the Crown into harmony with the Parliament'. There was 'in the whole history of England, no prouder circumstance' than the passage of the Act, reflecting as it did, not just the security of a constitutional settlement, but also the 'moderation' and 'humanity' of a people (Macaulay 1832, 563).

Macaulay would later serve in Melbourne's 1839 administration as Secretary of State for War. His primary responsibility however between 1832 and 1848 was to serve as champion of the 'reforming' Whigs and their 'Great' Act. 'Time after time', James Grant attested in his 1836 *Recollections of the House of Commons*, 'the House listened to him as if entranced' (Hamburger 1976, 156). His services came at a price. Lord Melbourne, not by temperament the kind of Whig who appreciated a lecture on the finer points of constitutional propriety, dreaded Macaulay's appearance in Cabinet. He would, he later confessed, ‘prefer to sit in a Room with a Chime of Bells, ten Parrots and one Lady Westmorland to sitting in Cabinet with Mr Macaulay’ (Mitchell 1997, 92). Macaulay was however necessary, his support in the Commons for the 1832 Act critical. As to what kind of Whig, Macaulay liked to identify himself as a ‘trimmer’. He was certainly keen to distance himself from any presumed affinity with the Radicals. Macaulay maintained a visceral distrust of the mob, the ‘human vermin’, informing Parliament that if the demands of the Chartists were ever met the ‘country’ would undoubtedly be ‘lost’ (Sullivan 2009, 236–8). The 1832 Act had been passed precisely to preclude any further ‘grant’ of electoral power, hopefully distracting about 250,000 of those who might otherwise have been tempted to wander along to a local Chartist meeting. At the same time, this did not mean that Macaulay was a reactionary Whig (Sullivan 2009, 53). Constitutions evolved, but they did so slowly. Macaulay’s Whiggism was moderate, innately conservative, essentially practical, and for precisely these reasons reflective of the political opinion of the majority of his countrymen. There was nothing, in the final analysis, particularly great about the ‘Great’ Reform Act, just as there was nothing that grand about Russell’s ‘Grand Whigs’. And deep down Macaulay knew it.

In terms of enfranchisement, except for the 250,000, the significance of the Act was largely symbolic. Constituency reform had a variable impact. For some MPs it meant little. For others, it was thoroughly inconvenient. Macaulay, ironically, was one of the more inconvenienced. He had been the MP for the pocket borough of Calne, in the gift of his friend Lord Landsdowne. They got on well. But then Calne vanished from the electoral map, and Macaulay found himself successively representing the voters of Leeds and then from 1838 Edinburgh. Both proved to be rather more capricious, the latter especially so as Macaulay discovered in 1847. Disapproving his support for the Maynooth grant the gentlemen of Edinburgh disinclined to re-elect their esteemed representative. In rather churlish tones Macaulay wondered, in an open letter, how he had ‘incurred your displeasure’ notwithstanding his unarguable commitment to the ‘fundamental principles of the Constitution’ (Edwards 1988, 44). But he had, momentarily at least. A peeved Macaulay returned to the drafts of his projected *History*, begun a decade before. Five years later he was back in favour and back in the Commons as MP for Edinburgh, the celebrated author of the now published *History of England* evidently forgiven his earlier transgression.

For the previous twenty years, Macaulay had written almost exclusively for the Whig *journal de combat*, the *Edinburgh Review*. But the audience and the ambition was now all the greater. 'Cocksure Tom' intended to re-write the history of England, and not just for his Whig friends and patrons, but for the enlightenment of the entire nation.[5] It was certainly intended to be a big history, no 'less than an entire view of all the transactions which took place between the revolution which brought the Crown in harmony with the parliament and the revolution which brought parliament into harmony with the nation', or so Macaulay envisaged when he set off sketching the first volumes in 1838 (Sullivan 2009, 190–1). Most importantly of course it would also be a Whig history, a necessary corollary of which would be a pointed rebuttal of those 'Court' histories which had seduced so many eighteenth-century Tory gentlemen. Prominent amongst these was David Hume's six-volume *History of England*. Whilst Hume had likewise made much of the 'revolution' of 1688, the suggestion that the constitutional settlement which followed owed more to the calming offices of Church and Crown cast an unacceptable aspersion. The Hanoverians had not secured the constitution; the constitution had secured the Hanoverians. Macaulay admired some Tory writers, including the poet Southey. But he took serious issue with Hume, as was evidenced in his earlier essay on Hallam's *Constitutional History of England*. He was obliged to deal judiciously with Hallam, indisputably Whig and thoroughly Burkean in his reverence for the 'wisdom of our ancestors' (Lang 1995, 47–51). But Hallam had not much liked reform in 1832, suggesting that it smacked rather more of 1640 than 1689, and he had displayed rather too much deference to Hume. Macaulay was determined to validate 1832 as a reform cast in the mould set a hundred and forty years earlier; and in this, as the German historian Ranke would later attest in 1875, his 'victory' would be total (Firth 1938, 15).

For obvious reasons, he had to be equally judicious in regard to Burke too. Whilst at times Macaulay was evidently troubled by the sheer force of Burke's passion, he was still 'the greatest man since Milton'. The power of Carlyle's *History of the French Revolution* could not be denied. But it was still to Burke's chronicle that gentlemen of a Whiggish disposition turned. Both were terrifying in their respective ways. The

[5]The epithet 'cocksure' appears to have been first bestowed on Macaulay by Lord Melbourne (Firth 1938, 54).

revolution found in Burke's *Reflections*, Macaulay reminded readers of the *Edinburgh Review* in the spring of 1832, was 'the most horrible event recorded in history', a signal warning of what might happen if reform was to fail (Macaulay 1832, 560). The difference was that ultimately Burke reassured; Carlyle did not. In his 1841 essay on Hastings Macaulay declared his visceral admiration for Burke, a 'man in whom compassion for suffering, and hatred of injustice and tyranny, were as strong as in Las Casas or Clarkson' (Macaulay 1841, 232; Sullivan 2009, 301–2). Burke, Macaulay averred, should be read like Thucydides, as an artist stimulating the 'imagination'. Sadly, as Macaulay had already observed, the present generation of historians now 'miserably neglect' the Burkean 'art of narration, the art of interesting the affections and presenting pictures to the imagination' (Macaulay 1828, 96, 331, 336–9, 361; Knowles 1960, 12–13; Sullivan 2009, 140).

For equally understandable reasons Macaulay also preferred Burke to his contemporary Jeremy Bentham. He did not dismiss Bentham's significance as the 'father of jurisprudence', the man who found the law a 'gibberish, and left it a science' (Macaulay 1832, 553). But he was far too much the romantic to be persuaded by the march of utility, still less the apparent affinity of utility and radicalism; as readers of his various *Edinburgh Review* essays were time and again reminded. Like Burke, Macaulay shared a visceral distrust of metaphysical 'cant' of whatever variety. The attempt to turn the study of economics into a 'science' was an 'object of disgust to the majority of the community', and the same fate would befall 'reform' if it was sequestered by the Benthamites (Macaulay 1829, 177–80; 1832, 559; Sullivan 2009, 52) The great mistake of men like Mill was to presume a generality of human nature on such deductive speculation, deploying 'sleight of tongue' and 'abject sophisms' in place of historical insight. It is, Macaulay affirmed, 'utterly impossible to deduce the science of government from the principles of human nature' (Macaulay 1829, 185). In his essay on Mirabeau, Macaulay reiterated Burke's conclusion, that the French revolution was violent precisely because it was animated by 'speculators' (Macaulay 1832, 572–3). The alternative to the 'cant' of speculative 'deduction' is the science of historical or philosophical 'induction'. The great philosopher of induction was Francis Bacon. Engaging the more immediately political consequences, Macaulay suggested that the 'latent principle of good government ought to be tracked, as it appears to us, in the same manner as Lord Bacon proposed to track the principle of Heat'.

'Our creed', he concluded, 'is, that the science of government is an experimental science, and that, like all other experimental sciences, it is generally in a state of progression' (Macaulay 1829, 101).

Macaulay wanted to be accounted a 'philosophical historian' like Bacon, one whose narratives 'began in observations and ended in arts' (Macaulay 1837, 80). At the same time, however, his history was different again, for alongside Burke and Bacon loomed the equally considerable presence of Sir Walter Scott. Scott was the most successful writer of his generation, and Macaulay was again an avowed admirer. His 1842 *Lays of Rome* was clearly indebted. It was, Macaulay had argued in his Hallam essay, the responsibility of the historian to 'reclaim those materials which the novelist' such as Scott had 'appropriated' (Macaulay 1828, 97). He must embrace the 'affecting and picturesque', to 'intersperse the details' of his history with 'the charm of historical romances' (Macaulay 1828, 331, 365). The 'past in my mind', he would again confirm in testamentary tones, 'is soon constructed into a romance'; for which reason he was never averse to deploying the likes of Dryden, Addison or Swift, even Laurence Sterne as historical authorities (Levine 1968, 100). There is, as later critics have noted, a distinctly Hogarthian sensibility in Macaulay's historical writing (Burrow 2007, 372–3). Charles Firth later concluded that Macaulay appeared to have gleaned his appreciation of the military campaigns of William III from nothing more elevated than *Tristram Shandy* (Firth 1938, 109–10). 'Facts' on the other hand 'are the mere dross of history'. It is not facts that the historian must excavate, but the 'gold in the ore' (Macaulay 1828, 340). Revisiting the metaphor in his Hallam essay Macaulay averred that 'History, at least in its ideal perfection, is a compound of poetry and philosophy' (Macaulay 1828, 96).

Macaulay determined that his history would be painted in variegated tones; a layered history of sweeping narrative, grand set-pieces and intimate anecdote. 'The perfect historian', the young Macaulay observed in his 1828 essay 'is he in whose work the character and spirit of an age is exhibited in miniature', in pictures of 'ordinary men as they appear in their ordinary business and in their ordinary pleasures' (Macaulay 1828, 364; Plumb 1963, 265–6). In his review of Macaulay's *History*, Walter Bagehot admired precisely this ability to reveal the 'nation' alongside the 'court, the camp, the senate', as well as the 'anecdote' which might, to other historians, have seemed too 'insignificant' (Bagehot 1965, 414). Time again, in his essays and in his *History*, Macaulay would transport his readers to a place in the past, perhaps magnificent, perhaps intimate, where they might like Adam Smith's famed 'judicious spectator' be guided, ever so gently, to reach a 'judgment of events and men'. 'The poet', he averred, should always try to 'place his readers, as nearly as possible, in the situation of the sufferers or the spectators' (Macaulay 1828, 97). They must be made to 'mingle in the crowds of the exchange and the coffee-house' (Macaulay 1828, 364). No historian, as Bagehot again appraised, had ever mastered the art of 'spectacle' as well as Macaulay. Thus in his essay on Milton, Macaulay opened with an image of the poet sat in his 'small lodging' with a 'quick twinkle in his eyes'. It might seem a little 'foolish', as Macaulay confessed (Macaulay 1825, 339–40). But it was also brilliant.

There was, of course, a price to pay as Macaulay had acknowledged in his 1828 *Essay on History*:

> History cannot be perfectly and absolutely true… No picture then and no history, can present us with the whole truth: but those are the best pictures and the best histories which exhibit such parts of the truth as most nearly produce the effect of the whole. (Macaulay 1828, 338)

It was not an admission which would sit comfortably with later critics, or later historians. Chapter eleven of Firth's *Commentary* is simply entitled 'Macaulay's Errors'. It is not short. But such criticisms did not, rather too obviously for some, appear to bother Macaulay that much at the time. He would later acknowledge a difference between the 'flippant' license which might be accorded the essayist and the more sober responsibilities of the writer of epic history. The 'natural life' of an essay, he once observed, was no more than 'six weeks' (Edwards 1988, 90, 93). The *History of England*, in contrast, was intended to educate generations to come. Macaulay never suggested that history should ever abandon the faculty of reason. But neither should it allow itself to be 'seduced' by metaphysics or utility, and thus reduced to 'dross', for which reason he 'cheerfully' admitted in the Preface to the *History* that his 'narrative' might when reason demanded descend below the customary 'dignity of history' (Macaulay 1986, 53). It would be evocative, romantic in the sense that Scott was romantic, and above all entertaining. The 'talent which is required to write history thus', Macaulay confirmed, 'bears a considerable affinity to the talent of the great dramatist' (Macaulay 1828, 351).

A Peculiar Revolution

One of the most immediately striking features of Macaulay's *History of England* is the presence of the law and the constitution. As we have already noted, the opening lines of the *History* had sought to reassure readers in terms of political and constitutional certainty. The English were 'saved', at least from further revolution, precisely because they already had a judicious 'settlement' (Macaulay 1986, 51). The younger Macaulay had already mined the earlier decades of the seventeenth century in order to excavate the foundations of this settlement. Like so many of his contemporaries, he was fascinated by the English civil war, thrilled by the romantic engagement of cavalier and roundhead, just as puzzled by the necessary ambiguities collected in the figure of Oliver Cromwell. Accordingly when Macaulay contemplated the events of 1688–1690, it was hardly surprising that he did so in jurisprudential terms. He had of course already written on the 'revolution' of 1688, most notably in his Hallam essay where he had concluded that it was 'assuredly, a happy revolution, and a useful revolution; but it was not, what it has been called, a glorious revolution' (Macaulay 1828, 159). The tone might have seemed rather deflating. But Macaulay, as we shall see, put a lot of stock on what was useful, still more perhaps on what made his readers happy. The *History* is not, of course, wholly about law and the constitution. But each page that Macaulay wrote was intended to reaffirm the historical legitimacy of the constitution which would find an eventual and seemingly definitive statement in the 1701 Act of Settlement; and to refine popular perceptions about what constitutions were for too. Constitutions are 'not power', but they are the 'symbols of power'; an insight which was as distinctly Burkean as it should have been already familiar, at least to those gentlemen whose tutors had properly appreciated that Burke on the consequence of 1790 was rather more valuable than Hobbes on the consequence of 1642 (Macaulay 1829, 110).

Macaulay's sweeping narrative is built around a series of often familiar set-piece events, a mixture of parliamentary speeches, wars, conspiracies and trials. As such legal and constitutional commentary can be found scattered about the narrative, assuming an evidently greater presence in certain of these set-pieces; three in particular. The first is the serial abuse of judicial process instigated by Lord Chief Justice Jeffreys. Critics have long noted that Macaulay was happier narrating events than he was contemplating human complexity. Bagehot wanted to 'love and hate'.

But Macaulay did not do love and hate; just heroic and evil, right and wrong (Bagehot 1965, 427). His Jeffreys, plainly evil and plainly wrong, assumes a demeanour of melodramatic familiarity, a man of 'insolence' and 'angry passions', heartless and brutal, but perhaps most significantly, the arch-corrupter of the constitution (Macaulay 1986, 74–7, 117–21). Firth would later suggest that a lot of Macaulay's Jeffreys was drawn from the necessarily unreliable accounts of contemporary caricaturists. The aspersion is quite credible. But it is doubtful whether it would have bothered Macaulay too much. What mattered was the grander drama in which Jeffreys must play his part. It is he who, assuming the classic guise of the evil counsellor, advises the new King James II within 'not many hours' of his ascending the throne, to rule by 'edict'; a strategy only too resonant of that preferred by his father and his similarly perfidious advisers (Macaulay 1986, 77). Possessed of the worst kind of legal mind, one of cunning and 'sophistry', Jeffreys's propensity to judicial corruption crosses a critical constitutional boundary when he 'obtained a seat in Cabinet and a peerage', for 'since the judicial system of the realm had been remodelled in the thirteenth century, no Chief Justice had been a Lord in Parliament' (Macaulay 1986, 77). It might seem to be a narrow constitutional point, but to a historian writing in the classical Whig tradition any infringement of the doctrine of separate powers assumed altogether greater significance. As it would any historian writing in the tradition of Algernon Sidney whose 'judicial murder' is also attributed to Jeffrey's corruption (Macaulay 1986, 77).

Jeffreys assumes an increasingly demonic theatricality as Macaulay's narrative moves forward to the failed Monmouth rebellion, and the 'Bloody Assizes' over which the Chief Justice subsequently presided. In tones which would again have resonated with any Burkean devotee, Macaulay wrote:

> The Chief Justice was all himself. His spirits rose higher and higher as the work went on. He laughed, shouted, joked, and swore in such a way that many thought him drunk from morning to night. But in him it was not easy to distinguish the madness produced by evil passions from the madness produced by brandy. (Macaulay 1986, 123)

The maniacal laughter recurs throughout the narrative. A little later the reader is informed that he employed a 'crew of parasites' in order to extort money from the relatives of those convicted, demented minions who shared the same liking for 'drinking and laughing' (Macaulay 1986, 126). Dragged before Satan in his hellish scarlet-draped Assizes, men and women could be literally terrified to death. Alice Lisle however, whose trial had been long sanctified in Whig hagiography, was made of sterner stuff. Lady Alice, the reader is informed, fell victim to the 'disgraceful' inconsistencies of the law relating to 'principal and accessory', convicted and beheaded for the 'noble and benevolent' crime of giving a desperate man a 'morsel of bread'. A 'wise and good' magistrate would have punished her 'tenderly' (Macaulay 1986, 118–9). Jeffreys did not, and having 'strained' the law 'for the purpose of destroying Alice Lisle' then moved on to enact a roaming 'judicial massacre' across the rest of south-west England (Macaulay 1986, 120–2). Subsequent historians have cast doubt on various parts of Macaulay's narrative, not least the statistics he produces for the number of those executed or transported. And whilst we might express some procedural misgivings in regard to presiding judges serving as prosecutors it was not uncommon practice in cases of alleged treason. It might further be noted that in Alice Lisle's case Jeffreys deliberately stayed execution in the apparent expectation of a royal pardon. It was James who evidently demurred (Davies 1939, 189). Macaulay passed over this bit of the story. There was to be no mitigation of Jeffreys's guilt.

A second set-piece, which assumes a still larger presence in Macaulay's narrative, is the arraignment of 'the seven bishops' who petitioned against James's second Declaration of Indulgence in April 1688 and who were subsequently prosecuted for seditious libel. Anglican clergy does not always fare well in Macaulay's *History*. But in their defence of the principles of the established Church, the bishops are presented as heroic defenders of the constitution, meeting the neurosis of a king 'quick of temper' and screaming treason with an almost ethereal 'cheerfulness'; so much so that they were 'rapturously extolled by the general voice' (Macaulay 1986, 206–7, 212–3, 219). It was, as Macaulay pointedly observes, perhaps the 'first and last occasion' when a common 'love of freedom' seemed in 'perfect harmony' with a 'love of the Church' (Macaulay 1986, 237). Corruption of judicial process is again an animating theme. The Judges of King's Bench before whom the Bishops were arraigned were the 'tools' of the court (Macaulay 1986, 211). The 'odious' Crown prosecution tries, but fails, to pack the jury. In an account of proceedings which, as Macaulay advises, owes more to the 'interest of drama' than that of cool jurisprudential reflection, the fortunes of the

Bishops wax and wane. But, defended by the most 'eminent' legal minds of the generation, they are in the end gloriously acquitted, the forces of corruption vanquished (Macaulay 1986, 224–7). The nation rejoices, church bells ring, stuffed popes are placed on bonfires up and down the land, and everyone goes to the nearby tavern for a celebratory drink.

And the narrative moves on a couple of months, to the third and in purely constitutional terms most significant of Macaulay's set-pieces. The coronation of William Prince of Orange may not account for quite so many pages in the *History*, but it might be said that the entire narrative pivots around this one event; in much the same way as Burke's *Reflections* moves around the spurious 'rape' of Marie Antoinette. At the close of the tenth chapter of his *History* Macaulay places his readers amongst the entranced 'gazers' who 'filled' the streets surrounding Whitehall on 13th February 1689. And then he takes them within, to join the assembled Peers and Commons and Yeomen of the Guard in admiring the 'masterpieces of Rubens' which embellish the walls of the 'magnificent' Banqueting House, and watching as William and his wife, Mary Stuart, 'advanced a few steps' towards the throne before being invited to listen to the Clerk of the House of Lords read 'in a loud voice' the Declaration of Right. After which, and only after, Lord Halifax offers the crown. The terms are accepted, and the new King William III reaffirms his commitment to the common 'law of England' as articulated in the Declaration, promising that they 'should be the rules of his conduct' as would be the 'welfare' of his kingdom. And, just to be sure that he will be able to fulfil these commitments, William confirms that he 'should constantly recur to the advice of the Houses, and should be disposed to trust their judgment rather than his own' (Macaulay 1986, 287).

William, as Macaulay had previously averred in his youthful *Essay on William III*, was the saviour who did nothing:

> He outraged no national prejudice. He abolished no ancient form. He altered no venerable name. He saw that the existing institutions possessed the greatest capabilities of excellence, and that stronger sanctions and clearer definitions were alone required to make the practice as admirable as the theory. (Macaulay 1969, 469)

Firth later confirmed that William was the 'hero' of Macaulay's *History* for this precise reason; a man of 'phlegmatic serenity', possessed of a 'singular charm' in private, whose greatest devotions were to God and to his family (Macaulay 1986, 174; Firth 1938, 44). Not every hero was of the kind who made it into Carlyle's pantheon of square-jawed strongmen. Macaulay preferred his heroes to be temperate. His Cromwell is, accordingly, a moderate God-fearing man whose first instinct always is to tolerate difference, to 'heal and settle' and to cherish accommodation (Hamburger 1976, 150–1). And he was a good husband too, and a loving father. So was William; a hero in his own home; the same kind of hero indeed which Prince Albert, one of Macaulay's many admirers, aspired to be. By 1848, the idea of kingship had assumed a rather different aspect. For the generation that followed the madness of George III and the excesses of George IV, there much to be said for serenity, common sense and sound judgment. Macaulay's William ultimately was a 'trimmer', just like Cromwell, just like his creator indeed; and this was a thoroughly good thing.[6]

He was not the only hero of the story of course. Macaulay's admiration for Parliament, whether it was the Parliament of 1848 or 1832, or 1688 or 1642, was pretty much unalloyed. What distinguished the Parliament of 1688, was the innate pragmatism of its members, or at least the Whig ones, who 'judiciously abstained from mixing up the irritating and perplexing question of what ought to be the law and the plain question of what was the law'; an observation that would, in its scornful dismissal of metaphysical allure, have earned the common, if contrasting, approbation of both Benthamite and Burkean (Edwards 1988, 112). Less so Carlyle, who disparaged Macaulay's mystical fetish for Parliaments of whatever age or hue (Edwards 1988, 110). Unsurprisingly Carlyle and Macaulay did not get on; a relationship of 'mutual repulsion', according to the latter. Not one of Macaulay's ideas, Carlyle opined, 'has the least tincture of greatness or originality', and the fact that his *History* was perhaps 'the most popular history book ever written' was certainly not to its author's credit. Macaulay may have had a 'wonderful historical memory' and an even more wonderful ability to entrance his readers, but he did write the most fantastical nonsense

[6]Even if he was not, as Firth pointed out, that much of a Whig (Firth 1938, 347–50). Macaulay's William clearly owed much to the William cherished by Bishop Burnet. Another 'trimmer', for which reason he was also another of Macaulay's heroes was Lord Halifax, a man 'singularly unsusceptible of enthusiasm, and singularly averse to extremes' (Hamburger 1976, 85, 89–95, 101).

(Heffer 1996, 294; Sullivan 2009, 319). And nothing was more fantastical than his description of the 13th February 1689.

As William and Mary slowly depart the chamber accompanied by 'heralds and pursuivants', a 'shout of joy' is heard outside, 'kettle drums struck up, the trumpets pealed', and the Garter King of Arms invites every Englishman and woman to pray for the new king and queen. A moment for quiet reflection arrives. 'Thus was consummated', Macaulay concludes with ironic simplicity, 'the English revolution'. And:

> When we compare it with those revolutions which have, during the last sixty years, overthrown so many ancient governments, we cannot but be struck by its peculiar character. (Macaulay 1986, 288)

The reach of sixty years is just far enough, inviting readers to compare and contrast the sober events at Whitehall in February 1689 with those which Burke so graphically depicted in his account of the storming of Versailles a century later. Such 'calamities our Revolution averted'. The English revolution was a 'strictly defensive revolution', one which, as Burke had striven to emphasise, 'had prescription and legitimacy on its side', its purpose extending only to the 'vindication of ancient rights' (Macaulay 1986, 290, 292). It is here however that the tonal differences between Macaulay and Burke become apparent. Where Burke had relished the chance to terrify his readers with accounts of screeching Jacobins declaiming abstract rights to 'equality', Macaulay invited his to contemplate groups of sober Parliamentarians pouring over ancient rolls of legal 'parchment' in the weeks and months which followed the coronation. Burke wanted heroes who knew when to draw their swords. Macaulay invested his with pens and ink-wells and a keen knowledge of the common law. Even so, whilst the invocation of the sublime might be missing in Macaulay the conceptual resonance remains. In his *Reflections*, as we have already noted, Burke famously depicted an 'ancient' constitution, its veracity attested by the 'collected reason of ages' and embedded for generations in an English state of 'mind' (Burke 1986, 116–7, 132–3). Macaulay appraised the 'main principles of our government' in similar terms:

> They were not, indeed, formally and exactly set forth in a single written instrument; but they were to be found scattered over our ancient and noble statutes; and, what was of far greater moment, they had been

> engraven on the hearts of Englishmen during four hundred years. (Macaulay 1986, 290)

The coronation of William III, on the conditions laid down by Parliament, ensures that Macaulay's *History* will have a happy ending; one that will be confirmed in 1832. There may be a need for 'change', and Macaulay took a further moment to suggest a more particular necessity in regard to the established Church and the need to 'deprive' the Crown of its attendant 'mysterious attributes' (Macaulay 1986, 291). But a 'realm of which these', by which he meant the common law principles of liberty now enshrined in the Declaration, 'were the fundamental laws stood in no need of a new constitution' (Macaulay 1986, 290). In 1688 or, the implication very obviously ran, in 1848. 'Now, if ever', Macaulay concluded, it must be apparent to 'all honest and reflecting minds' that the 'highest eulogy which can be pronounced on the revolution of 1688' is 'that it was our last revolution' (Macaulay 1986, 294). 'And if it be asked what has made' England 'different' from other less fortunate nations:

> It is because we had a preserving revolution in the seventeenth century that we have not had a destroying revolution in the nineteenth. It is because we had freedom in the midst of servitude that we have order in the midst of anarchy. For the authority of law, for the security of property, for the peace of our streets, for the happiness of our homes, our gratitude is due, under Him who raises and pulls down nations at his pleasure, to the Long Parliament, to the Convention, and to William of Orange. (Macaulay 1986, 295)

Apostle of the Philistines

It may, as Carlyle observed disparagingly and with perhaps a note of bitterness, have been the 'most popular history book ever written', but a century and a half later both the *History* and its author have rather faded from critical view. When he gave a lecture on Macaulay on the centenary of his death, David Knowles felt obliged to adopt a justificatory almost apologetic tone (Knowles 1960, 3–4). In 1967 Ronald Weber lamented a writer who had 'fallen into general oblivion' (Weber 1967, 210). Raymond Williams reached the same conclusion, with less evidence of the same regret (Williams 1965, 76). Faint praise was a common form of damnation.

AJP Taylor concluded that whilst Macaulay 'had a very simple outlook' no historian 'ever told a story better' (Taylor 1976, 57). In like tones, Trevor-Roper recommended history written by an essentially 'practical politician', his mind uncluttered by 'abstract thought' (Trevor-Roper 1957, 252–3). Others, rather more seriously, had begun to cast aspersions at perceived 'misrepresentations' of historical 'fact' (Davies 1939, 180–3, 197–204). Similar suspicions could be read into Sir Charles Firth's corrective *Commentary on Macaulay's History of England* published in 1938; even if, or perhaps because, it acknowledged that no subsequent historian had so well appreciated the 'art of telling a story'. Interestingly, whilst there may have been increasing doubts as to the acuity of Macaulay's *History* Firth felt similarly moved to conclude that it was 'still *the* authority' on late seventeenth-century English constitutional history (Firth 1938, 1–2). But the intellectual mood was already turning against the Whig epic. Whilst Firth poured over the minutiae of Macaulay's *History*, Butterfield was setting his sights on an entire genre of historians who displayed a similar propensity to wilful 'over-dramatisation' (Butterfield 1931, 34, 39).

It was, as we have noted, left to a band of loyal disciples to keep the flame of Whig history flickering. Plumb paid tribute to a historian whose real genius lay in the depth of 'his own sympathy with his age', suggesting that 'his success must partly lie in the fact that the men and women who read him so eagerly, felt as he felt and believed as he believed: his truth was their truth'. There had not been, he concluded, an historian of equivalent 'stature' in the past hundred years (Plumb 1963, 251; Gilley 1983, 328–9, 338–9). Friedrich Hayek was not so obviously Whiggish. But he paid similar tribute to Macaulay's singular 'success in making the achievements of the constitutional struggles of the past once more a living possession of every educated Englishman' (Hayek 1960, 469). Rather more recently John Burrow has surmised that Macaulay was the 'last great neoclassical historian' (Burrow 2007, 371). It is not quite the same as being the last Whig historian, but it gestures that way. Conversely as the twentieth century drew on, revisionist Macaulays began to appear. Joseph Hamburger, writing in 1976, reinvested Macaulay the conservative 'trimmer' as a corrective to Macaulay the liberal Whig (Hamburger 1976, ix, 110–1, 137–44).[7] Richard

[7] Concluding that 'Macaulay's contribution was to apply systematically the trimmer's outlook to nineteenth-century problems' most notably during the Reform Bill debates and

Sullivan's recent biography of Macaulay is written around the same premise, confirming in passing that what is most notable about Macaulay today is how little he is noted (Sullivan 2009, 1). In sum, the problem with Macaulay, and his *History*, is that it is all a bit 'easy', a bit too happy, maybe a bit too complacent too (Brantlinger 1977, 19).

It was all very different a century earlier of course, uncle Tom's reputation burnished by his nephew Sir Otto Trevelyan's hagiographic 1876 *Life and Letters* and then again in the various writings of great-nephew George Macaulay Trevelyan, who saw himself as the flame-carrier for that 'poetic' tradition of Whig history, and whose monumental *England under Queen Anne* was written as a reverential sequel to his uncle's *History*. The later Victorian generation grew up with Macaulay and his *History*, quite literally given its ubiquitous presence in its nurseries and classrooms. And it did so in large part uncritically. In commercial terms, the *History* remained a phenomenal success. In its first three months the first two volumes of the *History* had sold 13,000 copies. At the end of the year Macaulay received his first royalty cheque, for £5500. When the second two volumes appeared in December 1855, the publishers Longmans had budgeted for a print-run of 25,000. It was sold out within ten weeks. Even Macaulay was taken aback. 'Of such a run I had never dreamed' he wrote in his diary in mid-January. In March they paid £20,000 into the author's account; a sum equivalent today to around £1.5 million. A single volume edition published in 1858 sold 35,000 copies. By 1876, it was estimated that 140,000 copies had been sold in the UK, and very probably in excess of 200,000 in America (Firth 1938, 8; Mowat 1995, 62; Sullivan 2009, 315–6).

The plaudits of immediate contemporaries were many, various and loud. An admiring Prince Albert urged Macaulay to accept the Regius Professorship of Modern History at Cambridge. Lord Acton thought the *History* 'wonderful' (Firth 1938, 3). Fitzjames Stephen paid tribute to 'the greatest, and indeed, almost the only great advocate and expounder of Whig principles since the time of Burke' (Stephen 1860, 9). Detecting the same intellectual genesis, Lord Salisbury expressed himself a great admirer of Macaulay's 'picturesque narrative' (Sullivan

then again in the writing of his *History*, 'thereby significantly contributing to the shaping of national consciousness about the role of trimming' in 'the distinctively British approach to politics' (Hamburger 1976, 144).

2009, 475). No less significant in its way was the decision of assorted 'gentleman' of Dukinfield near Manchester to write to Macaulay in order to express their gratitude 'for having written a history which working men can understand' (Plumb 1963, 250). In sum, according to Gladstone at least, Macaulay assumed a 'monarchy over the world of readers' (Hamburger 1976, 163). Gladstone was himself a rather ambivalent admirer. The *History* he admitted was 'a true and high work of art', its author possessed of a 'rare and marvellous' ability to present images of 'ordinary life' alongside larger perceptions of historical moment. But there was, he detected, 'a pervading strain of exaggeration' too. More worrying still, the great historian did not seem sufficiently committed to 'Christian dogma' (Gladstone 1876, 14–15, 21, 31, 49). It is certainly true that Macaulay was an inconsistent churchgoer. It is also true that he had written a less than flattering review of Gladstone's *The State and its Relations with the Church* a decade earlier.

Even less impressed were the Benthamites. Given Macaulay's demolition of his father's *Essay on Government*, John Stuart Mill's hostility was perhaps unsurprising. Mill was above all troubled by the thought that the *History* will 'continue popular' (Sullivan 2009, 319). The same fear haunted Tory critics such as Matthew Arnold who railed against 'the great apostle of the Philistines', and Disraeli who, rather earlier in 1835, had dismissed Macaulay as the 'prescient flashman' of the reformist Whigs (Arnold 1968, 181; Hutcheon 1913, 46). John Morley doubted whether historians should seek to align themselves with 'the common average sentiment' (Morley 1886, 267). Lecky sniffily dismissed a historian whose writing seemed to 'influence' the 'the temper of modern journalism' (Firth 1938, 33, 81–5). Carlyle, as we have already noted, assumed a similarly contemptuous tone, likening the popular idolisation of 'the Right Honourable Tom' to that of a 'molten calf' (Sullivan 2009, 368). The *History*, he concluded, was far 'too popular' and far too Whig; in contrast to Lord Russell who, equally predictably perhaps, thought it not nearly Whig enough (Sullivan 2009, 319).

One of the most incisive critics, and for our purposes most intriguing, was Walter Bagehot. In an obituary he wrote in the days following Macaulay's death in December 1859 Bagehot placed Macaulay within the Burkean 'tradition' (Bagehot 1965, 2.429–31; Hamburger 1976, 188; Ritchie 1989, 324–8; Brantlinger 1977, 16). An earlier more substantive review of the Macaulay's *History* however betrayed a rather deeper ambivalence. Whilst Bagehot admitted that the *History* was a 'marvellous book', he noted that Macaulay seemed to eschew a more refined Burkean 'sensibility'; something all the more marked given that the temporal focus of his *History* was one of the 'most passionate eras of our history'. Macaulay is an eminently 'sensible' historian, but 'he has no passionate self-questionings, no indomitable fears, no asking perplexities' (Bagehot 1965, 2.397, 401, 405, 411). The criticism has stuck. It clearly played on Plumb's mind, a century later suggesting in very similar tones that, despite his undoubted 'moral passion', Macaulay 'never penetrates to the heart of human existence' (Plumb 1963, 255, 257). There is neither sufficient romance to make the *History* a cavalier chronicle, nor sufficient zeal to make it a puritan polemic. There is instead a pervasive tone of 'pleasant geniality' and 'easy cheerfulness'. The reason, he averred, was that despite his 'vivid fancy' Macaulay was ultimately a lukewarm Roundhead rather than a romantic 'Cavalier', a Baconian rather than a Burkean (Bagehot 1965, 2.400–2, 408–13). Like Scott, but unlike Burke, Bagehot supposed, Macaulay wrote to 'charm' rather than to impassion. Moreover, 'still the man of '32', Macaulay was trapped by his own inability to look beyond the constitutional settlement he had set in historical aspic (Bagehot 1965, 2.410, 415–7, 428).

Not of course that this affected sales figures, as Bagehot acknowledged. Macaulay knew his readers. If Bagehot was indeed the 'greatest Victorian', as GM Young later averred, then Macaulay was perhaps the quintessential one. He did not relish 'perplexities' and neither did his readers; so they got none (Bagehot 1965, 2.411, 425). What they wanted was calm reassurance, the comfort of black and white. Accordingly, as chapter eighteen of the *History* draws to its close, having witnessed the massacre of Glencoe followed swiftly by the allied victory at La Hogue, readers of his *History* could reflect on the events of chapter eighteen grateful that, unlike the perfidious French and the primitive Highlanders, they had an 'ancient constitution' which was forever, and forever cautiously, 'adapting itself, by a natural, a gradual, a peaceful development, to the wants of modern society'. For which reason then, and by implication, now:

> There was a sense of relief everywhere, from the Royal Exchange to the most secluded hamlets among the mountains of Wales and the fens of Lincolnshire. The ploughmen, the shepherds, the miners of the Northumbrian coalpits, the artisans who toiled at the looms of Norwich and the anvils of Birmingham, felt the change, without understanding it;

> and the cheerful bustle in every seaport and every market town indicated, not obscurely, the commencement of a happy age. (Macaulay 1986, 486)

Macaulay, as Bagehot appreciated, gave his readers what they wanted, the ability to 'pass a day of easy thought, of pleasant emotion' in the company of a good, if very long, book. An evening of 'easy, pleasant reading', Carlyle concluded in tones where were again not intended to compliment (Mowat 1995, 63). It was this which, of course, distinguished Macaulay from Carlyle. Both might have preferred their histories to be picturesque and dramatic. But where Carlyle dealt in doom, Macaulay bestowed a Whiggish faith in hope and charity. He gave an anxious mid-Victorian England what it so desperately craved, a happy ending (Heffer 2013, 577).[8] Macaulay knew his audience, precisely. The English were still chosen, their constitution the envy of the world, and it was all thanks to the 'great' Revolution of 1688 and the 'great' Act of 1832; and of course to men like Macaulay who ensured that the latter was passed and the former held in suitably awed remembrance. The essential mythology would survive, for a little longer at least.

References

Aldous, R. (2007). *The Lion and the Unicorn: Gladstone v Disraeli.* London: Pimlico.

Arnold, M. (1968). *Essays in Criticism.* Chicago: Chicago University Press.

Bagehot, W. (1965). *The Collected Works of Walter Bagehot* (St. John Stevas, Ed.). London: The Economist.

Bentley, M. (1996). *Politics Without Democracy 1815–1914.* London: Fontana.

Brantlinger, P. (1977). *The Spirit of Reform: British Literature and Politics 1832–1867.* Cambridge, MA: Harvard University Press.

Briggs, A. (1959). *The Age of Improvement.* London: Longmans.

Brown, D. (2010). *Palmerston: A Biography.* New Haven: Yale University Press.

Burke, E. (1986). *Reflections on the Revolution in France.* London: Penguin.

Burrow, J. (1988). *Whigs and Liberals: Continuity and Change in English Political Thought.* Oxford: Oxford University Press.

Burrow, J. (2007). *A History of Histories.* London: Penguin.

Butterfield, H. (1931). *The Whig Interpretation of History.* London: Bell & Sons.

[8]As Plumb concludes, praising Macaulay's sensitivity to the fact, the 'men and women of his time loved to hear certainties, confidence was a part of the air they breathed (Plumb 1963, 257).

Cannon, J. (1973). *Parliamentary Reform 1640–1832*. Cambridge: Cambridge University Press.

Carlyle, T. (1986). *Selected Writings*. Harmondsworth: Penguin.

Davies, G. (1939). The Treatment of Constitutional History in Macaulay's *History of England*. *Huntington Library Quarterly, 2*, 179–204.

Dicey, A. (1914). *Lectures on the Relation Between Law and Public Opinion in England During the Nineteenth Century*. London: Macmillan.

Dransfield, S. (1998). Reading the Gordon Riots in 1841: Social Violence and Moral Management in *Barnaby Rudge*. *Dickens Studies Annual, 27*, 69–95.

Edwards, O. (1988). *Macaulay*. London: Weidenfeld & Nicolson.

Erskine May. (1861). *The Constitutional History of England Since George III*. London: Longman.

Firth, C. (1938). *A Commentary on Macaulay's History of England*. London: Macmillan.

Frye, L. (1997) "Great Burke", Thomas Carlyle, and the French Revolution. In L. Crafton (Ed.), *The French Revolution Debate in English Literature and Culture*. London: Greenwood Press.

Gash, N. (1965). *Reaction and Reconstruction in English Politics 1832–1852*. Oxford: Oxford University Press.

Gaunt, R. (2010). *Sir Robert Peel: The Life and Legacy*. London: I.B. Tauris.

Gilley, S. (1983). Macaulay as Historian. *Australian Journal of Politics and History, 29*, 328–343.

Gladstone, W. (1876, July). Review of Trevelyan's *Life and Letters*. *Quarterly Review*, pp. 14–49.

Halperin, J. (1977). *Trollope and Politics*. London: Macmillan.

Hamburger, J. (1976). *Macaulay and the Whig Tradition*. Chicago: University of Chicago Press.

Hawkins, A. (1989). Parliamentary Government and Victorian Political Parties c.1830–c.1880. *English Historical Review, 104*, 638–669.

Hayek, F. (1960). *The Constitution of Liberty*. Chicago: Chicago University Press.

Heffer, S. (2013). *High Minds: The Victorians and the Making of Modern Britain*. London: Random House.

Hibbert, C. (1997). *Wellington: A Personal History*. London: HarperCollins.

Hibbert, C. (2001). *Queen Victoria: A Personal History*. London: HarperCollins.

Hutcheon, W. (Ed.). (1913). *Whigs and Whiggism: Political Writings by Benjamin Disraeli*. London: John Murray.

Knowles, D. (1960). *Lord Macaulay 1800–1859*. Cambridge: Cambridge University Press.

Lang, T. (1995). *The Victorians and the Stuart Age*. Cambridge: Cambridge University Press.

Levine, G. (1968). *The Boundaries of Fiction: Carlyle, Macaulay, Newman*. Princeton: Princeton University Press.

Longford, E. (1998). *Victoria RI.* London: Weidenfield & Nicolson.
Macaulay, T. (1825, August). Milton. *Edinburgh Review*, pp. 304–346.
Macaulay, T. (1828, September). Hallam's Constitutional History. *Edinburgh Review*, pp. 96–169.
Macaulay, T. (1829, March). Utilitarian Logic and Politics. *Edinburgh Review*, pp. 159–189.
Macaulay, T. (1832, July). Dumont's *Recollections of Mirabeau. Edinburgh Review*, pp. 552–576.
Macaulay. (1837, July). Montagu's *The Works of Francis Bacon. Edinburgh Review*, pp. 1–52.
Macaulay, T. (1841, October). Warren Hastings. *Edinburgh Review*, pp. 160–255.
Macaulay, T. (1969, May 1). William III. *Times Literary Supplement*, pp. 469–470.
Macaulay, T. (1986). *The History of England.* London: Penguin.
Mandler, P. (1990). *Aristocratic Government in the Age of Reform: Whigs and Liberals 1830–1852.* Oxford: Oxford University Press.
Mather, F. (1959). The Government and the Chartists. In A. Briggs (Ed.), *Chartist Studies.* London: Macmillan.
Mitchell, L. (1997). *Lord Melbourne 1779–1848.* Oxford: Oxford University Press.
Morley, J. (1886). *Critical Miscellanies* (Vol. 1). London: Macmillan.
Mowat, R. (1995). *The Victorian Age.* London: Senate.
Newsome, D. (1998). *The Victorian World Picture.* London: Fontana.
Parry, J. (1993). *The Rise and Fall of Liberal Government in Victorian Britain.* New Haven: Yale University Press.
Plumb, J. (1963). *Men and Places.* London: Cresset.
Ritchie, D. (1989). Burke's Influence on the Imagination of Walter Bagehot. *The Modern Age, 32,* 324–328.
Royle, E. (1996). *Chartism.* London: Longman.
Royle, E. (2000). *Revolutionary Britannia? Reflections on the Threat of Revolution in Britain 1789–1848.* Manchester: Manchester University Press.
Smith, E. (1990). *Lord Grey 1764–1845.* Oxford: Oxford University Press.
Smith, E. (1999). *George IV.* New Haven: Yale University Press.
Stephen, F. (1860, January 7). Lord Macaulay. *Saturday Review*, p. 9.
Sullivan, R. (2009). *Macaulay: The Tragedy of Power.* Cambridge, MA: Harvard University Press.
Taylor, A. (1976). *Essays in English History.* Harmondsworth: Pelican.
Thompson, E. (1991). *The Making of the English Working Class.* Harmondsworth: Penguin.
Trevor-Roper, H. (1957). *Historical Essays.* London: Macmillan.
Weber, R. (1967). Singer and Seer: Macaulay on the Historian as Poet. *Papers on Language and Literature, 3,* 210–219.
Williams, R. (1965). *The Long Revolution.* London: Pelican.
Woodward, L. (1962). *The Age of Reform 1815–1870.* Oxford: Oxford University Press.

CHAPTER 4

The Greatest Victorian

Death mattered to the Victorians, peculiarly so. It was in part a consequence of doubt. But it mattered in a different rather more prosaic sense too. Particular deaths of particular people could herald revolutions. It was the death of Swellfoot, the Tyrant that opened up the possibility of parliamentary reform in the 1830s. And it was another death, just as momentous in its own way, which opened up the possibility of another Reform Act thirty-three years later. It was entirely appropriate that Henry John Temple, 3rd Viscount Palmerston, suffered a heart attack whilst trying to grope a maid over the billiard table at Brocket Hall in October 1865. Whig peers were supposed to die scandalously and 'Lord Cupid', as he was known to friend and foe alike, had form (Brown 2010, 78). Only two years earlier, he had been cited in a 'criminal conversation' action brought by an Irish journalist. Lord Clarendon expressed a grudging admiration that the 'old lad' had it in him (Brown 2010, 475).[1] Palmerston may not have been the last Whig peer to grope a maid. But he was the last Whig peer to serve as Prime Minister in what

[1]The journalist was Timothy Joseph O'Kane, a well-known Radical. He alleged that his wife had, rather improbably, visited Palmerston to discuss politics, but had then, rather less improbably, been seduced. He claimed £20,000 damages. Clarendon blamed his 'unscrupulous attorney' and shared the common opinion that it was little more than a crude attempt at extortion. Needless to say, the action did nothing to dent Palmerston's popularity in the country; quite the contrary. Disraeli wondered if the entire affair had not been concocted for precisely this reason.

I. Ward, *Writing the Victorian Constitution*, Palgrave Modern Legal History, https://doi.org/10.1007/978-3-319-96676-2_4

would prove to be the last Whig Cabinet (Brown 2010, 385). And with Palmerston's passing, so historians have commonly presumed, passed not just the last Whig premier and the last Whig administration, but so too the Whig party itself. 'We shall never', an admiring Bagehot concluded, 'see his like again' (Bagehot 1965, 3.278; Brown 2010, 482).

Nearly eighty-one, beset according to his doctors with gout, haematura, 'abdominal and dorsal pains', an irregular heartbeat, 'furring of the tongue', 'catarrh of the bladder' and discoloured urinary 'secretions', death should not have come as much of surprise. But it seemed to all the same. Acclaimed the 'coming man' as late as 1854, aged nearly seventy, Palmerston had dominated the English political landscape for six decades, twice Prime Minister, nineteen years as Secretary of State for War, fifteen more as Foreign Secretary, and two as Home Secretary. 'Death', as Gladstone observed, had 'indeed laid low the most towering antlers in all the forest' (Brown 2010, 1). Contemporaries quickly recognised the passing of a Palmerstonian 'age'. They did not, however, seem to know quite what to do. Lord Russell staggered on for a tortuous nine months before resigning the last Whig administration. He was succeeded in June 1866 by a minority Tory administration cobbled together by Lord Derby, with Disraeli as Chancellor. It lasted just long enough to pass the 1867 Reform Act. But it did not survive the consequences. In February 1868, Derby resigned. Disraeli struggled on as Prime Minister until December 1868, at which point Gladstone won a convincing victory at the General Election. If Disraeli had thought the 1867 Act would secure a Tory future, he was badly mistaken. Gladstone would serve a full term. Disraeli would be left with a fair bit of explaining to do, not least to his Queen.

But if the country had turned distinctly Gladstonian and Liberal, the electors of Bridgwater and Beverley had not. Having declined the opportunity stand for London University in 1860 and then Manchester in 1865, Walter Bagehot had finally been persuaded to put himself forward as a Liberal candidate at the Bridgwater by-election in 1866. He should have won. But he did not, in large part because Bridgwater was eminently corruptible, and Bagehot was rubbish at corrupting people. Chastened he declined the opportunity to stand in the 1868 election for Mid-Somerset which, ironically, he would probably have won, and then again, despite Gladstone's pleading, for Liverpool in 1873. Bagehot was not the first to be frustrated at the hustings, or to vent his frustrations. Back in 1806, William Cobbett had railed against the 'insoluble chain of venality' which bound parliamentary candidate to elector (Briggs 1959, 104–5). Much later Alfred Lord Tennyson would lament a system of election which rewarded the 'practised hustings-liar' over 'nobleness of mind' (Tennyson 1991, 337). Carlyle's contempt was predictable and rather more prosaic. The 'mass of men consulted at hustings upon any matter whatsoever, is as ugly an exhibition of human stupidity as the world sees' (Carlyle 1986, 302). The Bishop of Peterborough blamed the 1832 Reform Act. The pre-1832 voter had been 'stolid and bovine', but the newly enfranchised 'half-taught, newspaper-reading, platform-hunting, discussion-club frequenter, conceited, excitable, nervous product of modern town artisan life is a most dangerous animal'. His Worship feared the worst. England would soon be 'the nastiest residence conceivable for anyone save infidel pigs and unsexed women' (Bentley 2001, 153–4).

Certainly, the first Reform Act had done nothing to reinvest the reputation of Parliament. The House returned in 1841 became known as the 'Bribery Parliament', for reasons that were entirely self-evident. The 1854 Corrupt Practices Act, for the 'better discovery of bribery and corruption', made little difference in this regard, and certainly not in Bridgwater. The idea of still further reform, Palmerston advised Russell in the same year, was accordingly perverse. 'A low class of electors may naturally be expected to chuse a low class of representatives', whilst no gentleman could be expected to 'play for the shilling gallery' (Brown 2010, 359). Lord Salisbury agreed; 'Educated men do not like going round, hat in hand, begging for votes from the mob' (Bentley 2001, 147–8). John Stuart Mill suggested that a secret ballot might help. Few others were keen. Trollope thought the idea both 'unmanly' and un-English (Halperin 1977, 121). Bribery was easier, and there were still bargains to be found. Alighting on Tiverton in 1835, Palmerston credited himself 'singularly fortunate' in finding such a 'quiet borough which gives me very little trouble', and which was so cheap (Brown 2010, 194). And the mob, it was becoming apparent, were not particularly keen on electoral reform either. They liked being bribed, just as they liked a day off to attend the hustings and get themselves blind drunk at someone else's expense. The 1872 Ballot Act introduced a secret ballot. It did not stop electoral 'fraud', as the later Tory Chancellor Michael Hicks-Beach predicted. It just made it a bit more 'organized' (Heffer 2013, 407).

Whilst Bagehot was still licking his wounds in Bridgewater, far away in East Yorkshire, Anthony Trollope was proving himself to be just as rubbish at corrupting voters. Trollope had long fancied being a Member of Parliament, but had never much fancied standing for election. In 1868, however, he allowed himself to be put forward as a Liberal candidate at Beverley. In his *Autobiography*, he later commented that his 'desire' to become an MP was 'almost insane', a signal 'weakness of my ambition'. He claimed that he had sought election because he 'always thought that to sit in the British Parliament should be the highest object of ambition to every educated Englishman' (Trollope 1996, 186, 190–1). The fancy was quickly dispelled. Beverley was a thoroughly chastening experience, from the very moment when his agent, a local solicitor, confirmed that he had absolutely no chance of winning the seat:

> 'Oh no', continued he, with good humoured raillery, 'you won't get in. I don't suppose you really expect it. But there is a fine career open to you. You will spend £1000 and lose the election. Then you will petition and spend another £1000. You will throw out the elected members; there will be a commission, and the borough will be disenfranchised. For a beginner such as you are that will be a great success'. (Trollope 1996, 191)

And so it came to pass. As his agent had predicted Trollope came bottom of the poll, after which the Beverley Liberals duly petitioned Parliament to have the result set aside. The elected members were indeed thrown out, and Beverley was disenfranchised.

But Trollope extracted little satisfaction from his agent's perspicacity. Canvassing was an especial horror, 'I think, the most wretched fortnight of my manhood' (Trollope 1996, 192). He was even prevented from going hunting. Trollope was an avid hunter. But the burghers of Beverley, it was surmised, were not. So from 'morning to evening every day', he was obliged to traipse 'the lanes and byways of that uninteresting town, canvassing every voter, exposed to the rain, up to my knees in slush'. The distaste was evidently mutual, and Trollope, like Bagehot, spent far too little. The report of the electoral commissioners concluded that of 1100 electors at Beverley, 800 'were open to bribery and other corrupt influences', leaving a mere 300 'rolling stock' as respective agents termed them. Trollope invested a mere £400 in the rolling stock, though he was quick to assure the commissioners that none of it had been used 'to corrupt the electors' (Hall 1991, 328–9).

It was nothing like enough, though at least it furnished him with the consolation that he had not wasted as much as his opponent, who spent twice the sum only to have his election annulled.[2] And by precipitating the disenfranchisement of such an obviously rotten borough, he might even have 'done some good' (Trollope 1996, 192–4; McMaster 1986, 107).

Time healed, but not much. Uplifting accounts of electoral practice remained few and far between in the Trollopian canon. But none are quite as caustic as those which, still licking his wounds, Trollope wrote into his 1870 novel, *Ralph the Heir*. Beverley and the 'very old borough of Percycross', as he later admitted, are 'one and the same place', the same cynical and mendacious agents, the same misery of being 'dragged from door to door' canvassing for votes, the same coarse violence of the hustings, the 'tremenjous' bribery, even the petition and resultant commission (Trollope 1978, 145–8, 218–21, 292, 328–36, 386; 1996, 192–5). Trollope did not think much of *Ralph*, later supposing that it was 'one of the worse novels I have written' (Trollope 1996, 217). The critics were much more impressed, with the Percycross election especially, written 'so humorously and so truthfully', the *Times* gushed (Smalley 1969, 351; Halperin 1977, 128–9). Percycross had clearly hit a nerve.

As Asa Briggs famously observed, there was much else that Bagehot and Trollope had in common, aside from commonly frustrated parliamentary careers. Both esteemed themselves to be gentleman. There was, Trollope confirmed in his *Autobiography*, no higher estimation (Briggs 1990, 102). And both would certainly have identified themselves with what Lord Brougham had termed the 'intelligence of the country', with what Thackeray in similar terms identified as 'that class of lawyers and merchants and scholars, of men who are striving on in the world' (Newsome 1998, 64). The striving added something of course. Parentage might make for a gentleman, as it always had, along with education and breeding. But so, by the mid-nineteenth century, might

[2] The Commission heard evidence that the Tory agent had withdrawn £800 from the bank on the morning of the election, stationed under-agents around the town to direct voters and then settled comfortably into a corner of the Golden Ball Tavern placing a bag of coins ostentatiously on a table in front of him. Voters were asked to line up and wait to be ushered into his presence, to be given their reward and have their names recorded in a notebook.

admission to a profession (Lacey 2011, 611–4, 618–20). Having attended Harrow and Winchester, both of which he hated, but then failed to secure scholarships to either Oxford or Cambridge, Trollope had ended up in the civil service, working at the Post Office. Striving was his lot. And the same fate ultimately befell Bagehot. The scion of a well-to-do dissenting family, Bagehot took a slightly different course, attending Langport Grammar School, Bristol College and then University College London. But he too ended up striving for a living, as a journalist. As a profession, it just about counted, as did working in the civil service. And anyway the boundaries of social acceptance were moving, as a wistful Lady Amberley acknowledged. The very 'highest' sections of 'London society' were being daily infiltrated by more and more 'plebeians who were personally attractive' (Best 1979, 275). The same, as we shall see, was true of Parliament, increasingly full of plebs and strivers.

But there was more still that bound Bagehot and Trollope, a shared perplexity and a shared sense of foreboding, for which reason they were ultimately chroniclers of the same doom, the same loss of 'young hopefulness' which haunted George Eliot's *Middlemarch* (Briggs 1990, 95, 122–3; Pollard 1968, 16–18; Brantlinger 1977, 8–9). A 'consciousness of wrong', as Trollope termed it, was common amongst the 'intelligence'. But so was a paralysing uncertainty as to what might be done to alleviate it in world that was becoming ever more obviously Godless and Whig-less (Trollope 1996, 187). Neither Bagehot nor Trollope was Liberal in the emergent sense. 'I hate the Liberal enthusiasts' Bagehot once remarked, adding that he always felt 'inclined to say "Go home, Sir, and take a dose of salts, and see if it won't clean it all out of you"' (Briggs 1990, 108). Bagehot may have breakfasted with Gladstone, but he lived and died a conservative Whig. And precisely the same can be said of Trollope, 'both Whiggish and waggish' (Weintraub 1993, 362). The voters of Beverley were assured that Trollope was an 'active, constant and unwearied' supporter of Gladstone, not that they could care less (Hall 1991, 324). Affinity was more oblique in the later *Autobiography*, in which Trollope claimed to be an 'advanced but still conservative Liberal, which I regard not only as a possible but as a rational and consistent phase of political existence' (Trollope 1996, 186). The older Trollope got, the more confused became his politics. Here, again he was hardly alone.

Palmerston was of course a more particular, and more acquired, taste. There was much about 'Pam' that troubled the more fastidious. Queen Victoria loathed him. But to men like Bagehot and Trollope,

Palmerston and the past appealed in a way that Disraeli and the future did not. Trollope confirmed his continuing estimation in a short 1882 biographical essay, in which appraised a 'statesman for the moment' (Briggs 1990, 97; Hall 1991, 494–7; Halperin 1977, 132). In similar terms, Bagehot admired Palmerston's supremely Whiggish, 'quality' of 'animated moderation' (Bagehot 1965, 7.131). The opening of his *English Constitution* indeed invited readers to return to the 'time of Lord Palmerston', precisely so they could better appreciate what had been lost. In one sense, it was not much of a reach. To Bagehot, however, it was an age. Britain after Disraeli's 'mischievous and monstrous' 1867 Reform Act was a very different place and a much darker one. There had been 'great changes in our politics', changes more of 'pervading spirit' than of 'particular details'. The 1832 Act had merely enfranchised a generation of 'minor English shopkeepers'. The 1867 Act had done far more, and its consequences were still unknown. Bagehot was not hopeful. Peering into the future, he could see only 'calamity' and the further hideous spectre of socialism (Bagehot 2001, 194–5, 197–8, 201–2; Buchan 1959, 138, 144–5). The essays which would comprise the *English Constitution* were written as a prophecy of pending doom.

Leaping in the Dark

It had all seemed so much brighter just a decade earlier. The 'year of revolutions' came and went. Three years later, resplendent in pink and white, wearing the Koh-i-noor diamond and a very broad smile, Victoria had opened the Great Exhibition of the Works of Industry of All Nations at the Crystal Palace, or Paxton's giant 'cucumber frame between two chimneys' as Ruskin rather caustically described it (Heffer 2013, 305). It was, Victoria confided, the 'proudest and happiest day of my life', even 'more touching' that her coronation. Three thousand chosen subjects were in attendance. A further six million would pour through the turnstiles in the months that followed. Prince Albert, forever trying to find things to do, had energetically accepted the invitation to become patron and chief evangelist of a project which, he announced, would celebrate the 'wonderful period of transition' in which they were all lucky enough to live (Heffer 2013, 297–8). It was Albert who decided that Joseph Paxton, famed designer of very big greenhouses, was the right architect for the job. Albert and his wife would return to the Crystal Palace time and again over the summer.

There was a darker side to mid-Victorian England. 'Progress halts on palsied feet', as Tennyson would later put it in *Locksley Hall Sixty Years After*, 'Crime and hunger cast our maidens by the thousand on the street' (Tennyson 1991, 341).[3] But inside Paxton's giant greenhouse all was light, and profit. The Exhibition made in excess of £200,000. Visitors gawped in admiration and amazement, whilst dodging the defecating pigeons which took to nesting in the rafters and the sparrowhawks brought into hunt them down but which proved to be messier still. There was much on display which might seem odd today, along with just as much which is more familiar, including an early sewing machine, steam turbines and locomotives, a telegraphic link to Edinburgh, various air pumps and microscopes, and a 'cricket catapulta for propelling the ball in the absence of a first-rate bowler'. The nation seemed to be entranced, its leading minds appropriately awed and reflective, in the main at least. Carlyle typically was not worrying rather more about the danger of bringing lots of boisterous Englishmen together in one place. The Whig historian Buckle however preferred to meditate on the 'bright promise of reward to man's genius' (Briggs 1959, 400). Macaulay was enraptured. 'I made my way into the building, a most gorgeous sight; vast; graceful; beyond the dreams of Arabian romances. I cannot think the Caesars ever exhibited a more splendid spectacle. I was quite dazzled, and I felt as I did on entering St Peters' (Plumb 1963, 258).

The editor of the Times gestured to the larger implication: 'We have committed ourselves to the general laws of Providence, and Providence now rewards us with a vista of social improvements, and unexpected blessings, which men had not dreamt of ten years ago' (Parry 1993, 168). Six years later, John Stuart Mill gestured similarly, aligning Providence and industry with constitutional settlement:

> The triumph of the Reform Act of 1832 consists not so much in the recognition of certain abstract principles, or in the readjustment of the franchise, as in the fact that for a quarter of a century parliamentary government has been established in a country with greater purity and efficiency than it ever possessed before, that during this period innumerable

[3]The immediate context here being the publication of W.T. Stead's incendiary articles on child prostitution in London, the 'Maiden Tribute to Modern Babylon', in the *Pall Mall Gazette* in the summer of 1885. The veracity of the articles would be later questioned, but their immediate impact was nothing short of sensational.

> measures of unequalled public importance have been adopted in rapid succession by the legislature, and that whilst discord has shaken, and despotism subdued, almost every other great nation in Europe, the people of England have never been more heartily attached to their institutions, or more happily at peace amongst themselves. (Hawkins 1989, 614)

It was all part of living in an 'age of progressive improvement', as Palmerston liked to put it. Not all the 'public' measures were equally well received, as we shall see. As the century drew on, however, it became increasingly commonplace to look upon the mid-century as something of a golden age. Looking back at the end of the century WEH Lecky supposed that the 'world' had never 'seen a better constitution than England enjoyed' in the three decades which lay between the first and second Reform Acts (Lecky 1899, 1.21). But then it all went wrong. The age of 'equipoise' passed into something very different.

It would be a mistake to suppose that everything was blissfully settled up until the moment that Palmerston's heart finally gave out. Disraeli had sensed 'tempestuous times' since 1860 (Briggs 1959, 497). Carlyle could always sense tempestuous times. His world had been 'sick and out of joint' since 1829 (Himmelfarb 2007, 48). October 1865 simply sharpened concentration. Two particular constitutional questions had already begun to assume a threatening aspect, and there had been a second death, the consequences of which were starting to assume worrying proportions. The questions related to the future of the monarchy and the functionality of Parliament. The second death occurred at the very end of 1861. In late November of that year, Prince Albert contracted typhoid. His condition quickly deteriorated. Increasingly unable to recognise his wife, he could be found constantly wandering around the corridors at Windsor hallucinating and rattling door-handles. No one, the doctors included, appeared to have the courage to tell him to rest. Victoria fretted manically, following him around sprinkling eau-de-cologne on his shoes and thrusting smelling salts under his nose. All strength finally dissipated, Albert took to his bed, to be given half-hourly doses of brandy and liberal amounts of opiate. It was all his doctors, led by the famed William Jenner, recently appointed Royal Physician, seemed able to do. A thoroughly unimpressed Lord Clarendon made it known that, in his opinion at least, they were 'not fit to attend a sick cat' (Longford 1998, 295). Albert died on 14 December. He was just forty-two.

Death came earlier in nineteenth-century England of course. Even so Albert had died young. He looked a lot older, but then being married to Victoria was an exhausting business. In more lucid moments during his final days, Albert suggested that his demise was wrought by 'over work'. In truth, he had been unwell for sometime, probably afflicted by Crohn's disease, possibly by early-stage stomach cancer. Windsor moreover was damp as well as cold, an incubator for typhoid bacteria. To his wife, however, Albert's death was unexpected and devastating, not least because, until the very last hours, the doctors had been sure that there was 'no cause for alarm'. For four days, she could not write a line in her diary. On the 14th, she wrote 'Oh God! Oh God! Oh God!' Two days later, her entry was more explicit: 'How am I alive after witnessing what I have done?' (Longford 1998, 307) Entries for the following weeks and months adopted the same tone. 'The loss of her husband', Lady Lewis confided to Clarendon, 'has changed her from a powerful sovereign' into 'a weak and desolate woman with a weight of duties she has not the moral and physical power to support' (Briggs 1959, 460).

Victoria went into mourning, which was entirely to be expected. The royal family was bedecked in weeds for months. Victorian stayed bedecked for years. Mourning, the *Times* observed, became a 'sort of religion' at court. At first, patience was the order of the day, and no one demurred at the expense incurred as various Albert memorials began to pop up across the country, few of which earned Victoria's approval, blighted apparently by an inability to capture the sheer majesty of her recently departed's expression. The Albert Memorial did not impress. She did, however, approve the construction of the Albert Hall opposite. 'It looks like the British Constitution' she declared rather gnomically on the visiting the site a few months before its opening much later in 1871 (Heffer 2013, 336). Patience had long worn thin by then. In April 1864, the *Times* had published an April Fools headline which suggested that 'Her Majesty's loyal subjects will be very pleased to hear that their sovereign is about to break her protracted seclusion'. A teasing poster was pinned to the gates of Buckingham Palace. 'These commanding premises to be let or sold', it read, 'in consequence of the last occupant's declining business'. Victoria was advised to turn a blind eye. Instead, she chose to publish a sober contradiction in the same paper, alongside a doctor's note. 'The Queen', the letter confirmed, 'heartily appreciated the desire of her subjects to see her'. But:

> There are other and higher duties than those of mere representation which are now thrown upon the Queen, alone and unassisted – duties which she cannot neglect without injury to the public service, which weigh increasingly upon her, overwhelming her with work and anxiety. (Strachey 1971, 184)

She would continue to serve 'Society' as best she could, but 'More than that the Queen cannot do'.

Her percipient uncle, King Leopold, sought to remind her that it was not simply a matter of doing stuff, but of being seen to do it. The English, he observed, 'are very personal; to continue to love people they must see them' (Longford 1998, 321). Mere representation was everything. As a gesture, she agreed to attend an occasional horticultural show here and there, inspect troops at nearby Aldershot now and again, and even host an 'alarming' breakfast party or two. In February 1866, she reluctantly agreed to open Parliament, albeit in a foul humour, pointedly refusing to wear her robes of state or the crown, preferring instead a mourning cap and black tulle veil designed to hide her face and remove the need to acknowledge, still less smile at, any of the 'staring people' inside or outside Parliament.[4] The Prime Minister Lord Russell was chastised for forcing a 'broken-hearted widow' to present herself in such way on 'Show'. All in all a 'wretched day', her diary recorded in blunt tones (Hibbert 2001, 312; Homans 1998, 64). But that was pretty much it. 'Where is Britannia?' the satirical *Tomahawk* magazine asked, before casting a series of aspersions regarding the role of her Highland gillie John Brown. *The Times* struck a sober, but no less ominous, note. It is 'impossible for a recluse to occupy the British Throne without a gradual weakening of that authority which the Sovereign has been accustomed to exert' (Homans 1998, 70, 160).

By the end of the decade, the situation had become critical. Republican clubs were springing up again, all over the country. Away in Newcastle, the Radical MP Sir Charles Dilke invited an audience in early

[4]The robes were draped across the back of the throne. She refused to read the address, instead just staring blankly ahead. Victoria was bribed by the offer of £30,000 from Parliament to help cover the expense of Princess Helena's wedding to Prince Christian of Sonderburg-Augustenburg. Subsequent invitations were generally rebuffed for reasons of health and climate; sometimes too cold, sometimes too hot, occasionally too windy. The idea that she should open Parliament 'as a matter of course, year after year', Lord Derby was informed, was entirely mistaken, only if the weather was right.

1871 to contemplate the virtues of a republic. 'I say for my part', he concluded, 'and I believe that the middle classes in general will say - let it come'. There was, *The Times* reported, 'great enthusiasm' in the room (Jenkins 1965, 69–70). Back in London, Lady Ely confirmed Victoria had been reduced to 'crying a lot' (Longford 1998, 388). Whilst Dilke harangued his audience of disgruntled shopkeepers at the Newcastle 'Lit and Phil', a few miles to the west George Otto Trevelyan wandered the gardens at Wallington correcting drafts of a pamphlet entitled *What Does She Do With It?* which inferred that the Queen was squirreling away large amounts of civil list money which was intended to cover expenses incurred in her conspicuously non-existent public engagements. Gladstone despaired. 'I cannot help continually revolving the question of the Queen's invisibility', he moaned to Lord Granville, 'in rude and general terms, the Queen is invisible and the Prince of Wales is not respected' (Wilson 2002, 360). Pressed to open Parliament in 1870, Victoria threatened to abdicate. Abdication was, however, out of the question. Even mad George III had been kept on the throne; the prospective coronation of his son, the Prince Regent, raising as hideous a spectre as that which accompanied visions of King Bertie swaggering up the nave of Westminster Abbey to be invested with the Orb and Sceptre.[5]

In summer 1871, an exasperated Gladstone responded sharply to Victoria's insinuation that she was being dragged back and forth to attend various public events just to prop up his government. It was a 'sickening' aspersion. 'Worse things', he added, 'may easily be imagined; but smaller and meaner cause for the decay of Thrones cannot be conceived' (Jenkins 1995, 345–6). On a different occasion, he complained to the Queen's long-suffering secretary Ponsonby that such 'woes of fancy' could do every bit as much harm as 'the most fearful dispensations of Providence' (Longford 1998, 383). In the end, as we shall see, the monarchy would be saved; in large part, the consequence of the same malignant bacteria that did for Albert. Throughout much of the 1860s, however, it seemed as though Carlyle's earlier prognostication would prove to be right. 'Even amongst the lowest classes of the people', he had foretold back in 1842, 'Queenship and Kingship are fast growing

[5] A vision which horrified Victoria as much as anyone, 'If only our dear Bertie was fit to replace me', she moaned on one occasion as she contemplated retiring, apparently, to a 'cottage in the hills' (Arnstein 2003, 135). But he was not.

out of date' (Jenkins 1965, 68). With the passing of 'age of equipoise', many increasingly feared, must come the passing of monarchy.

Meanwhile, and just as concerning, some were beginning to conjure the barely less dreadful prospect of further parliamentary reform. Charles Dickens tried to be patient with his Queen, sensitive to her misery. He was nothing like so patient with his Parliament. As early as 1855, he had mused that there was 'nothing in the present time at once so galling and so alarming to me as the alienation of the people from their own public affairs', adding in sober tones that contemporary 'discontent' was 'extremely like the general mind of France before the breaking out of the first Revolution' (Jones 2009, 10). By then, he was already contemplating the idea of writing a novel about the 'wild' events of 1789. Dickens would also have noted the tabling of a series of Reform Bills in Parliament, beginning in 1849 and continuing right through the 1850s and into the 1860s. But he would also have noted that they all failed. *Punch* took a different view of the public mood, publishing a cartoon in which John Bull was depicted falling asleep whilst trying to read newspaper reports of parliamentary reform debates. So did Disraeli's ally Lord Stanley, who reported that whilst there was some 'political excitement' at Westminster, it was not evidently 'shared to any considerable extent by the people' (Bentley 1996, 187). Palmerston had voiced the same opinion in Cabinet in late 1859. The people had no evident 'wish' for further reform and seemed to appreciate that political matters were best left to those with 'wealth and intelligence' (Brown 2010, 465).

The mood shifted as the 1860s unfolded. The Radical press adopted an increasingly belligerent tone. The Chartist *Leader* sought to rally the 'old' cause, announcing that the 'blood of the Chartists of forty-eight is the seed of the Reform Movement of 1866' (Royle 1996, 89). The Universal League for the Material Elevation of the Industrial Classes, the original purpose of which had been to promote the better education of East Anglian agricultural workers, had morphed into a full-blown Reform League in 1865, its cause being energetically argued by the likes of John Stuart Mill. Sensing that the time might be ripe for a larger expression of public discontent, and maybe another picnic, the League decided that the coming July in Hyde Park would be ideal. The Metropolitan Police Commissioner was not sympathetic and asked the Home Secretary Spencer Walpole to issue a prohibitive proclamation, which he did. The League was, however, undeterred, and in the late afternoon of July 18, its leaders arrived in a fleet of Hansom cabs to address what the *Times* reported as being 'vast crowds' of supporters. At some point, there was a 'surge' and a handful of railings were torn down. Mrs Disraeli, who had been shopping and found herself marooned for a while in Curzon Street, reported some collateral damage to the flower beds.[6]

But that was about it. No one really wanted a riot, least of all the League leaders. Charles Bradlaugh, who had appointed himself deputy-marshal, rode around wearing a 'tricolour scarf and armlets' urging his compatriots not to annoy the policemen (Cowling 1967, 37). When a troop of Horse Guards arrived, the putative Jacobins cheered wildly and settled down to eat their sandwiches, after which they all went home. Westminster was all the same unsettled, and when the League announced its intention to hold another gathering in the same place the following May, the Home Secretary issued the same proclamation. On this occasion, he had misread the public mood, or at least the mood of those who read the *Times*, which first criticised him for failing to clarify the source of his assumed constitutional authority, and then when he subsequently backed down, criticised him for backing down. The May gathering meanwhile, as the same readers were informed, duly 'passed off with the quietness and good order of a temperance meeting', enlivened only by the presence of 'acrobats, cardsharps' and 'ballad singers without number' (Heffer 2013, 401). The Young Tory Lord John Manners could not help expressing a tincture of disappointment; 'no hooting, hardly any cheering' (Cowling 1967, 25).

It might have been ready for a bit of a party, but England in 1866 and 1867 was evidently no more inclined to revolution than it had been in 1848. The 'question' of constitutional 'settlement', the *Times* confirmed, had indeed become supremely 'tedious' to all but the most radical of Radicals. Disraeli calculated, correctly, that it had moved from being a 'public question' to an essentially 'Ministerial question' (Bentley 1996, 168; Heffer 2013, 394–5, 401). Sir Henry Bulwer appreciated the pragmatics. There were three considerations facing Tories asked

[6]The Disraelis lived at nearby Grosvenor Gate. On hearing of the disturbance Disraeli, who was at Westminster, asked his secretary Montagu Corry to report. Corry was reassuring. The crowd had made no especial effort to vandalise his house. Mrs Disraeli was meanwhile quite safe and 'wishes me to add that the people in general seem to be thoroughly enjoying themselves' and Corry added 'I really believe she sympathises with them' (Hibbert 2004, 253).

to support further reform proposals: 'First what is best for your party with a view to retaining office, secondly what is best for returning to it, and lastly what is best for the country generally' (Bentley 1996, 191). A case could be made, though not particularly in terms of realising natural 'rights' to anything. By 1867, the rhetoric of rights had anyway given way to that of 'trust', of who might be properly entrusted with the franchise. The case that convinced Disraeli was rather more prosaic. Dizzy the 'conjuror', as *Punch* liked to despise him, did the figures, second-guessed how redistribution might, if done properly, secure a House of more obedient Tory MPs, chuckled inwardly at the consternation it would cause on the opposition bench, and decided that another Reform Act might after all be a good idea.

The question of efficacy also pressed. It was not just League leaders such as Bradlaugh and Bright who suggested that Parliament was no longer properly functional. In 1856, Gladstone had published an essay pointedly entitled *The Declining Efficiency of Parliament*. Carlyle referred disparagingly to 'the national Palaver' (Heffer 2013, 155). Dickens despaired of an institution which 'does so little and talks so much that the most interesting ceremony I know of in connection with it was performed by one man, who just cleared it out, locked up the place, and put the keys in his pocket' (Goldberg 1972, 64). A few years later he confirmed his 'hope' to 'have every man in England feel something of the contempt for the House of Commons that I have', adding 'We shall never do anything until the sentiment is universal' (Forster 1966, 2.386). When he heard that Trollope was considering standing for election in Beverley in 1868, Dickens confessed himself to be baffled. The decision was 'inscrutable' (Halperin 1977, 113). Given Trollope's own disparaging observations in regard to the 'collection' of parliamentary 'windbags that puff and blow, and crack to the annoyance of honest men', it was a reasonable inference (Trollope 1995, 132). It was not only the Whig party which appeared to have lost the will to govern. The Tory party too had become possessed by what Lord Stanley termed, an 'entire apathy'. 'Too much hunting and shooting, eating and drinking', Peel concluded of his shire MPs. Disraeli agreed. They 'wanted culture' (Briggs 1959, 332; Gaunt 2010, 14–15; Bentley 1996, 147, 159, 163). They also wanted manners, as Macaulay observed of parliamentary proceedings in 1840; too often a cacophony of 'beastly bellowings' (Le May 1979, 153). Bagehot, as we shall see, reached precisely the same conclusion. Parliament had become the refuge of boors and 'bores'. It was certainly not the place to look for heroes, as Carlyle inferred ruefully. Matthew Arnold agreed. The 'British Constitution' itself, he observed, had become nothing more than a 'colossal machine for the manufacture of Philistines' (Heffer 2013, 595).

The more optimistic supposed that passage of another reform statute might restore a measure of institutional credibility.[7] Bagehot was not of their number, neither was Carlyle. And neither, unsurprisingly, were many of Disraeli's lobby-fodder. Robert Lowe, leader of the irredeemably recalcitrant Adullamites, loudly questioned how another reform bill was supposed 'to save the Constitution from the hands of a multitude struggling with want and discontent'.[8] Moreover, if they were to be given the vote, Lowe continued, Parliament had better make some provision for the better education of 'our future masters', something that was no longer a merely 'religious' matter but upon which the 'existence of our Constitution' would henceforth depend (Briggs 1959, 511, 521; Heffer 2013, 412–3). Arnold was doubtful. The Philistines who ran the local Mechanics Institutes could hardly be trusted to properly inculcate the newly enfranchised in the deeper cultural as well as political responsibilities. The 'best self' needed to know Greek (Arnold 1993, 182; Heffer 2013, 595–600). Lord Cranborne was more worried by the closet Jacobins lurking in the corridors of Westminster. Further reform, as the Tory MP Roundell Palmer supposed, could only promote a still greater degree of 'constituent-worship', a 'thing opposed to all real Conservatism'. Salisbury was simply 'disgusted' (Bentley 1996, 150; 2001, 259). And it was not just Tories. Lord Grey had early set his face against any further reform. There had to be a 'stop somewhere', he had advised back in 1837, 'unless we mean to keep the country in a state of continual agitation' (Smith 1990, 321). His protégé agreed. 'Power in the Hands of the Masses', Palmerston advised, only 'throws the Scum of the Community to the Surface' (Bentley 1996, 161).

[7] In his *A History of the Reform Bills of 1866 and 1867*, published in 1868, Cox suggested that reform was necessary if Parliament was to avoid being branded as an 'utterly incapable and incompetent assembly' (Briggs 1959, 508).

[8] The nomenclature Adullamite was taken from the Old Testament story of David. It was deployed in Parliamentary debate by John Bright, who suggested that Lowe and his supporters had retreated to the 'political cave of Adullam', the last refuge for 'everyone that was in distress and everyone that was discontented' (Aldous 2007, 158).

Bagehot agreed entirely. As readers of his essay on Lord Brougham were reminded the first Reform Act had already 'abolished' the more iniquitous politics of 'Toryism', for which reason it was not at all obvious why there needed to be a second (Bagehot 1965, 3.179). The Prime Minister Lord Derby famously confessed that it was something of a 'leap in the dark', but ventured that the 'extended franchise' might bring 'contentment' to the nation (Heffer 2013, 402–3). Carlyle, predictably enough, despaired:

> Let it come when it likes, since there are Dizzies, Gladstones, Russells, &c., triumphantly prepared to bring it in. Providence truly is skilful to prepare its instrumental men. Indeed, all England, heavily though languidly averse to the embarking on Niagara rapids, is strangely indifferent to whatever may follow… Newspaper editors, in private, I am told, and discerning people of every rank, as is partly apparent to myself, talk of approaching 'revolution', 'Common wealth', 'Common illth', or whatever it may be, with a singular composure. (Heffer 1995, 358)

Carlyle entitled his essay, *Shooting Niagara: And After?* It sold 4000 copies in three weeks. Carlyle had the answer too. There must be a fight to the death between the forces of 'Anarchy and anti-Anarchy'. Gladstone took a more positive view. Promoting the 1866 bill Gladstone had suggested that they were 'making History', and 'laying the foundations of much to come' (Heffer 2013, 388, 578–80). But he did not say what the coming might be. Disraeli, typically, eschewed both the messianic and the apocalyptic. A House of more obedient Tory MPs was the extent of his ambition; that and annoying Gladstone. Varying the common metaphors of leaping and shooting things, *Punch* famously carried a cartoon entitled 'The Derby 1867: Dizzy Wins with "Reform Bill"'. A sour looking Gladstone is depicted coming in second.[9] There was never much chance of anyone claiming that the second Reform Act was 'great'. Hardly anyone, it seemed, really wanted it.

The provisions of the 1867 Representation of the People Act, which received royal assent in August 1867, doubled the electorate, raising

[9] On the night of the crucial second Reading division, Disraeli looked in on the Carlton Club. Sir Matthew Ridley proposed a toast on the same theme: 'Here's the man who rode the race, who took the time, who kept the time, and who did the trick!' (Weintraub 1993, 448–9).

it to around 3.5 million, enfranchising more specifically all borough householders and lodgers paying £10, reducing the property threshold in counties, and rather more notoriously investing so-called 'fancy franchises' which granted extra votes to those who were graduates, had savings of £50 or who might otherwise be esteemed as 'professional' gentlemen. It was estimated that where Russell's failed 1866 bill might have added around 600,000 to the electoral roll, Disraeli's added half as much again. It also continued the process of redistribution, disenfranchising fifty-eight constituencies. The maths still looked a bit odd, very odd in places. The Lake District had a representation six times that of the north-east. Manchester, with a population of 350,000 and an electorate of 48,000 had three Members, the same number as the boroughs of Knaresborough, Petersfield and Andover, with a combined electorate of 2500. But then the second Reform Act was never intended to be a democratising measure, any more than was the first, whilst the logic of redistribution was driven by a desire to entrench a Tory *cordon sanitaire* in the provinces rather than create a 'hovel suffrage' in the cities (Cowling 1967, 47–8, 55, 68–74, 78). As was the case in 1832 the greater significance of the 1867 Act did not lie in ratios of redistribution, at least not directly.

Dignity and History

And no one appreciated this more sharply than Walter Bagehot. In much the same way as Burke and Macaulay, Bagehot mattered because he was the kind of man whose opinions mattered to other men who mattered. In the 'age of discussion', it was men like Bagehot, gossiping their evenings away in the Athenaeum and Brook's, who set the political tone. And who, in journals such as Trollope's *Fortnightly Review*, in which his celebrated essays on the English constitution originally appeared, engaged the masses, or at least masses of similarly minded middle-class English gentlemen. Burke and Macaulay had written for journals too of course, and frequented the same clubs. But neither earned their living in quite the same way. Bagehot was a journalist by profession, serving as editor of *The Economist* from 1861 until his death in 1877. The journal was renowned for its stance on market reform, its editor revered as a leading financial commentator. When the financial house of Overend Gurney collapsed on 11th May 1866, it was to Bagehot that Gladstone, then Chancellor the Exchequer, extended an urgent invitation to breakfast.[10] A natural free trader, Bagehot was innately more supportive of market than franchise reform. At the same time, as readers of his later *Lombard Street* would have noted, he was above all conscious of the need to calibrate the extent of reform by its capacity to reinvest public confidence. Breakfast with Gladstone, tea with George Eliot, dinners with friends and acquaintances such as R.H. Hutton, Matthew Arnold and Lord Acton, Bagehot moved in elevated circles. If the task of the progressive intellectual in mid-Victorian England was to furnish a 'polished Liberalism', as Bagehot alleged, then he was just the man to do the burnishing.[11]

Moreover, this polishing was not simply a matter of applying a further coating of utilitarian common sense. The polished liberal was also a man of letters. The younger Bagehot took considerable pride in his reputation as a literary critic. Shelley was his 'restorative', his 'passion for reforming mankind' thrilling, and a little terrifying (Bagehot 1965, 1.436–8, 449–50, 454–5, 474–5; Buchan 1959, 32, 84–5). He loved Wordsworth because he wrote about the 'human' rather than the 'abstract'. It was because of Wordsworth that 'all cultivated men speak differently' (Bagehot 1965, 1.3210).[12] The future Mrs Bagehot received copies of their respective collected works as engagement presents. As his various literary essays confirmed, it was the writer as much as the writing which fascinated Bagehot; the humanity of Wordsworth, the 'experiencing nature' of Shakespeare. These earlier essays moreover clearly left an imprint on Bagehot's own literary style. The art of political writing, the young Bagehot concluded, should be 'like the art of Rembrandt';

[10]Overend and Gurney enjoyed a solid reputation, and was popular amongst investors when it became a limited company in 1865. It had, however, been making increasingly speculative investments for much of the previous decade, and finally collapse in spring 1866. Banking legislation passed in 1844 was supposed to have prevented collapses of such magnitude.

[11]Bagehot advanced the merits of 'polished liberalism' in his 1855 essay *The First Edinburgh Reviewers* (Bagehot 1965, 1.332). In the words of Brian Hanley, Bagehot wrote for an audience of 'successful bankers, lawyers, shopkeepers, and the like – highly finished instruments of the economy' (Hanley 2004, 172–3).

[12]Wordsworth dominates what is perhaps Bagehot's most famous literary essay, *Wordsworth, Tennyson and Browning or Pure, Ornate and Grotesque Art in English Poetry*, published in 1864. Wordsworth and Milton are identified as the greatest of the 'pure' poets, with Tennyson and Browning respectively taking the honours for the 'ornate' and the 'grotesque' (Bagehot 1965, 2.333–66).

and there was one writer above all who had written in such a way (Best 1979, 260, 266). Bagehot was another considerable admirer of Burke. Macaulay may have been a great historian, but Burke was much the 'greater' writer, even if he would occasionally evince a too 'cavalier feeling of deep idolatry for the ancient realm'. It was the 'fierce living interest' which redeemed, the appreciation that politics is 'warm', that political 'institutions are shifting things, to be tried by and adjusted to the shifting conditions of a mutable world', that politics itself is a 'mutable business', a matter of 'sense and circumstances' (Bagehot 1965, 2.298–400, 406–10, 416–7; Ritchie 1989, 324–8; Burrow 1988, 171). This Burke assumed a familiar form in Bagehot's various essays on Whiggery and its heroes, populating many of his earlier essays such as *The First Edinburgh Reviewers.* Men such as Romilly and Sydney Smith, appraised for their 'character' as much as their 'creed', who disdain the Tory 'devotion' to the cult of monarchy, who are instead 'constitutional by instinct' and who hold, above all, to a 'steady belief' that 'the present world can, and should, be quietly improved' (Bagehot 1965, 1.315, 318–23). The young Bagehot liked to think he was such a man.

And he wrote his history accordingly, eschewing any trace of 'historic twaddle about the rise of liberty' (Bagehot 1965, 4.99). Accordingly whilst recommending Macaulay's *History* as 'a marvellous book', Bagehot counselled readers against too naive an acceptance of its most egregious complacencies; the all 'too perfect' William III, the 'too imperfect' James, the serried ranks of revered Whig revolutionaries all depicted a 'trifle like angels' (Bagehot 1965, 2.397, 427). Bagehot never questioned the importance of history, merely the mistake of making a fetish of it. Constitutions had their histories, but they were not only histories. The final chapter of the *Constitution* is entitled 'Its History and the Effects of that History'. The narrative, such as it is, rattles along; Greeks city-states, Norman kings, medieval parliaments, Tudor councils, all gone in a flash, along with any hint of whimsy. Neither Magna Carta nor Cromwell somehow 'founded the English constitution'. The Revolution of 1688 was more 'weak' than 'glorious', an internecine squabble between rival aristocratic families and their acolytes, for which reason the 'rule of Parliament' which somehow emerged as a collateral consequence is relegated to the chance of 'curious oddities' which pepper the 'curious' history of the English constitution (Bagehot 2001, 177–83). As for the Hanoverians, the least said the better, literally.

Any reader who anticipated a more leisurely progress had clearly not spent long enough contemplating the title of this final chapter, nor indeed the reason why it came at the end. It is the use of history which interests Bagehot, how it leads and misleads contemporary understanding, what it does. We have already noted the renowned introduction to the *Constitution*; the depiction of 'an ancient and ever-altering constitution' as being 'like an old man who still wears with attached fondness clothes in the fashion of his youth: what you see of him is the same, what you do not see is wholly altered' (Bagehot 2001, 3). Sceptical, ironic, Whig; Burke might have written it. The tone is set. The greater 'effect' of history lies in the moulding of minds, not the shaping of institutions. The settlement of the English constitution is located in the 'preservative habit' of its people, an 'inbred principle of discipline and order' which over centuries has proved itself to be 'nature's favourite resource for preserving steadiness of conduct and consistency of opinion' (Bagehot 1965, 7.37–8, 52–4, 70–5; Spring 1983, 524–31).

Burke might have been rather less pejorative in his dismissal of the 'stupidity' of the 'bovine masses', the 'crowds of people who are scarcely more civilised than the majority of two thousand years ago' (Bagehot 2001, 6–7, 30). But he would certainly have agreed with the more measured supposition that the 'calm national mind' of the English owed much to the 'homage' and 'deference' habitually exhibited by the 'ruder sort of men' (Bagehot 2001, 7, 24, 183–5). In this belief, Bagehot never wavered. His 1848 *Letters* had accredited the stability of the English constitution to the 'work of old-fashioned generations', to the 'dull care' and 'stupid industry' of some many 'slumberers in the churchyard' (Bagehot 1965, 4.36). And the same would be disinterred twenty-four years later in *Physics and Politics*. Here, engaging more fully the emergent science of social anthropology, Bagehot reached the comfortingly Whiggish conclusion that the best constitutions are those which enjoy the closest cultural fit, those which express most acutely the 'national character', something which allowed Burkean and Darwinian alike to recognise the singular blessing of being English (Bagehot 1965, 7.34, 37; Brantlinger 1977, 207).

English constitutional history mattered, but only insofar as it shaped the constitution in 1865. There was nothing intrinsically significant about 1688 or 1642 or 1215 for that matter. The *Constitution* was intended to describe a 'living constitution – a constitution that is in actual work and power' (Bagehot 2001, 193). Here again, the Burkean resonance is immediate. What concerned Bagehot was functionality. It was the same attitude evinced by a generation of 'professional' historians, as we have already noted (Tosh 1985, 98–9). 'What grows upon the world', as he confirmed in the closing passages to the 1867 edition, 'is a certain matter-of-factness' (Bagehot 2001, 167). It is no coincidence that a number of Bagehot's earliest published essays invited contemplation of John Stuart Mill, whose determination to contemplate utilitarianism in social practice, rather than reflecting on abstractions such as the 'calculus of felicity', attracted particular approval (Ford 1970, 315–6). As we have already noted, where Burke and Macaulay had invited their readers to travel back to the seventeenth century, Bagehot merely asked them to reach back a year or so, to 'the time of Lord Palmerston' (Bagehot 2001, 193). There was no need to excavate any more remote causation in order to comprehend why things were not working quite as well as they should, nor to resurrect ancient 'principles' in order to ascertain what to do. The problems were self-evident and immediate; one was Victoria, the other was Parliament. This did not mean that England would be better off with a republic, or with an extended franchise. The failings of republican government were evident to anyone who cared to glance across either the Channel or the Atlantic, and Bagehot was no more a natural reformer than he was a democrat. Even so in regard to both cases, it was very obvious that 'something will have to be done' (Bagehot 2001, 191).

The essays which comprised his *English Constitution* were written to this end. And Bagehot established a famous demarcation which was intended to aid the reader in their contemplation of the alternative functions of Crown and Parliament. There were, he suggested, two 'parts' to the constitution. There were the 'dignified parts', being those which 'excite and preserve the reverence of the population', and the 'efficient parts', being 'those by which it, in fact, works and rules' (Bagehot 2001, 5). Whilst the 'efficient parts' of the constitution were comparatively modern and comparatively 'simple', the 'dignified' were comprised of various 'historical, complex, august, theatrical parts, which it has inherited from a long past' (Bagehot 2001, 8). The greater delusions of history are evident in the latter, their consequences in the former. Raising an image familiar from Adam Smith's *Theory of Moral Sentiments* as well as Burke's *Reflections*, Bagehot suggested that history fashions a 'spectacle' which 'acts as a disguise' for the more prosaic necessities of government (Bagehot 2001, 46).

And the centrepiece of the 'dignified' constitution is the monarchy, steeped in history, designed to delude and distract. In his second essay on the role of monarchy, Bagehot observed:

> The apparent rulers of the English nation are like the most imposing personages of a splendid procession: it is by them the mob are influenced; it is they whom the spectators cheer. The real rulers are secreted in second-rate carriages; no one cares for them or asks about them, but they are obeyed implicitly and unconsciously by reason of the splendour of those who eclipsed and preceded them. (Bagehot 2001, 31)

In his *Essay on the History of the English Government and Constitution* also published in 1865 Russell reached much the same conclusion. There was no more compelling proof that the English constitution was an expression 'of imagination as well as of reason' than the 'passionate' and peculiar 'reverence paid to Royalty' (Smith 2001, xx). But Bagehot was nothing like as confident as Russell. As early as 1831, John Stuart Mill, like Carlyle, had wondered if the 'charm' of the 'ancient constitution' was beginning to wear off (Himmelfarb 2007, 53–4). Bagehot wondered the same. Context, and demeanour, was everything. Passionate reverence could come and go. A sad Queen might find herself removed from office at the whim of a few hundred jeering Geordies. A happy Queen could rule an Empire. There was nothing in the constitution to preclude either eventuality. In the matter of monarchy, as in so much else to do with the English constitution, there was 'no authentic explicit information as to what the Queen can do, any more than of what she does' (Bagehot 2001, 49).

Or at least there was not until Bagehot decided to redress the absence in the two essays which opened his *Constitution*. And what the monarch 'does' was simple; she performs. 'There is in England', Bagehot confirmed, 'a certain charmed spectacle which imposes on the many, and guides their fancies as it will' (Bagehot 2001, 31). Guiding these 'fancies' is the principle responsibility of the reigning monarch, and as many of her progeny as can be safely let loose in public. Even the much-maligned Bertie appreciated this much. 'We live in radical times', he urged in late 1870, 'and the more People see the Sovereign the better it is for the People and the Country' (Hibbert 2001, 332). So did Lord Halifax: 'The mass of the people expect a King or Queen to look and the play the part. They want to see a Crown and a Sceptre and that sort of thing.

They want the gilding for the money. It is not wise to let them think', he concluded ominously 'that they could do without a sovereign who lives at Osborne and Balmoral as any private lady might do' (Hibbert 2001, 336). And so of course did Bagehot. The entire purpose of the monarchy is to furnish the constitution with a 'theatrical' masque, one which can distract the 'ruder' multitude, and inspire its 'reverence' (Bagehot 2001, 7). A monarch in retirement was no use to anyone.

There is no evidence that Victoria ever read Bagehot. But it is sometimes claimed that every subsequent monarch has been pointed towards the *English Constitution* as a kind of primer on what to do (Wheare 1974, 188–90). Bertie, whose preference was for the bodice-ripping sensation novels of Ellen Wood and Mary Elizabeth Braddon, would probably have found it rather hard work. Quite what he or his mum might have made of the following notorious observation must therefore remain moot:

> The use of the Queen, in a dignified capacity, is incalculable. Without her in England, the present English government would fail and pass away. Most people when they read that the Queen walked on the slopes at Windsor – that the Prince of Wales went to the Derby – have imagined that too much thought and prominence were given to little things. But they have been in error; and it is nice to trace how the actions of a retired widow and an unemployed youth become of such importance. (Bagehot 2001, 34)

Two verbs in this famous passage warrant particular attention. Both engage the idea of perception. The first is to walk. The perambulatory image had been deployed, in rather more respectful terms, seventy years earlier in Dorothy Wordsworth's diary, recording a visit to Windsor where she espied the periodically deranged King George III walking on the terrace accompanied by his grotesquely bloated son, the future Prince Regent. 'I fancied', she wrote, 'myself treading on Fairy-Ground, and that the gay company around me was brought there by enchantment'. Intermittently mad he may have been, but George III was a notably popular monarch; certainly in comparison with his son. His carefully choreographed strolls along the terrace and Windsor were calculated to entrance, and they did, or at least they worked on Dorothy.

The second verb that Bagehot preferred is just as significant; to read. By 1865, it was no longer merely a matter of making a trip to Windsor to see the Queen wandering about, or to Epsom to see Bertie attending race meetings. It was also a matter of reading about it; even if it did mean that accounts of Bertie attending the Derby meet in 1869 jostled for column inches with those which described the delightfully salacious proceedings in the Mordaunt case. Bertie was called as a 'witness' in the divorce proceedings which followed in 1870.[13] It was reported that the Prince's appearance at Epsom that summer has, as a consequence, been accompanied by rather a lot of distasteful jeering. Those who had also taken their trouble to read Bagehot would have remembered a further piece of advice in regard to the 'performance' of majesty: 'Its mystery is its life. We must not let in daylight upon magic' (Bagehot 2001, 50). There was way too much daylight in the Divorce Court, as Gladstone curtly informed Bertie.

The whole purpose of a Queen, as Disraeli had so brilliantly appreciated, is to spread a bit of fairy-dust. Bagehot loathed Disraeli. But on this matter, he was entirely in agreement. The function of monarchy is to 'disguise' the real workings of government:

> Most do vaguely know that there are some other institutions besides the Queen, and some rules by which she governs. But a vast number like their minds to dwell more upon her than on anything else, and therefore she is inestimable. A republic has only difficult ideas in government; a constitutional monarchy has an easy idea too; it has a comprehensible element for the vacant many, as well as complex laws and notions for the inquiring few. (Bagehot 2001, 37)

Characterised by a 'decorous dullness' peculiar to themselves, the English are a 'deferential' people 'by imagination, not reason' (Bagehot 2001, 70, 185). They are also a credulous people. They like living in fairyland. The monarchy provides 'a visible symbol of unity to those still so imperfectly educated as to need a symbol' (Bagehot 2001, 41). The 'ruder sort of men' has little interest in 'the plain, palpable ends of government'. Society is animated by the 'theatrical show of society', by 'a

[13] Bertie was not directly cited in the case of *Mordaunt v Mordaunt, Cole and Johnstone* and he vigorously denied any 'improper familiarity' when the insinuation arose during cross-examination. But the mere fact that he was called to give evidence was enough for the press. In the end the petition was denied for reason of Lady Mordaunt's 'puerperal mania'; an ending which would have resembled so many of the sensation novels of the time. Bertie, a devotee of the genre, might have appreciated the irony.

certain pomp of great men' and 'a certain spectacle of beautiful women'. The 'higher world, as it looks from without, is a stage on which the actors walk their parts much better than the spectators can', and the 'climax of the play is the Queen' (Bagehot 2001, 30–1). Or it should be.

John Stuart Mill had vouched the same conclusion in 1831. The security of the monarchy rested on the continuing gullibility of the 'vulgar' (Himmelfarb 2007, 75). Charles Kingsley did not deploy the same pejorative tone, but his suggestion that monarch and 'ruder' subject existed in a state of mutual dependency, one which rendered a monarch 'more or less elected' by public appreciation, was acute (Homans 1998, 146–7). The idea of a constitutional monarchy, understood in these terms, as one who reigns rather than rules, imported a series of collateral representational responsibilities. Most importantly, as Bagehot confirmed, in political terms a constitutional monarch must appear 'aloof and solitary'; something which had the additional virtue of precluding the 'great danger' of a 'prejudiced' monarch (Bagehot 2001, 41, 54). Casting around for a sobering example of the latter, Bagehot alighted, predictably enough, upon the much-maligned Swellfoot. A constitutional monarch retained the 'right to be consulted, the right to encourage' and the 'right to warn' and, Bagehot famously concluded, a monarch of 'great sense and sagacity would want no others' (Bagehot 2001, 60).

Though rarely short of an opinion, and prone to taking offence, Victoria was considerably more sagacious than Swellfoot. She was also informed. Her teenage reading had included lots of Blackstone. And following her marriage to Prince Albert it had broadened further, evenings passed 'doing cross-stitch' which her beloved 'read aloud to her Hallam's *Constitutional History of England*' (Strachey 1971, 102–3). Some responsibilities were more palatable than others. Opening Parliament was one of the least palatable, dispensing trinkets under her personal prerogative as the 'fount of honour' one of the more. Victoria clung to her personal constitutional prerogatives with a peculiar tenacity; in essence the limited power to appoint generals and priests, and rather greater license to harass ministers. Peel was not the first Prime Minister to weary of having to reply to his monarch's incessant queries 'several times a day'. Gladstone gave up bothering, earning a predictable rebuke; the Queen was not to be 'kept in the dark' (Le May 1979, 105, 119). Foreign Secretaries were peculiarly exercised. Palmerston proved to be as recalcitrant as Gladstone, finding himself dismissed in late 1851 for failing to keep the Queen informed of events surrounding the coup which dismissed Napolean III. He was back a few months later.

Otherwise, however, there was not a lot for a monarch to do. The ambit of constitutional prerogative was diminishing. That of dismissing administrations or dissolving Parliaments had, as Bagehot confirmed, 'almost, if not quite, dropped out of the constitution' (Bagehot 2001, 161–2). The last pertinent example of a monarch touching the edges of this prerogative, Bagehot supposed, was William IV's dismissal of Melbourne's administration in 1834. And the days when a monarch might decline legislative assent were long gone. Bagehot was characteristically pithy; 'she must sign her own death-warrant if the two Houses unanimously send it up to her' (Bagehot 2001, 48). As to the appointment of Prime Ministers, the limitations there were made very apparent in 1880 when Victoria tried to prevent the return of the 'entirely mad' Gladstone to office. She could not, as Disraeli gently reminded her. The 'spirit of the Constitution' described a greater duty (Heffer 2013, 810–1). More and more it was a matter of appreciating the 'recondite' difference between reigning and ruling; which meant, in prosaic terms, turning up at 'nice and pretty events' and sprinkling a little fairy-dust around, and not getting too much in the way of government (Bagehot 2001, 25).

It was of course the lack of fairy-dust which concerned Bagehot in 1867, even if he was keen to reassure his readers that 'no one proposes' seriously to remove the Queen (Bagehot 2001, 167). In a sense, as Bagehot conceded, England already resembled a 'disguised republic', one that had 'insinuated itself beneath the folds of monarchy'; a renowned observation which inspired an equally renowned repost from Leslie Stephen, that Bagehot had made 'the rarest kind of discovery, that which is already known' (Bagehot 2001, 44, 187; Buchan 1959, 160). Most importantly, however, it was still a republic with a Queen at its head, for which reason it was immune from the tensions evident elsewhere, at which point Bagehot gestured across the Atlantic. Much of the second essay on the monarchy was given over to convincing readers that a 'wise' monarch was an alternative to be cherished; even if the realities of 'hereditary' in-breeding and recent, particularly Hanoverian, history suggested that the country was just as likely to be landed with a 'meddling maniac' or a grotesque wastrel. Victoria, Bagehot insinuated, might be perplexing indeed, even maddening at times. But she seemed, in broad terms at least, to appreciate the nature of constitutional monarchy.

Interestingly Bagehot appraised Albert on these terms, a prince possessed of the 'rare gifts of a constitutional monarch' (Bagehot 2001, 61, 66–7). He mused briefly on what might have been. But Bagehot rarely surmised for long, and by the time of the 1872 edition of the *Constitution*, it was evident that his concern with the meddling monarchs had given way to a much greater concern regarding the misuse of Crown prerogatives by unscrupulous politicians.

The Efficient Secret

During the mid-1860s, the subject of public governance was inextricably bound up in the broader question of parliamentary reform. Bagehot's complaint was familiar. Parliament should be the 'great instructor of the nation'. Instead, it had become little more 'than a big meeting of more or less idle persons', the natural habitat of boors, bores and buffoons. He was particularly bothered by the quality of parliamentary debate. 'As soon as bore A ends, bore B begins', he observed in tones of evident contempt, 'Some enquire from genuine love of knowledge, or from a real wish to improve what they ask about; others to see their name in the papers' (Bagehot 2001, 12, 125). And the rot set in at the top of the greasy pole. Amongst the many criticisms written into his essay on *The Character of Sir Robert Peel* was his subject's predilection for the rhetorically 'specious'. Too many wasters, too many fools, too little getting done; in this sense, there was indeed a case for reform. It was not, however, a matter of principle or even practice, but of 'gross appearances'. Parliamentary representation did not 'look right' (Bagehot 2001, 121). In the first edition of the *Constitution*, he was prepared to concede that the new class of 'town artisans' were entitled to have their opinions heard, and voiced, in Parliament. He justified the 1832 Act in similar terms, not as the fanciful realisation of revolution 'principles', but precisely because it quieted 'agitation' whilst also extending the vote to those who could be trusted to return 'moderate' men of 'moderate' opinions (Bagehot 2001, 104–5, 109, 113–5). Bagehot evinced a very Whiggish faith in the right kind of chaps, in Parliament and in government; and an equally Whiggish anxiety regarding the possibility that it might all be about to change.

By 1872 his worst fears had been realised. The aspiring Parliamentarian must now be content 'to utter common thoughts, and to bind himself to the formularies of common creeds, or he will not succeed in his candidature' (Buchan 1959, 116–7). Disraeli's Act had been a 'mischievous and monstrous' deceit, and a reckless gamble. England 'is a very small and very crowded country to try experiments in', he concluded in an essay on Dilke published in the *Economist*, and until education has made them a little safer 'they are better let alone' (Buchan 1959, 165). The same tone pervades the *Constitution*. The working-class is generally 'ignorant', readily corruptible, and 'contribute almost nothing to our corporate public opinion' (Bagehot 1965, 116, 188). Ignorance precluded trust, and much hope. The 'difficulty' of 'amplifying parliamentary institutions' was evident in the sheer ignorance of those who existed at the bottom of the social scale'. Only the naive could really believe that 'our constitution' is based on 'equality, or on an avowed and graduated adjustment to intelligence and property' (Bagehot 1965, 191–2). There are 'rude' men and there are 'delicate' men. The latter are fit to vote, the former are not, and a 'happy state' is one in which this simple reality is commonly appreciated (Bagehot 1965, 1.202–3; Bagehot 2001, 29). The notorious preface to the 1872 edition of the *Constitution* was written in these darker tones. Parliament was in need of reform. But it was not in need of the kind of reform which Disraeli proposed.

Like any other institution, Parliament had a 'dignified' and an 'efficient' aspect. And the same was true of each constituent chamber. The greater responsibility of the House of Lords tended towards the former, a 'dignified torpor'; not that attendees at Victoria's coronation would have been easily persuaded (Bagehot 2001, 70). Bagehot quoted Gladstone; every Englishman retains a 'sneaking kindness for a lord', however inebriated. As regards the practice of passing legislation though the consequence of the 1832 and 1867 Acts was to confirm that the Lords must concede to the 'opinion' of the Commons, no matter how distasteful. Back in 1829, Lord Grey had adopted an apocalyptic tone in urging his fellow peers to approve the Catholic Emancipation Act. The alternative was 'absolute destruction' (Gash 1965, 30–1). Much the same could be detected in Wellington's similarly sober advice in 1846. Peel's Repeal Act was indeed a 'bad' Bill. But 'we must all vote for it. The Queen's government must be supported'. There was no future, the Duke added, in just 'rejecting' things (Gash 1965, 51; Le May 1979,

129).[14] Occasionally though, things just had to be rejected. 'What are you good for then?' Carlyle raged when the House demurred and failed to reject the 1867 Act, 'Show us, show us, or else disappear' (Heffer 2013, 580). Bagehot evinced an equivalent disdain. The House had 'ceased to be one of latent dictators, and has become one of temporary rejectors and palpable alterers' (Bagehot 2001, 75, 204–6). In due course, Lord Salisbury would refine a strategy of aristocratic recalcitrance, founded on the traditional Tory idea of a constitution of balanced 'interests', wherein the Lords served as a mediator between the innate conservatism of the nation and the radical propensities increasingly evident in the Commons.

The idea of a 'revising' second chamber, Bagehot conceded, had much to recommend it; most obviously as a check on the 'pernicious' tendency of the Commons. Unfortunately, the Lords too commonly disappointed. It was not simply a matter of 'apathy' and indolence (Bagehot 2001, 83–5). There was also arrogance, the temptation, as Rosebery said of Salisbury, to behave like 'a King of Hungary on his coronation, who rides around to an eminence and brandishes his sword to the four corners of the globe' (Le May 1979, 138). And bloody-mindedness and sheer stupidity too, as Bagehot noted in 1869 when the Lords threatened to reject the Irish Church Bill. The House had made itself look 'ridiculous' (Buchan 1959, 174). The advice was not heeded. When their Lordships threatened to refuse assent to the third Reform Bill in 1884, the Radical Labouchere proposed a resolution in the Commons which asked for 'such alterations in the relations of the two Houses of Parliament' which would in the future make it impossible for the second Chamber 'to alter, defeat, or delay legislation'. When she heard rumour that Gladstone might be tempted, Victoria was horrified, pointedly taking the trouble to loudly defend the 'existence of an independent body of men acting solely for the good of the country, and free from the terror which forces so many Commoners to vote against their consciences' (Arnstein 2003, 162). Labouchere made a habit of proposing things which horrified his Queen, as we shall see in the next chapter. In the

[14] Bagehot quotes extensively from Wellington's 'very curious letter' to Lord Derby on the subject of 'rejecting things' written in 1846 in the context of Peel's Repeal Act. Wellington's warning touched upon a more particular convention. The 1846 Repeal Act was presented as a money bill, which even then was hedged by a convention which was supposed to prevent its rejection in the Lords (Bagehot 2001, 75–8).

end, a compromise Redistribution of Seats Bill was agreed. Two years later the House brought down Gladstone's third administration when it rejected his Home Rule bill. A decade on in 1893 it would do the same again, rejecting another Home Rule bill by 419 votes to 41. Revenge, as we shall see later, would be served cold in 1911, by a later Liberal government long of memory, and shorter of patience.

In comparison with their Lordships, the 'dignified' aspect of the Commons, according to Bagehot, was 'altogether secondary to its efficient use' (Bagehot 2001, 94, 126). Bagehot identified five particular 'functions' of the House, conjured with the possibility of a sixth, and then with a magician's flourish produced a seventh to which he duly devoted an entire essay. The first, which is the 'elective' function, the 'choosing' of 'our President' or Prime Minister is, in fact, the complement to the seventh, 'for at any moment' the Commons 'can' both 'choose a ruler' and also 'dismiss a ruler'. This reciprocal power, Bagehot goes on to explain at some length, must be comprehended within the broader political context of mid-Victorian politics, and more particularly the consolidation of parliamentary power in political parties. Discussing the emergence of party in 1846 the *Quarterly Review* had pondered the question 'And are not gratitude and fidelity due at least equally to the Party as to the Sovereign?' (Le May 1979, 174). It had also pondered the consequence; that a minister, or indeed an MP, who disagreed with the party line should resign. Bagehot asked pretty much the same question and reached pretty much the same resolution. Party was by 1865 the 'essence' of the House of Commons, the 'bone of its bone, and breath of its breath' (Bagehot 2001, 101). It was in sum the first fidelity.

Whilst Bagehot treats the second, third and fourth functions, the 'expressive', the 'teaching' and the 'informing', with comparative brevity, their significance should not be underestimated. And the immediate political context is again critical; for each plays a part in regulating something which was of great concern to men like Bagehot, the shaping of public opinion. The 'expressive' function is essentially 'lyrical'. The Commons 'pours out in characteristic words the characteristic heart of the nation' (Bagehot 2001, 117). The 'teaching' function is complementary. The Commons 'ought to teach the nation what it does not know'. It is an 'altering' function, and what it should alter is of course public opinion. Unfortunately, however, as we have already noted, Bagehot here shared a common opinion; that the Commons had long disappointed. The third function is the 'informing'. Through its various procedures, the Commons addresses the 'grievances' of 'special interests, special opinions, special prejudices' (Bagehot 2001, 95–6). Here again, the Commons plays an inter-active role, receiving and expressing particular public concerns, whilst also seeking to ameliorate, address and reshape them. It can do this, Bagehot adds, precisely because it is a 'real electoral body', its members a 'chosen people, a picked and selected people' (Bagehot 2001, 19, 112). In regard to the 'informing' function of the Commons, as in so much else, there was at least as much Whig in Bagehot as there was new liberal.

The fifth 'function' of the Commons is the legislative. So too is the sixth, which Bagehot terms the 'financial', and which as a species of legislation is not, on reflection, deemed worthy of special consideration. Here Bagehot engages the first of two tenets of Whig constitutional faith; the sovereignty of Parliament. It is important first to distinguish parliamentary sovereignty from political sovereignty. Bagehot never doubted the reality of the latter, after all 'Hobbes told us long ago and everybody now understands that there must be a supreme authority, a conclusive power in every state on every point somewhere' (Bagehot 2001, 150). The principle of parliamentary sovereignty is however different, and Bagehot eschews the rather grander suppositions articulated by the likes of Hume, that the Commons 'absolutely commands all other parts of the government'. Parliament is an 'ultimate' political authority, and in terms of its legislative capacity assumes a complementary constitutional authority. But the supposition that the Commons 'commands' government is too simplistic. Rather it 'appoints' and then 'watches' government, and then occasionally 'from day to day' it 'seats and unseats ministries' (Bagehot 2001, 154–5). This latter aside, almost casual in tenor, assumes far greater import in the chapter which follows, on 'changes of ministry'. At this point, Bagehot's focus shifts to a rather more concerted consideration of government. The unseating of ministries represents a sharp point in the 'peculiar' relation of legislative and executive. Much of the chapter is given over to excavating examples of the 'evils' that flow from 'sudden' changes in ministry.[15]

At the same time, however, this same contemplation requires Bagehot to engage a second fundamental tenet of Whig constitutional faith; the

[15] Bagehot identified three of these 'evils', bringing in 'untried persons' all of a 'sudden', promoting a sense of transience amongst incumbent ministers, and removing safeguards against any 'mischievous change of policy' (Bagehot 2001, 122–3).

separation of powers, the responsibility to 'ensure' as Lord Durham put it in 1838, 'harmony, in place of collision, between the various powers of the state' (Vile 1967, 212). But this too can be misunderstood. Whig historians such as Hallam invariably liked to guide their readers back to 1688 in order to find the origins of a principle which, they impressed, was peculiarly English. The same writers liked to write the history of 1832 in much the same terms. Lord Grey did, in his 1858 essay *Parliamentary Government Considered with Reference to Reform of Parliament*. So did Erskine May in his *Constitutional History of England*, published a couple of years later between 1861 and 1863. The genius of the Reform Act lay in the fact that 'while the undue influence of the crown' had been 'restrained, democracy has been also held in check' (Erskine May 1861, 2.236–7; Hawkins 1989, 662). Tories took a slightly different approach, but ended up in pretty much the same metaphorical place. Thus Peel recommended a system of checks and balances as a means to limiting the excesses of parliamentary sovereignty. Emphasising that the 'office' of the Prime Minister should never be one of 'servile tenure' in regard to Parliament, he saw in 'the quiet good sense of the people of this country' an ally which 'an Executive Government may rely for neutralizing the mischievous energies of the House of Commons' (Jenkins 1996, 35; Hawkins 1989, 655). According to Bagehot, however, the idea that constitutional powers should be either 'divided' or 'balanced' was entirely 'erroneous'; as he pointed out on the very first page of the very first chapter of the *Constitution*, not least because it militated against the idea of Parliament as an 'ultimate' authority (Bagehot 2001, 1–2). If anyone had any doubts as to the chaos that might ensue from the establishment of three separate sovereignties they need only consider the recent history of France or America.[16] The attendant notion that anyone might look to the 'good sense of the people' in order to preserve the constitution against the machinations of Parliament was moreover hardly to Bagehot's taste. Certainly, the dissolution of Parliament serves as a 'regulator', but it is not part of some grand scheme of 'checks and balances'.

[16]Thus contemporary France 'vacillates' wildly, and violently, between revolutionary and parliamentary government, whilst a century of American history has confirmed the inherent dangers in establishing a constitution wherein there is 'no ready, deciding power'. 'The splitting of sovereignty into many parts' experience confirms, simply 'amounts to there being no sovereign' (Bagehot 2001, 139–140, 153).

Bagehot was not into what he termed 'fancied' checks (Bagehot 2001, 162–3, 167).

He was however into fancy metaphors. The 'efficient secret of the English constitution', he opined, 'may be described as the close union, the nearly complete fusion of the executive and legislative powers', and this fusion was achieved in the institution of Cabinet which, he elsewhere confirmed, was best described as 'a combining committee', a 'hyphen which joins, a buckle which fastens, the legislative part of the State to the executive part of the State' (Bagehot 2001, 8–9). Bagehot liked to suppose that he was the first to have identified the true significance of the Cabinet, hitherto a body the 'most curious point about which' is that 'so very little is known about it' (Bagehot 2001, 10–11). The opacity was however commonly noted. The very word Cabinet, according to Homersham Cox, writing in 1854, was 'foreign to our language and our law' (Le May 1979, 97). Famously in 1851, the House of Commons had rejected the suggestion that Cabinet ministers be given precedence in parliamentary ceremonial, on the simple grounds that the Cabinet was 'unknown' to the constitution. In fact, Macaulay had explained twenty years earlier how the Cabinet had come into existence after 1688, as a device necessary to make 'parliamentary government' work, and had defined it as a 'committee of leading members' of the two Houses. John Austin had directed his readers similarly, towards the functional and growing importance of Cabinet, describing it as 'virtually a standing committee of the two houses of Parliament'. Bagehot was in partial agreement. The measure of Cabinet was certainly its utility. He also characterised it as a species of 'committee elected by the legislature'. But the comparator he preferred was that of a 'board of control chosen by the legislature' (Bagehot 2001, 10). And the final choice as to membership belonged, not to the members of the House, but to the Prime Minister.

Not that the Prime Minister enjoyed an absolute discretion, his choice of ministerial colleagues limited in practice to a 'charmed circle' of suitably educated men possessed of 'a cool, moderate, resolute firmness, not gifted with high imagination, little prone to enthusiastic sentiment', men who enjoyed a 'clear view of the next step, and a wise inclination to take it', men in other words who were born and bred to govern (Bagehot 1965, 1.318–9). The 'position of most men in Parliament forbids their being invited in cabinet; the position of a few men ensures their being invited' (Bagehot 2001, 10). Bagehot, for whom the credibility of a political institution was always measured in human terms, cast no aspersion. The system of cabinet government nurtured a collective 'character' that was distinctly Whiggish, and for this reason, despite the ironic tone, Bagehot liked it; an institution quite literally custom-made to ensure that the right kind of chaps ran the country. Thus comprehended, even if the electorate preferred Tory MPs there was a reasonable prospect that the Cabinet would be populated by lots of closet Whigs. Of course, if the wrong people were allowed to vote, the danger of the wrong people popping up in Cabinet necessarily increased; a concern which reinforced Bagehot's anxieties regarding further franchise reform. We shall shortly see what could happen when the wrong kind of chap turned up in Parliament.

Interestingly, Bagehot had less to say regarding the office of Prime Minister, the head of the 'efficient' part of the constitution. In truth, as Richard Crossman observed in his introduction to the 1963 edition of Bagehot's *Constitution*, the true nature and scale of 'prime ministerial government' has only subsequently become apparent. The 'hyphen which joins', we could now see, had become 'one single man' (Crossman 1963, 51; Marshall 1999, 262–4). It was not so obvious in 1865. 'Nowhere in the wide world', as Gladstone admitted, 'does so great a substance cast so small a shadow; nowhere is there a man who has so much power with so little to show for it in the way of formal title or prerogative' (Le May 1979, 118). It certainly confused Prince Albert's tutor Baron Stockmar, who suggested that the Prime Minister was merely the 'temporary head of Cabinet'; supposing conversely that the incumbent monarch might be considered the 'permanent Premier' (Hibbert 2001, 367; Strachey 1971, 147–8).

But if the precise relation of Cabinet and Prime Minister remained allusive, the respective power of both was becoming ever clearer. Morley recognised that office had become one of 'exceptional and peculiar authority' (Le May 1979, 118). So too did Disraeli, who famously celebrated reaching the 'top of the greasy pole'. And so did Bagehot, even if he did have rather less to say. He was particularly sensitive to the fact that the power to dissolve Parliament was 'yearly ebbing from the sovereignty and centring' instead in the Prime Minister, as indeed was the 'peer-creating power'. A closer appreciation of Bagehot's view of the premiership is perhaps more readily gained from reading his individual essays on particular 'constitutional statesmen', and indeed from his later *Physics and Politics*, in which he confirmed that the greatest responsibility of any minister, prime or otherwise, is to set the right 'tone' (Bagehot

1965, 7.72). Brougham set the right tone, even if the extent of his 'passion' precluded him from the very highest office. So did Palmerston, 'distinguished' by his appreciation that the best government was that of 'animated moderation' (Bagehot 1965, 7.131–2). In contrast Peel, the epitome of the 'new breed' of 'statesman', chosen 'representative of a transacting and trading multitude', possessed of 'the powers of a first rate man, and the creed of a second rate man', incontrovertibly did not (Bagehot 1965, 3.165, 170).

Whilst Bagehot was broadly approving of Cabinet as an 'efficient' mechanism of governance, there is a sense that he was also troubled by its accretion of power, and to a degree by the evident lack of transparency. Melbourne, predictably enough, cherished the 'veil of secrecy' (Le May 1979, 107). But not Bagehot, who bemoaned the likely consequences of a 'committee which unites the law-making power to the law-executing power' but which is 'wholly secret'. Its meetings are 'not only secret in theory, but secret in reality' (Bagehot 2001, 11). The potential for abuse should 'sinister interests' ever come to power was only too evident (Bagehot 2001, 80). In theory, lack of transparency did not preclude accountability. Administrations could still be dismissed by Parliament, just as a Cabinet might indeed dismiss a Parliament. Moreover, the dismissal of both Parliament and Prime Minister lay within the notional remit of monarchical prerogative. But it was the practice of politics that interested Bagehot, not the fictions of prerogative. The idea that a monarch might dismiss a Parliament without the authority of the Prime Minister was 'dubious' at best. Again Bagehot was not opposed to the fiction in principle. The exercise of prerogatives by Cabinet on behalf of the Crown was a vital part of 'efficient' government. Here again, there was much to be said for a system of government which, under the guise of constitutional monarchy, allowed the right sort of chaps to run the country, 'sensible men of substantial means' (Bagehot 2001, 209).

By the time of the 1872 edition, however, Bagehot's mood had darkened. More than ever troubled by the thought that Cabinet might in course of time be populated by the wrong sort, Bagehot devoted vast tracts of his Introduction to the subject of prerogative and the possibility of its misuse, especially in the realm of foreign and imperial affairs. Aside from good breeding, there was nothing in the English constitution designed to preclude the politics of 'sharp practice', something that was becoming increasingly apparent in a nascent age of antagonistic party politics (Bagehot 2001, 213–5). Bagehot accordingly recommended a new convention which would require foreign 'contracts' and treaties to be presented to Parliament for approval. The idea was credible. The exercise of prerogative commonly rests on such conventions. Unfortunately, the older he got the more Bagehot worried about conventions too. Gentlemen's agreements only worked if there were gentlemen about.

In regard to the more particular conventions of Cabinet government, foremost was that of ministerial responsibility, that 'wholesome doctrine', as Lord Holland put it, which held 'every member of the Cabinet in some degree responsible for the measures adopted by the government' (Hawkins 1989, 651). The sanctification of the convention of collective ministerial responsibility in the form of a Cabinet minute, drafted at Gladstone's insistence in 1869, was representative of an emergent professionalism in government. Towards the end of the century, Salisbury would confirm the status of the convention as a 'great constitutional law', the breach of which would be a considerable 'inconvenience' (Le May 1979, 108–9; Heffer 2013, 765). The same sentiment, if not quite the same gravitas or tone, could be discerned in Lord Melbourne's notorious inquiry half a century earlier in 1834, when trying to bring some order to Cabinet discussion of proposed import duties: 'What are we to say? Is it to make our corn dearer or cheaper, or to make the price steady? I don't care which, but we had better all be in the same story' (Le May 1979, 104; Hawkins 1989, 651). The management of Cabinet, 'at all times a delicate and fragile Machine', was in Melbourne's opinion thoroughly tiresome (Mitchell 1997, 146). Bagehot would have sympathised.

Conventions were just too allusive in principle, too troublesome in practice. The deleterious consequences which tend to flow from 'sudden' changes of ministry could be ascribed to the limitations of a second Cabinet convention, ministerial accountability. The idea that ministers should give account to Parliament was laudable; the fact that fractious Commons might then move for their dismissal, and in so doing quite possibly facilitate the dismissal of an entire administration, was not (Bagehot 2001, 129–31). In fact, ministers rarely resigned on a point of responsibility; only seven between 1855 and 1914. But it was once again all a bit flaky. Bagehot did not go so far as Disraeli who, being asked the deeper significance of the principle of ministerial responsibility, responded that it was 'only a piece of Parliamentary gossip' (Longford 1998, 437). But he veered pretty close.

The Greatest Victorian

Bagehot's critical reputation has endured. Dicey struck a minor note of discord, acknowledging the influence of the most incisive political commentator since Burke, but suggesting that his more particular 'work on the constitution is marred by an excessive ingenuity which degenerates into a kind of dodginess' (Dicey 1986, 79–80). Dicey did not much appreciate irony. As we will shortly see, he envisaged a rather different kind of constitution, and a very different kind of constitutionalism. But aside from Dicey, contemporaries were commonly effusive in their praise of Bagehot and his writing. Disraeli bestowed the sincerest form of flattery by plagiarising shamelessly from Bagehot's chapters on monarchy in drafting his famous 1872 Manchester Free Trade Hall speech. The Queen, Disraeli argued, retained her place in the hearts of all her subjects because she ruled over an essentially 'domestic country' where the 'home is revered and the hearth is sacred' (Heffer 2013, 772). A little later in 1899, Mountstuart Grant Duff concluded that Bagehot's *Constitution* was 'one of the best things that has ever been written about that strange abstraction' (Duff 1986, 148). Half a generation later, US President Woodrow Wilson suggested that Bagehot's 'genius' lay in the fact that he was a 'literary politician', someone to whom 'by reason of knowledge and imagination and sympathy, governments and policies are open books'. Blessed with a 'Chaucerian insight', a 'conceiving imagination' as opposed to an 'imagination of fancy', Bagehot appreciated the serious 'play' of politics. He knew that in order to understand the workings of a constitution it is necessary 'to stand with the poets as well as the lawgivers' (Wilson 1986, 161, 165, 168). It was conversely Bagehot's pragmatism which attracted the praise of AJ Balfour, 'his ceaseless endeavour to discover how public business was in fact transacted' (Balfour 1928, vi).

For much of the twentieth-century Bagehot's intellectual stock remained high, finding famous expression in GM Young's seminal 1937 study *Victorian England: Portrait of an Age*. Looking 'for a man who was in and of his age and who could have been of no other', Young concluded that Bagehot was indeed the 'greatest Victorian'. Notably, Young's Bagehot is also a great Burkean, his *Constitution* written as a paean to the 'the tradition of Burke', the 'true English tradition' of liberal and open conversation (Young 1986, 209, 212). Subsequent mid-century accolades were no less effusive. David Easton admired a liberal thinker who, sensing the prospective demise of a political philosophy founded on abstract principles and distant history, tried to reinvest a sense of 'realism'. The same term could be found in Kitson Clark's 1962 *Making of Victorian England*. 'Nothing could be better', Clark's readers were informed, 'than the humane and brilliant realism of Bagehot's ringside account of Parliamentary life' (Clark 1962, 49). His biographer Buchan appraised Bagehot for talking 'nothing but the baldest common sense' (1959, 163). It might seem a little flat, but it was meant as a compliment. And nothing could be more conclusive than Kenneth Wheare's declaration eight years later that Bagehot had 'invented' the English constitution: 'by breathing life into it; he created it' (Wheare 1974, 195).

Wheare was further struck by Bagehot's apparent immunity from critical disapproval. Doubtful voices could be discerned. Literary critics noted that Bagehot seemed rather less interested in poetry than in poets. In like terms, John Maynard Keynes supposed noted that Bagehot seemed rather more interested in economists than in economies. Richard Crossman suggestion, that Bagehot tended to write what he thought ought to happen rather than what actually perceived as happening, is resonant and suitably ironic (Crossman 1963, 26–9). More recent critics have found the reactionary Bagehot a less comfortable presence; especially the Bagehot who evinces such contempt for his witlessly deferential compatriots (Jenkins 1996, 12–13; Vile 1967, 224–5). John Burrow suggests that such 'liberal impatience' is testimony to an irreducible tension which men like Bagehot could never really overcome; between a desire to manage 'practical' reform whilst retaining a Whiggish scepticism as to the likely consequence (Burrow 1988, 68–9).

But all things considered, and more especially in regard to his analysis of the political workings of the constitution, Bagehot's reputation has remained largely intact, subsequent generations of political scientists, as Peter Hennessy has recently suggested, seemingly unable to liberate themselves from the same kind of 'thrall' into which Wilson, Wheare and Young happily bound themselves. It is Bagehot's 'ghost' that haunts the collective narrative of modern British government (Hennessy 1995, 41–3). No one, Paul Smith concludes, has 'exerted more influence' than Bagehot in shaping modern perceptions of the relation between government and constitution (Smith 2001, xxv). We have already noted Bogdanor's suggestion; that Bagehot's spectre might be discerned lurking in the shadows of the 'new' British constitution. It was Bagehot, Simon Heffer infers, who in writing his *English Constitution* 'codified' it (Heffer 2013, 378). The tangential supposition that Bagehot was writing against the looming despotism of Diceyan jurisprudence is perceptive, and intriguing; for reasons that will become apparent shortly (Burrow 1983, 164–5).

And yet there is something slightly odd here, as perhaps there is in similar regard to Burke and Macaulay. If Macaulay has tended to be damned by praise that is rather too faint, Bagehot seems to be damned by praise that is rather too polite. Frank Prochaska concludes his recent, and curious, faux-*Memoirs of Walter Bagehot* with the prospective conclusion that, even if he was not quite as important a figure as some of his earlier admirers liked to think, Bagehot was still 'the Victorian with whom you would most want to have dinner' (Prochaska 2013, x). Even if Bagehot was not the 'greatest' Victorian, the man who for so long was credited with 'creating' the modern constitution ought perhaps to attract a rather more agitated critic. Here is it worth contemplating more closely what made Young conclude that Bagehot was indeed the 'greatest' Victorian. In Bagehot, Young had located:

> A man with sympathy to share, and genius, to judge, its sentiments and movements: a man not too illustrious or too consummate to be companionable, but one, nevertheless, whose ideas took root and are still bearing, whose influence, passing from one fit mend to another, could transmit, and can still impart, the most precious element in Victorian civilization, its robust and masculine sanity. (Young 1986, 209)

As Norman St. John Stevas argues, when Young supposed that Bagehot was the 'greatest' Victorian he actually meant the 'truest'; that whilst he was no ordinary writer Bagehot was in many ways a very ordinary mid-Victorian, moderately liberal in terms of political allegiance, temperamentally conservative, a Whig of the roundhead rather than cavalier variety (St. John Stevas 1987, 1–2). There are echoes here; of Birrell's conclusion, that Bagehot was, like so many of his heroes, himself a man of 'animated moderation'; and Jacques Barzun's, that Bagehot was the consummate philosopher of political 'equilibrium' in an age of equipoise (Birrell 1986, 202–3; Barzun 1986, 26); and of the Bagehot appraised in John Buchan's studiously polite 1959 biography. In his essay on Peel, Bagehot famously suggested that 'A constitutional statesmen is in general a man of common opinions and uncommon abilities' (Bagehot 1965, 3242). If there was ever a general man possessed of uncommon abilities it is Buchan's Bagehot, the consummate intellectually engaged mid-Victorian 'conservative Liberal' (Buchan 1959, 135). This particular affinity is of course familiar. It has a Gladstonian ring for sure. From the converse perspective, John Gardiner has recently suggested that the Grand Old Man was a 'sensible Bagehotian' (Gardiner 2002, 143).

But it has a still sharper resonance, most obviously familiar to Trollopians. Not only is it the affinity which Trollope claimed for himself in his *Autobiography*, but it echoes the 'intelligent voice' of middling mid-Victorian England which Briggs identified in both Trollope and Bagehot (Briggs 1959, 514). The assumption at the heart of Briggs's essay is that the kind of person who read Trollope's novels was also the kind of person who read Bagehot's essays. The supposition is perfectly credible, not least because of the sheer number of people who read both. Identifying a typical Trollope reader is of course difficult for the precisely the same reason. Victoria was an unimpressed one, finding *Barchester Towers* to be rather lacking in romance. And there was nowhere near enough bodice-ripping for Bertie. Thousands of others were however charmed. Mrs Arbuthnot was the kind of woman who would have enjoyed a Trollope. In her diary, she recorded a pleasant ride round the Surrey countryside accompanied by her husband and the Duke of Wellington. It was, she observed, a 'beautiful ride'. Everyone 'looking rich and happy', she added, 'altho' we are told every day that we are ruined and starving' (Bentley 1996, 55). It might be supposed that Trollope wrote for much the same audience as Macaulay, one that preferred an afternoon of 'easy, pleasant reading'. There are darker shades in Trollope, the doubting clergymen, the unhappy marriages, and so very many politicians whom Dicey might have found dodgy. Overall however it can be supposed that no Victorian novelist made a larger fortune from making middle England feel a bit better about itself (Brantlinger 1977, 223).

Certainly no Victorian novelist wrote quite so much about politics, or at least depicted quite so many politicians; for Trollopian politics, as the *Autobiography* famously affirmed, is a human endeavour far more than it is a metaphysical one, a matter of sympathies and empathies rather than 'doctrine' or ideology (Trollope 1996, 188; Lansbury 1970, 214–5, 218–9; McMaster 1986, 92–3; Hughes 1986, 33–4). This does not mean that no one believed. Faith and creed is as pivotal in the Palliser novels as it is in the Barset. Indeed the entire series can be read as eulogy to the passing of the 'creed' of Whiggery (Hughes 1986, 42, 48). What Trollope liked was what Charles Kingsley also liked, the 'practical good sense' of Whiggism, a species of what Bagehot termed 'dullness' and which was, despite the apparent pejorative, a good thing (Heffer 2013, 379). In his *Autobiography* Trollope admitted that the character of Plantagenet Palliser, eponymous Prime Minister in the fifth of the Palliser novels, was intended to describe 'the perfect gentleman', and if 'he be not then I am unable to describe the perfect gentleman'. Plantagenet was crushingly dull. And Trollope was proud of him for the very reason (Trollope 1996, 229; Hall 1991, 267; Brantlinger 1977, 209–13). Whilst so many of his political caricatures are readily identifiable, Disraeli as variously Daubeny and Beeswax, Gladstone as Gresham, 'Planty' Palliser has always seemed that bit more elusive (Lansbury 1970, 213). It has been suggested that there might be a bit of Palmerston in Plantagenet Palliser. Trollope was as much an admirer as Bagehot, and there is a nice symmetry in the coincidence of Pam's death and Planty's literary birth. And there is certainly a shared appreciation that politics is about getting stuff done, rather than dreaming of what might happen in an ideal world (Halperin 1977, 215–7; Briggs 1990, 96–7). There again Planty would never have been discovered groping a maid on a billiard table. Trollope thought too much of him, and if Plantagenet Palliser is representative of any particular 'set of political intuitions' they are more probably Trollope's (Butte 1981, 225; Halperin 1977, 221). He is certainly invested with an enviable ethic of public service, of simply being 'useful' (Trollope 1996, 186). It might mean reluctantly agreeing to become Prime Minister of an unstable coalition administration, as Planty does, or it might mean hours spent working for the Post Office, as Trollope did. Either way it was commendable.

Perfect gentleman, ideal Statesman and quintessential Whig too, by temperament, and by birth; Plantagenet Palliser is the kind of man perhaps that only his creator could really love (Laski 1960, 339–40). In his *Autobiography*, Trollope acknowledged that political caricatures are too easily 'shorn' of 'those little touches of humanity' which make them interesting. The early Plantagenet certainly seems a little shorn. The later, however, acquires a greater depth. Seeds are planted in the *Prime Minister*, in the very fact of Plantagenet's 'failure'. He was 'scrupulous, and being scrupulous – weak' (Trollope 1996, 228; Halperin 1977, 224–7, 232). But it is in the sixth and final Palliser novel, *The Duke's Children*, published in 1879 three years after the *Autobiography*, that Plantagenet becomes a character that readers too might to come to love, or least admire. As the novel opens, Planty is out of office, mourning his wife's passing, and contemplating what to do with his variously rebellious children. Politics still matters of course. The Pallisers are defined by their politics. But there is more to politics than wandering around Westminster trying to cobble together coalitions; as critics of *The Prime Minister* had insinuated. It was the marriage of the private with the political which elevated the final Palliser chronicle (Halperin 1977, 211–3, 246–7; Berger 2003, 315–7, 320–3). Planty's children marry all the wrong matches. His daughter marries a Tory. His eldest son Lord Silverbridge even becomes one; a decision which comes as a 'terrible blow' to his father (Trollope 1995, 19). He should 'stand for the county in a proper constitutional spirit', and allow his father to spend £10,000 to secure the seat (Trollope 1995, 49). Instead, he prostrates himself before the 'politicians' of Silverbridge borough; a seat which has, as a consequence of reform, become increasingly independent-minded, and conspicuously Tory. He cannot understand why he should 'remain with a party so utterly snobbish', and which is 'down' with the Radicals, just 'because his father happened to be so before him' (Trollope 1995, 57).

In the end the Duke is reconciled to his children's choices, for which reason they are likewise reconciled to him. Silverbridge returns to the political faith, having dwelt more deeply on the nature of public service and more particularly the responsibilities which attach to being a Palliser. There is, he resolves, nothing contradictory in cherishing the 'conservative feeling' of a Carlylean gentleman and the 'propriety' of a Whig peer of the realm (Trollope 1995, 140, 349–50; McMaster 1978, 147–9; Halperin 1977, 264–5). Trollope had laid the ground for Silverbridge's conversion in his *Autobiography*, in the appreciation of public 'duty' rather than narrow political affinity (Trollope 1996, 188). It is again the kind of fictive resolution of which Macaulay would have approved, written in a 'genial spirit' as the *Athenaeum* concluded and most importantly ending 'happily'; or as happily as might be hoped in an increasingly Whig-less world (Smalley 1969, 467, 471; McMaster 1978, 154).[17] His liberalism may have been of the 'resistant' kind, and he may

[17]The *Westminster Review* famously observed that Plantagenet Palliser was now the 'only duke whom all of us know'; a suggestive observation (Trollope 1995, vii). At the very end of the novel, Trollope leaves Plantagenet considering whether he should agree to return to government as President of the Council. The position is more honorific than real; a dilemma which is every bit as suggestive (Halperin 1977, 268).

have retained some darker suspicions regarding the coming generation, but in the end Trollope inclined to be optimistic (Anderson 2007, 531). In the final chapter of the *Autobiography* he chastised the 'wailing and gnashing' of unthinking Carlylism and its presumption of inevitable 'deterioration' (Trollope 1996, 224–5; Hall 1991, 136–7; Butte 1977, 723, 726). Here of course Bagehot and Trollope diverged. The author of *The Duke's Children* might have been able to imagine a sunny prospect. The author of the 1872 Preface to the second edition of his *English Constitution* could not.

Ultimately the coincidence of Trollope and Bagehot represents a significant adjustment in the propagation of Whig constitutionalism, their divergence a finer adjustment still. To the familiar historicism of Burke and Macaulay could be added two further strategic, and complementary, interventions; the poetic whimsy of the Pallisers and the seeming seriousness of Bagehot. The advance of a politics that was becoming ever more responsive to public opinion demanded both. It wanted to be entertained, but it also wanted to be taken seriously. Trollope did the first, as contemporary reviewers readily appreciated. A novel such as the *Duke's Children* presented in 'thoroughly readable' form a 'dramatic essay' on the consequences of a 'reformed' constitution; betraying the reality of parliamentary government whilst also engaging the defining political 'struggle' of the age, between the 'caste' of Whiggery and the 'creed of progress'. It also laid bare the realities of managerial 'government' (Smalley 1969, 468, 470–1).

Bagehot did the same but differently, in a series of essays which purported to investigate the supremely pragmatic science of government, but which in the end betrayed precisely the same Whiggish prejudices and predilections. Those who preferred their constitutions to be historical and nostalgic could still revisit their copies of Macaulay. For those of a still more whimsical inclination, there were, alongside Trollope, the 'political' novels of Disraeli and Dickens and Thackeray. There were more sober 'scientific' and historical accounts too, the consequence of the more 'professional' historical attitude we encountered earlier. The Whig constitution would live on, as indeed would its more sceptical Tory alternative. We have encountered their respective mutations too. But there was, by the final quarter of the nineteenth century, something else; a new constitutional perception to be narrated, and a new constitutional jurisprudence to be explored.

References

Aldous, R. (2007). *The Lion and the Unicorn: Gladstone v Disraeli.* London: Pimlico.

Anderson, A. (2007). Trollope's Modernity. *ELH, 74,* 509–534.

Arnold, M. (1993). *Culture and Anarchy, and Other Writings.* Cambridge: Cambridge University Press.

Arnstein, W. (2003). *Queen Victoria.* Basingstoke: Palgrave.

Bagehot, W. (1965). *The Collected Works of Walter Bagehot* (St. John Stevas, Ed.). London: The Economist.

Bagehot, W. (2001). *The English Constitution.* Cambridge: Cambridge University Press.

Balfour, A. (1928). Introduction to W. Bagehot, *The English Constitution.* Oxford: Oxford University Press.

Barzun, J. (1986). Bagehot as Historian. In St. John Stevas (Ed.), *The Collected Works of Walter Bagehot* (Vol. 3). London: The Economist.

Bentley, M. (1996). *Politics Without Democracy 1815–1914.* London: Fontana.

Bentley, M. (2001). *Lord Salisbury's World: Conservative Environments in Late-Victorian Britain.* Cambridge: Cambridge University Press.

Berger, C. (2003). Partying with the Opposition: Social Politics in *The Prime Minister. Texas Studies in Literature and Language, 45,* 315–336.

Best, G. (1979). *Mid-Victorian Britain 1851–75.* London: Fontana.

Birrell, A. (1986). Walter Bagehot. In St. John Stevas (Ed.), *Collected Works of Walter Bagehot.* London: The Economist.

Brantlinger, P. (1977). *The Spirit of Reform: British Literature and Politics 1832–1867.* Cambridge, MA: Harvard University Press.

Briggs, A. (1959). *The Age of Improvement.* London: Longmans.

Briggs, A. (1990). *Victorian People.* London: Penguin.

Brown, D. (2010). *Palmerston: A Biography.* New Haven: Yale University Press.

Buchan, A. (1959). *The Spare Chancellor: The Life of Walter Bagehot.* London: Chatto & Windus.

Burrow, J. (1983). Sense and Circumstances: Bagehot and the Nature of Political Understanding. In S. Collini, D. Winch, & J. Burrow (Eds.), *That Noble Science of Politics: A Study in Nineteenth Century Intellectual History.* Cambridge: Cambridge University Press.

Burrow, J. (1988). *Whigs and Liberals: Continuity and Change in English Political Thought.* Oxford: Oxford University Press.

Butte, G. (1977). Ambivalence and Affirmation in *The Duke's Children. Studies in English Literature, 17,* 709–727.

Butte, G. (1981). Trollope's Duke of Omnium and "The Pain of History": A Study of the Novelist's Politics. *Victorian Studies, 24,* 209–227.

Carlyle, T. (1986). *Selected Writings.* Harmondsworth: Penguin.

Clark, K. (1962). *The Making of Victorian England.* Cambridge: Harvard University Press.

Cowling, M. (1967). *1867: Disraeli, Gladstone and Revolution*. Cambridge: Cambridge University Press.
Crossman, R. (1963). Introduction to W. Bagehot, *The English Constitution*. London: Fontana.
Dicey, A. (1986). Walter Bagehot. In St. John Stevas (Ed.), *Collected Works of Walter Bagehot* (Vol. 15). London: The Economist.
Duff, M. (1986). Walter Bagehot. In St. John Stevas (Ed.), *The Collected Works of Walter Bagehot* (Vol. 15). London: The Economist.
Erskine May. (1861). *The Constitutional History of England Since George III*. London: Longman.
Ford, T. (1970). Bagehot and Mill as Theorists of Comparative Politics. *Comparative Politics, 2*, 309–324.
Forster, J. (1966). *The Life of Charles Dickens*. London: Chapman & Hall.
Gardiner, J. (2002). *The Victorians: An Age in Retrospect*. London: Hambledon.
Gash, N. (1965). *Reaction and Reconstruction in English Politics 1832–1852*. Oxford: Oxford University Press.
Gaunt, R. (2010). *Sir Robert Peel: The Life and Legacy*. London: I.B. Tauris.
Goldberg, M. (1972). From Bentham to Carlyle: Dickens' Political Development. *Journal of the History of Ideas, 33*, 61–76.
Hall, N. (1991). *Trollope: A Biography*. Oxford: Clarendon Press.
Halperin, J. (1977). *Trollope and Politics*. London: Macmillan.
Hanley, B. (2004). The "Greatest Victorian" in the New Century: The Enduring Relevance of Walter Bagehot's Commentary on Literature, Scholarship and Public Life. *Papers on Language and Literature, 40*, 167–199.
Hawkins, A. (1989). Parliamentary Government and Victorian Political Parties c.1830–c.1880. *English Historical Review, 104*, 638–669.
Heffer, S. (1995). *Moral Desperado: A Life of Thomas Carlyle*. Weidenfeld and Nicolson.
Heffer, S. (2013). *High Minds: The Victorians and the Making of Modern Britain*. London: Random House.
Hennessy, P. (1995). *The Hidden Wiring: Unearthing the British Constitution*. London: Gollancz.
Hibbert, C. (2001). *Queen Victoria: A Personal History*. London: HarperCollins.
Hibbert, C. (2004). *Disraeli: A Personal History*. London: HarperCollins.
Himmelfarb, G. (2007). *The Spirit of the Age: Victorian Essays*. New Haven: Yale University Press.
Homans, M. (1998). *Royal Representations: Queen Victoria and British Culture 1837–1876*. Chicago: University of Chicago Press.
Hughes, T. (1986). Spontaneous Order and the Politics of Anthony Trollope. *Nineteenth Century Literature, 41*, 32–48.
Jenkins, R. (1965). *Dilke: A Victorian Tragedy*. London: Macmillan.
Jenkins, K. (1995). *On 'What Is History?' From Carr and Elton to Rorty and White*. London: Routledge.

Jenkins, T. (1996). *Parliament, Party and Politics in Victorian Britain.* Manchester: Manchester University Press.
Jones, G. (2009). Introduction. In G. Jones (Ed.), *Charles Dickens, A Tale of Two Cities and the French Revolution.* Basingstoke: Palgrave.
Lacey, N. (2011). The Way We Lived Then: The Legal Profession and the 19th Century Novel. *Sydney Law Review, 3,* 599–621.
Lansbury, C. (1970). *The Reasonable Man: Trollope's Legal Fiction.* Princeton: Princeton University Press.
Laski, A. (1960). Myths of Character: An Aspect of the Novel. *Nineteenth Century Fiction, 14,* 333–343.
Lecky, W. (1899). *Democracy and Liberty.* London: Longmans.
Le May, G. (1979). *The Victorian Constitution: Conventions, Usages and Contingencies.* London: Duckworth.
Longford, E. (1998). *Victoria RI.* London: Weidenfield & Nicolson.
Marshall, G. (1999). The Analysis of British Political Institutions. In J. Hayward, B. Barry, & A. Brown (Eds.), *The British Study of Politics in the Twentieth Century.* Oxford: Oxford University Press.
McMaster, J. (1978). *Trollope's Palliser Novels: Theme and Pattern.* London: Macmillan.
McMaster, R. (1986). *Trollope and the Law.* London: Macmillan.
Mitchell, L. (1997). *Lord Melbourne 1779–1848.* Oxford: Oxford University Press.
Newsome, D. (1998). *The Victorian World Picture.* London: Fontana.
Parry, J. (1993). *The Rise and Fall of Liberal Government in Victorian Britain.* New Haven: Yale University Press.
Plumb, J. (1963). *Men and Places.* London: Cresset.
Pollard, A. (1968). *Trollope's Political Novels.* Hull: University of Hull Press.
Prochaska, F. (2013). *The Memoirs of Walter Bagehot.* New Haven: Yale University Press.
Ritchie, D. (1989). Burke's Influence on the Imagination of Walter Bagehot. *The Modern Age, 32,* 324–328.
Royle, E. (1996). *Chartism.* London: Longman.
Smalley, D. (1969). *Trollope: The Critical Heritage.* London: Routledge.
Smith, E. (1990). *Lord Grey 1764–1845.* Oxford: Oxford University Press.
Smith, P. (2001). Introduction to W. Bagehot, *The English Constitution.* Cambridge: Cambridge University Press.
Spring, D. (1983). Walter Bagehot and Deference. *American History Review, 81,* 524–531.
St. John Stevas, N. (1987). *The Omnipresence of Walter Bagehot.* Oxford: Oxford University Press.
Strachey, L. (1971). *Queen Victoria.* London: Penguin.
Tennyson, A. L. (1991). *Selected Poems.* London: Penguin.

Tosh, J. (1985). *A Man's Place: Masculinity and the Middle-Class Home in Victorian England*. Yale University Press.
Trollope, A. (1978). *Ralph the Heir*. New York: Dover.
Trollope, A. (1995). *The Duke's Children*. London: Penguin.
Trollope, A. (1996). *An Autobiography*. London: Penguin.
Vile, M. (1967). *Constitutionalism and the Separation of Powers*. Oxford: Clarendon Press.
Weintraub, S. (1993). *Disraeli: A Biography*. London: Hamish Hamilton.
Wheare, K. (1974). Lecture on a Master Mind: Walter Bagehot. *Proceedings of the British Academy, 62*, 173–197.
Wilson, A. (2002). *The Victorians*. London: Hutchinson.
Wilson W. (1986). A Literary Politician. In St. John Stevas (Ed.) *The Collected Works of Walter Bagehot* (Vol. 15). London: The Economist.
Young, G. (1986). The Greatest Victorian. In St. John Stevas (Ed.), *The Collected Works of Walter Bagehot* (Vol. 15). London: The Economist.

CHAPTER 5

Dicey's *Law*

In the election of 1880, Northampton chose Charles Bradlaugh as one of their two MPs. In doing so, they precipitated a constitutional crisis that would run for six years. A number of similarly 'dreadful people' were returned in 1880, Disraeli noted (Heffer 2013, 810). Bagehot had warned middle England about men like Bradlaugh in his 1874 essay on *The Advantages and Disadvantages of Becoming a Member of Parliament*. Bradlaugh was radical, republican and loudly atheist. In 1858, he was made President of the London Secular Society, and two years later became editor of its house-journal the *National Reformer*. In 1868, he was prosecuted for blasphemy and sedition and acquitted. Eight years later, he was back in court, this time prosecuted for publishing Charles Knowlton's notorious pamphlet advocating birth control, *The Fruits of Philosophy, or the Private Companion of Young Married People*. The book, the court concluded, was clearly 'calculated to deprave public morals'. A sentence of six months imprisonment and a fine of £200 were overturned on a legal technicality in the Court of Appeal. His co-defendant, and companion, was the equally notorious activist for women's rights, Annie Besant. Unsurprisingly, they were not married.

They liked their MPs to be loud, radical and republican in Northampton. Alongside Bradlaugh in 1880, they elected Henry Labouchere. Labouchere was, in many ways, very different from Bradlaugh; a rabid anti-semite and homophobe, whose chief claim to

I. Ward, *Writing the Victorian Constitution*, Palgrave Modern Legal History, https://doi.org/10.1007/978-3-319-96676-2_5

legislative record lay in the notorious 1884 amendment which became known by his name and which criminalised 'gross indecency'.[1] The fact that he campaigned against female suffrage suggested that his relations with Besant were rather less cordial than those he apparently enjoyed with Bradlaugh. Labouchere did not make friends easily. Like Bradlaugh, however, he did make constitutional history. When Gladstone proposed that Labouchere might join his 1892 Cabinet Queen Victoria threw a fit; the last occasion upon which, constitutional historians commonly agree, a Prime Minister acceded to a prerogative veto of a prospective Cabinet member.[2] She was no more impressed by Bradlaugh, 'horrid and repulsive' (Longford 1998, 434). Her Prime Minister agreed, at least in private. Gladstone detested Bradlaugh's 'loathsome and revolting opinions' (Arnstein 1962, 306). In public, however, Gladstone was obliged to be more temperate. Amongst his backbenchers, there were an increasing number of men like Bradlaugh and Labouchere; not necessarily atheist, but broadly indifferent to matters of theological nicety and in terms of parliamentary procedure inclined to be difficult.

On 3 May 1880, Bradlaugh marched into the chamber of the Commons and ostentatiously placed a letter on the table, addressed to the Speaker and 'begging respectfully to claim to be allowed to affirm' instead of taking the customary Oath of Allegiance. To add some jurisprudential sheen, he cited the 1866 Parliamentary Oaths Act which granted a right of affirmation to Quaker, Separatists, Moravians and 'every other person for the time being permitted by law to make a solemn affirmation or declaration', together with the Evidence Amendment Acts of 1869 and 1870. The Speaker expressed 'grave doubts' and referred the matter to the 'whole' House. Tory MPs sensed blood. A Select Committee was duly established to consider the case, and ten days later reported against Bradlaugh. Expecting as much Bradlaugh wrote an open letter to the *Times* explaining why as an atheist he had thought it hypocritical to mumble a few 'words of idle and meaningless character'. In deliberately provocative tones, he concluded by saying that he would

[1] It was under the Labouchere 'amendment' that Oscar Wilde was prosecuted in 1894.

[2] Labouchere's journal *Truth* was a consistent critic of both Victoria and the institution of monarchy. Victoria made it a condition of his appointment that it be either sold or preferably closed. The condition was refused. Labouchere ended his days in comfortable disgrace, declining to challenge an accusation of share-rigging, what today might be more familiarly termed insider-trading, and retiring to Florence where he died a millionaire.

now take the Oath, but would 'regard myself as bound not by the letter of its words, but by the spirit which the affirmation would have conveyed had I been permitted to use it'. Labouchere was more provocative still. Nothing more than the 'same superstitious incantation as the trash of any Mumbo-Jumbo among African savages', he declared the Oath he had just solemnly attested (Wilson 1999, 290).

The stage was set. On Bradlaugh's arrival in the Commons chamber next day, Sir Henry Drummond Wolff stood up and objected to the pending administration of the Oath. The Speaker upheld the objection, and Bradlaugh was prevented from assuming his seat. No one was especially surprised by the turn of events, least of all Bradlaugh and his Prime Minister, who had already resolved to move for the establishment of a second Select Committee to be tasked with inquiring whether it was possible to prevent a prospective Member from taking the Oath. The second Committee asked for advice from the Clerk of the House, Sir Thomas Erskine May, who managed to identify a variety of authorities in parliamentary history, but not unfortunately much consistency; MPs being disabled for refusing the Oath, others such as the Quaker Joseph Pease who was permitted instead to affirm, and others still such as the Jewish Members Lionel de Rothschild and David Solomons who were allowed to take re-drafted Oaths which excluded the words 'on the true faith of a Christian'.

Having listened to Bradlaugh reiterate his intention to take the Oath on 16 June the Committee resolved to 'prevent' him doing so. At this point, Labouchere intervened in the Commons to initiate a debate on a motion to allow Bradlaugh's affirmation. The motion failed, but Bradlaugh, as expected, turned up the following day to take his Oath anyway, at which point the Speaker asked him to withdraw. Invoking another piece of archaic parliamentary convention, Bradlaugh was, however, permitted to stand behind the 'bar' of the Commons and address the House. The drama was now coming to its height. Bradlaugh was summoned back to the Table, told that Labouchere's amendment had failed and ordered to withdraw once again from the chamber. He 'respectfully refused' to obey an order which he maintained was 'against the law'. The elderly Serjeant at Arms was summoned. Bradlaugh was led to the 'bar', at which point he turned round and walked back into the chamber. In uproar, the House voted by 274 to 7 that Bradlaugh be 'taken into the custody' of the Serjeant and placed in the small prison cell located under the Clock Tower.

It is pleasing to suppose that WS Gilbert might have contemplated the possibility of a comic opera. There are, as we shall see, intimations, and he found conspicuous space for Labouchere in *His Excellency*. Moreover, there was plenty that was ridiculous in Bradlaugh's case in summer 1880 and plenty more to come. The second Act would have covered the four subsequent by-elections at which the electors of Northampton, playing the Chorus, duly returned their chosen candidate to serve as their MP. It would, at the same time, have charted the difficulties experienced by both Gladstone and his Conservative opponents in trying to somehow explain to a bemused public what precisely was going on. The gravitas of the ensuing events would have been suitably enhanced by the quality of *dramatis personae*; Bradlaugh's supporters including, alongside a reluctant Gladstone, Henry James, George Bernard Shaw and a young Mohandas Gandhi, his detractors numbering, alongside a regiment of Tory MPs, the Archbishops of Canterbury and York. There would be a trial scene in the spring of 1881, the case of *Clarke v Bradlaugh*, in which a private prosecution was brought against Bradlaugh for voting in Parliament in breach of the provisions of 1866 Act, which required his prior affirmation. Bradlaugh was duly convicted and fined £500 for each of three particular offences. Undaunted Bradlaugh arrived at the House for the beginning of the new session in February 1882. A moment of farce ensued when Labouchere moved for Bradlaugh to vacate his seat and seek a specific vote of confidence from the Northampton electorate. The House refused, thus denying Bradlaugh the right to sit or the right not to sit. A few moments later Bradlaugh left his seat in the gallery and walked towards the Table carrying a copy of the New Testament. Realising that Bradlaugh intended to administer the oath himself the House was momentarily stupefied. The chief actor in this grand constitutional drama had suddenly gone off-script. The House erupted yet again. Bradlaugh then left. The following day, he was officially expelled from the Commons.

The 'infernal business', as Gladstone's secretary termed it, simply would not go away. The electors of Northampton returned Bradlaugh once again. By now, even the *Times* was arguing that there would need to be statutory reform. An Affirmation bill was introduced in 1883, to which Gladstone felt obliged to lend his support. The Tory MP Henry Chaplin invoked two spirits, the Holy and the Burkean. The bill, Chaplin declared, 'shocks, horrifies, and outrages every sentiment and every feeling nearest and dearest to the hearts of the people, in every family, in every home, by every fireside, from the palace of the noble and the rich, to the dwellings of the poor and the lowliest in the land'. Lord Randolph Churchill raised the same. 'Surely', he reminded Members, 'the horrors of the French revolution should give some idea of the effect on the masses of the State recognition of Atheism'. 'I have no fear of Atheism in this House', the Grand Old Man thundered in return (Wilson 1999, 288–9). But he did have a fear of losing the division, and he was right. The bill fell. Gladstone's preference was anyway for a judicial solution, leaving the courts to decide what should be done with his recalcitrant MP. Though initially reluctant, Lord Chief Justice Coleridge was finally persuaded to hear the matter alongside three fellow judges and a specially empanelled jury in early 1884. The court held that as Bradlaugh was an atheist the Commons was probably right in refusing to allow him to take his oath. But as the Lord Chief Justice made plain, it was not for the courts to impugn the sovereignty of Parliament in conducting its own business: 'If injustice has been done, it is an injustice for which the courts of law afford no remedy' (Arnstein 1962, 325). Following his re-election in 1885, a new Speaker refused to countenance any attempt to interfere with Bradlaugh affirming the oath and assuming his seat in the chamber. Three years later, with a tangible sense of anticlimax, Parliament passed an Affirmation Act.

The Bradlaugh case suggested a number of things about the state of Parliament in the 1880s, and indeed the state of the nation. In regard to the former, it impressed the fact that Parliament could very easily make itself look very silly. Perhaps more importantly, as Bagehot had feared it inferred that there was post-1867 little to stop the wrong kind of chaps getting into Parliament. Chamberlain the Birmingham screw-merchant was viewed by many, mostly though not exclusively on the Tory benches, as precisely such a chap.[3] So too were the shopping-magnates Richard Cross and WH Smith, or 'Marshall and Snellgrove' as Churchill liked to call them. When the Leeds leather merchant William Jackson was

[3]The story of the Chamberlain family fortune says much about the dynamics of mid and late Victorian England. In summer 1851, John Sutton Nettlefold, a Birmingham industrialist, visited the Great Exhibition. He was impressed by a new wood screw exhibited by an American inventor called Sloane and offered to buy the patent. Short of the necessary funds Nettlefold invited his brother-in-law Joseph Chamberlain senior to come into business with him. By 1865, Nettlefold and Chamberlain were producing 90,000 gross screws a week.

appointed to Cabinet in 1891, his predecessor Arthur Balfour sought to reassure unconvinced colleagues that the new Chief Secretary for Ireland might import some 'middle-class tact and judgement, but good of their kind' (Bentley 1996, 293). As it transpired, the later 1st Baron Allerton did not seem to import much of anything, leaving little imprint either in Ireland or in parliamentary history. But at least he behaved himself, unlike Bradlaugh and Labouchere. Parliamentary politics had changed, and it would continue to change. We will take a closer look at the implications of this shortly. We will also take a look at the broader state of the nation as the nineteenth century began to draw to its close. Both establish the context within which we must approach the fourth in our series of texts which wrote the Victorian constitution.

The Age of Reason and Unmuzzling

Making the 'establishment' look silly made the respective fortunes of WS Gilbert and his librettist Arthur Sullivan. In March 1885, perhaps their most famous comic opera went into production at the Savoy Theatre, another 'meaningful coincidence'. *The Mikado* was of course set in Japan. But it was written to the same purpose as Burke had written his *Reflections on the Revolution in France* a century earlier. The principle referent was England. Life in Titipu was evidently rather more fun than life in revolutionary France, but only because it was more ironic; and the same it could be supposed was true of life in late Victorian England. The opening scene is set in the courtyard of the Lord High Executioner's Palace. Poo-Bah enters and explains in conversation with Nanki-Poo the consequence of recent reforms in the governance of Titipu. There are now just the two men holding high office: Ko-Ko, who has been appointed the Lord High Executioner, and himself, the now Lord High Everything Else. Law students might have been expected to spot the problems in the latter regard, especially those who had attended Professor Dicey's lectures on the separation of powers. But what bothers Poo-Bah rather more is the idea that a 'cheap tailor' like Ko-Ko might be elevated to the office of Lord High Executioner (Gilbert and Sullivan 2008, 369–70). He is precisely the wrong sort of chap to be in government, not just because he is too kind-hearted but because he is too common.

Poo-Bah on the other hand is born to office, 'in point of fact, a particularly haughty and exclusive person, of pre-Adamite ancestral descent' who can trace his 'ancestry back to a protoplasmal primordial atomic globule' (Gilbert and Sullivan 2008, 370). The cultural referent here was just as familiar and did not require any closer jurisprudential insight. Twenty-six years earlier Charles Darwin had published his *Origin of the Species by Means of Natural Selection*, the Preface to which concluded that the Old Testament account of the Creation was entirely 'erroneous'. The supposition came as no surprise to those who had read Sir Charles Lyell's *Principles of Geology* published two decades earlier; the biblical flood was evidently nonsense too. The implications of evolution were, however, no less distressing for being more familiar, and neither Darwin nor his publisher was sure of sales. The first print run of 1250 was sold out in days. By the time the fifth edition had sold out in 1872, Darwin had achieved still greater notoriety with the publication, the year before, of his *The Descent of Man, and Selection in Relation to Sex*. It suggested that all its readers were descended from the apes.

Some hominoid descendants were more easily persuaded than others. Those of a more metaphysical bent, especially those who had read Harriet Martineau's recently published monograph on *The Positive Philosophy of Auguste Comte* or George Eliot's translations of Feuerbach or her essays on the 'religion of 'humanity', were already apprised. Lytton Strachey would later celebrate the publication of GE Moore's *Principia Ethica* in 1903 as the 'beginning of the Age of Reason'. He was a couple of generations late, at least. Burke blamed the French Revolution on 'atheists' and 'stock-jobbers' and the 'smugglers of adulterated metaphysics' (Burke 1986, 186–7). Back in the very first year of Victoria's reign, a young Tennyson had made pointed reference to 'the fairy tales of science' in *Locksley Hall* (Tennyson 1991, 97). He would return to the same setting and the same theme half a century later in *Locksley Hall Sixty Years After*: 'Science grows and Beauty dwindles' (Tennyson 1991, 342). Poetry provided consolation of a sort. *In Memoriam* was Victoria's favourite poem; she read it to the marble bust of her dear departed, kept next to the washstand in his room. But it was an agonised consolation. In *Sixty Years After,* it verges on the apocalyptic: 'Chaos, Cosmos! Cosmos, Chaos! Who can tell how all will end?' the poet exclaims, 'Forward, backward, backward, forward in the immeasurable sea,/Sway'd by vaster ebbs and flows than can be known to you or me' (Tennyson 1991, 336, 340). There is, it has been suggested, no more 'terrible' cry of despair in Victorian literature (Levi 1993, 308–9). There is though a resonance, spiritual and metaphorical.

As he wrote *Sixty Years After*, Tennyson was reading Matthew Arnold's *Dover Beach*. Arnold's elegy, first drafted in 1851, though not published until the year of the second Reform Act, left its reader bereft, contemplating the 'melancholy, long, withdrawing roar' of the 'Sea of Faith', on 'a darkling plain/Swept with confused alarms of struggle and flight,/ Where ignorant armies clash by night' (Arnold 1986, 136).

One such clash occurred in summer 1860, not on a 'darkling plain' but at the Oxford University Museum where the Bishop of Oxford, 'soapy Sam' Wilberforce, challenged 'Darwin's Bulldog', TH Huxley, to a debate on the meaning of evolution. Oddly enough Wilberforce and Darwin were close friends and would remain so despite the extent of their intellectual differences. Wilberforce did not, however, much like Huxley. Adopting a bluff and condescending tone, he wondered if Huxley was descended from apes on his mother's side or his father's. Huxley retorted that he would rather be descended from a 'miserable ape' than seek to 'obscure the truth' by making bad jokes (Wilson 1999, 195–6; Heffer 2013, 218–9). The audience erupted. Nothing is more deadly to the dogmatist than the sound of laughter, as the many devotees of Gilbert and Sullivan so readily appreciated. A couple of years later Kingsley would satirise the satire in his *Water Babies*. It was the 'Great Hippocampus Question' and whilst it was yet to be fully resolved, it was clear the 'great Fairy of Science' was 'likely to be queen of all the fairies for many years to come'. There was much in the Reverend Kingsley's fable about Christian redemption and the virtue of hard work. But there was also much that was written in admiration of Darwin and in hope for the future. The 'great Fairy', a generation of later Victorian toddlers was assured, 'can only do you good and never do you harm' (Kingsley 2013, 48).

It was left to a harder core of Churchmen to rail against rationalism, the 'great evil of the day' according to John Henry Newman. Newman had been on crusade before. Back in 1833, he had published the first of a series of *Tracts for the Times*. Another eighty-nine would follow before the publication of the incendiary *Tract XC* in 1841, which argued that there was nothing in the Thirty-Nine Articles which precluded Anglicans from adhering to Catholic doctrine. When Newman had converted to Rome, taking a number of similarly disaffected 'High' Anglicans with him, Victoria announced herself glad to be rid of such 'dreadfully aggressive people' (Arnstein 2003, 93–4). The shock to the Church was undoubted. But it was also oddly marginal. The crisis of the Victorian

Church was never going to be resolved by a handful of Oxford dons bickering their way through High Table dinner. A crisis in the Church, as Carlyle readily appreciated, was also a crisis of state, and not just of the mind. The thought that 'unbelief' might become the 'disease' of later Victorian England had been another of the Sage of Ecclefechan's dour prophecies (Himmelfarb 2007, 45; Wilson 1999, 8). And it could not be simply blamed on Darwin or Huxley either. There was also a matter of leaky roofs and lack of money and statistics. The 1851 census had made for sober reading. Beauty was not the only thing that was dwindling. Apparently, only one in ten regularly attended Sunday service. The English had become, in the word of the accompanying census report, 'habitual neglecters of the public ordinances of religion' (Best 1979, 197). GK Chesterton blamed demography. The *Times* agreed. The 'parochial system' and the 'manufacturing town' were incompatible (Wilson 2002, 168; Gilmour 1993, 66).

The fact that one in four who did not go to an Anglican service instead attended various dissenting chapels provided scant consolation. The association of dissent and Chartism, and urban deprivation, was firmly embedded in the reactionary mind. The Tory Church was never simply a place where people might go to worship now and again. It was, alongside the Crown and in the absence of much else, the foundation of the English constitution. Any reader of Burke's *Reflections* knew at least that much: 'Church and state are ideas inseparable' (Burke 1986, 198). 'What gentlemen is Conservatism?' asked Christopher Wordsworth, brother of William and later arch-Tory Bishop of Lincoln, to which the rhetorical answer was 'the adoption of principles of the Church of England as the groundwork of legislation'. And if Englishmen and women felt the need for a written constitution, they should look no further than the Book of Common Prayer (Heffer 2013, 203). Samuel Taylor Coleridge, the most penitent of apostates, had supposed precisely this in his 1826 *Constitution of Church and State* Samuel Taylor Coleridge. He had also made the same necessary inference as Carlyle; a crisis in the established Church must represent a broader crisis of constitutional governance. It would become a common Tractarian complaint, the intrusion of the state as a 'direct disavowal of the sovereignty of God' (Woodward 1962, 512–3).

Victoria agreed in part. But as Governor of the Church, it was her duty to intrude a lot. She clung tenaciously to her prerogative right to appoint bishops and declared it her mission to make sure that government was not full of atheists. 'Disbelief in God', she opined, 'leads to a lack of reverence for those in authority, including parents' (Hibbert 2001, 201). In her opinion, it was clear that the greater threat, by the 1870s at least, was no longer Jacobins rampaging about the streets of London, but men like Bradlaugh and Labouchere lounging about on the benches in the Commons loudly proclaiming their godlessness. The solution, she resolved, was another 'very sweeping Reformation' (Arnstein 2003, 137). In truth, a Victorian reformation was already underway. Peel's Ecclesiastical Commission had been established in 1834, with a broad remit that encompassed not just leaky chancels and declining congregations, but also and most urgently, lack of finance. The Commissioners may have been rather more polite than those which Thomas Cromwell had visited upon the country three centuries earlier, but their recommendations were barely more palatable; the removal of patent abuses, including the holding of plural benefices more than two miles apart, the division of impoverished sees and dramatic redistribution of diocesan grants. Church rates survived, just, but not for long. Gladstone abolished them in 1868 (Waddams 1992, 267–9). Unpalatable perhaps, but by the 1880s it was evident that the Church was in a better, if leaner, shape. Congregations were steady, finances stronger, and whilst it might have evinced little enthusiasm for internecine scriptural debate, much of middle England betrayed a residual affection for the rhythm of Church life. In its obituary for Charles Dickens in 1870 *Fraser's Magazine* noted that the great novelist had 'spent no thought on religious doctrines or religious reforms but regarded the Sermon on the Mount as good teaching, had a regard for the village church and churchyard, and quarrelled with nothing but intolerance'. It was meant to be representative, and it was meant to be a compliment.

In 1885, the Church authorised the publication of the first Revised Version of the King James Bible. It represented, in the opinion of many contemporary Churchmen, the culmination of their 'reformation'. It was the second of three texts published that year which describe another of our 'meaningful coincidences'. The first was *The Mikado*. The third is Albert Venn Dicey's *Lectures Introductory to the Study of the Law of the Constitution*. It is their difference which is so striking; satire, science and faith, all vying for the attention of an increasingly animated, and literate, audience. We shall take a closer look at Dicey's *Law of the Constitution* shortly. But first, we need to broaden the context further still. For despite his intellectual preference for the emergent science of jurisprudence, Dicey's writing on the constitution was entirely informed by his active intellectual interest in late Victorian politics. This is most evident, as we shall again see, in his *Lectures on Public Opinion*, published in 1905. Twenty years earlier, however, the political agenda was yet again dominated by further talk of reform. The 'coincidence' of reason and reform may have found a varied textual expression in 1885, but it was otherwise irreducible.

Intellectually, Dicey was very much the adherent of reason, as we shall see. But it comes as little surprise to learn that he was far less enthusiastic in regard to reform. He only grudgingly approved the 1832 Act (Dicey 1914, 115–9). The price had been high, perhaps too high:

> But the transcendent importance of the Act lay in its effect upon public opinion. Reform thus regarded was revolution. It altered the way in which people thought of the constitution, and taught Englishmen, once and for all, that venerable institutions which custom had made unchangeable could easily, and without use of violence, be changed. (Dicey 1914, 42)

It was the faintest of praise. He was even less enamoured of subsequent reform statutes. Where the 1832 Act had at least been 'carried by and for the benefit of the middle classes' the subsequent Acts of 1867 and 1884 had been passed 'in deference to the wishes' of an inchoate and incoherent working class. And in so doing, both had 'transformed' England into a 'democracy'; a 'revolution' which 'completely explains the increasing influence of socialism' (Dicey 1914, 218, 254). The 1832 Reform Act might have precluded Jacobinism, but in their apparent embrace of socialism the 1867 and 1884 Acts had achieved precisely the converse.

The 1867 Act had, as Bagehot prophesied, changed the face of British politics. But it had not changed it for the better, still less had it brought 'finality'. The age of 'indolence and corruption' might have come to an end, as Lord Stanley supposed. But it had been replaced by a still more corrosive politics of confrontation, and a Commons increasingly populated by men like Bradlaugh and Labouchere; men who, as Arnold rather sniffly observed, claimed to represent the 'Populace' (Arnold 1993, 183; Parry 1993, 62, 155–9). No one had really thought the Act would bring 'finality' of course, least of all Disraeli and Gladstone. Disraeli was left to convince his party, and his monarch, that the 1867 Act had prevented revolution. Gladstone meanwhile set about constructing a distinctively conservative liberalism, the 'solid permanent conviction of the nation' (Parry 1993, 1; Aldous 2007, 10). And he would align it once more with the cause of reform. Having lost the race to enact the second Reform Act, he did not intend to lose the race to enact the third. The mission statement was already drafted. In the debates which preceded the 1867 Act, Gladstone had 'ventured' to suggest that 'every man who is not presumably incapacitated by some consideration of personal unfitness or political danger is morally entitled to come within the pale of the constitution' (Jenkins 1995, 247).

When the third Reform Act arrived in 1884, it did so as part of a wider package of parliamentary reform which also included a Corrupt Practices Act in 1883 and a Redistribution Act in 1885 (Jenkins 1965, 123). The 1884 Act established a uniform franchise for all householders and lodgers and £10 occupiers. The electorate was further increased by around 80%; impressive enough until it is remembered that 40% of all men and 100% of all women were still disenfranchised. The supplementary 1885 Act provided for uniform constituencies with a minimum threshold of 15,000 voters, and left just twenty-three seats, those with over 50,000 voters, with dual representation. Gladstone's Home Secretary Harcourt articulated a familiar disquiet, bemoaning a 'frightfully democratic measure which I confess appals me' (Parry 1993, 287). The Radical Joseph Chamberlain boasted that 'government of the people by the people' had 'at last been effectively secured' (Wilson 2002, 479). Harcourt was unduly pessimistic, Chamberlain the converse. It was a kind of democracy. But it was hardly radical, and in terms of franchise at least it was something short of what Gladstone had threatened two decades earlier.

The widening of the franchise was not, however, the only aspect of the third Reform Act which distressed later Victorian conservatives. It was not even the most. There was also of course the question of make-up, not just in the Commons but around the Cabinet table. The younger Gladstone had declared himself to be a firm 'believer in the aristocratic principle' (Wilson 2002, 356). But the Cabinet which he formed on his return to power in 1886 was the first in parliamentary history to contain fewer than seven peers or their progeny. The decline of the aristocracy would of course be gradual, as well as grudging (Cannadine 1994, 35). Later Victorian England would still be ruled by grandees. Few grandees were grander than Robert Arthur Talbot Gascoyne-Cecil, 3rd Marquis of Salisbury. The last premier to serve from the red benches, Salisbury was in office for thirteen of the seventeen years that fell between 1885 and 1902, so dominant a presence indeed that Westminster became known colloquially as the 'Hotel Cecil'. Salisbury, who thought that formal party affiliation was 'great trash', formed Tory administrations (Bentley 2001, 20). But he spent much of his time trying to infuse them with 'common' Burkean 'principles' and fill them with disaffected Whigs, most notably perhaps Spencer Compton Cavendish, Marquis of Hartington and later 8th Duke of Devonshire (Bentley 2001, 25, 65, 251).[4] Scion of the most Whiggish of 'old' Whig families, 'Harty-Tarty' as his friends called him, and in whose opinion the role of a politician was to 'form the opinion and guide the destinies of the nation' rather than concede to its every passing whim, was Salisbury's kind of chap (Parry 1993, 11).

Gladstone most certainly was not. In due course, Hartington would lead the anti-Home Rule liberals out of Gladstone's party and into the clutches of Salisbury's, taking Dicey and a generation of similarly troubled 'little Englanders' with him. By then, the erstwhile hope of the 'stern and unbending' Tories, as Macaulay had famously termed the younger Gladstone, had changed not just his own party but the culture of British politics. And it was this which, for men like Dicey, caused the greatest consternation of all. Here, again it was the manner in which the 1884 Act passed which was significant. In 1832, it had been a matter of bullying a King and terrifying his Peers. In 1867, it was a matter of political calculation. The 1884 Act happened because Gladstone went to the people and asked their opinion. It was not just the people of course. There was also the 'great hand of God, so evidently displayed'. Gladstone was a crusader too. When he embarked on his famed 1879 Midlothian campaign, he did so with the immediate purpose of saving the chosen people from the 'obscene empires of Mammon and Belial'. Providence had entrusted him with a 'striking gift', and it was his God-given duty to use it (Shannon 1999, 335; Parry 1993, 251–3, 277). But his second purpose was to make himself popular: the 'People's William', as well as God's.

He had of course used his 'striking gift' before. 'At last my friends', Gladstone had thundered to an audience of 6000 at the Manchester

[4] He was not alone in his predilection. Lord Derby likewise preferred to populate his Cabinets with distinctly Whiggish Tories. By the end of the century, it was, paradoxically, Liberal practice to accuse the Tory party of having assumed the previously Whig mantle of being the party of aristocratic 'interest' (Parry 1993, 4–5; Hawkins 1989, 657).

Free Trade Hall one bright morning in July 1865, 'I am come among you and I am coming among you unmuzzled'. Later that afternoon, he came similarly unmuzzled before 5000 adoring supporters in Liverpool (Jenkins 1995, 251; Aldous 2007, 151). The adoration, moreover, seemed to be reciprocal. It is 'impossible', he purred following another of his provincial tours, 'not to love the people from whom such manifestations come, as meet us in every quarter' (Briggs 1959, 493). It was again a necessary consequence of 1832 and 1867. Constituencies needed to be cajoled rather than simply cowed. 'It is to the people and in the main the people only to whom we have to look', he observed (Shannon 1999, 347). Morley likened the Midlothian campaign to a royal progress; a far 'grander and more august spectacle' than any of the petty ceremonials periodically exhibited at Westminster or Windsor (Jenkins 1995, 424–7; Shannon 1999, 339). The highlight in 1879 was an address to 20,000 at Edinburgh Waverley market. By the end of the year, one statistically minded contemporary concluded that he had addressed precisely 86,930 in thirty speeches over fifteen days. Another equally statistically inclined contemporary supposed that he had during this time articulated 85,840 words (Jenkins 1995, 428).

Victoria took an unsurprisingly dim view of Gladstone's unmuzzling, expressing herself 'utterly disgusted with his stump oratory, so unworthy of his position'. He was anyway a 'dreadful man', and the idea of addressing the people directly was inherently 'absurd' (Longford 1998, 470). Tory opponents were unsurprisingly horrified too, as were Liberal Unionists such as Edmund Wodehouse, 'disgusted' with his erstwhile leader's 'unscrupulous demagogy' (Jenkins 1996, 129). Gladstone's Chancellor of the Exchequer, William Harcourt, though far from averse to a bit of unmuzzled demagoguery himself, expressed misgivings. The country 'becoming daily more democratic', and it would only get worse (Bentley 1996, 276). Salisbury agreed in terms that were rather more obviously apocalyptic. The 'hurricane that has swept us away', he advised a young AJ Balfour in 1880, must bring with it the prospect of a 'serious war of the classes' (Bentley 2001, 72). In the past, opinion had come to Parliament, articulated in reverential petitions or by supplicant client MPs. But not anymore; now, it seemed, Parliament went to the people and asked their opinion.

Much Shaken

And so when in 1904, Dicey was invited to give a course of lectures on Harvard University on a subject of pressing contemporary interest, he chose the history of public opinion in the nineteenth century. It was in effect a course of lectures on the dark side of reform, the purpose of which was not merely to chronicle the worst excesses so far, but to warn against any further. Constitutional reform had not merely extended the franchise. It had acted as an accelerating agent for the rise of the regulatory state. A vicious cycle had developed between the respective ages of 'progressive improvement' and reform and the advance of 'public opinion'. As we have already noted, the age of 'improvement' was multiform, everything from screw manufacture to cricket ball catapult. But two particular improvements had nurtured the mutant growth of public opinion especially: the press and the railway. In the former case, it was a mixture of print technology along with various parliamentary statutes designed to promote the industry. Stamp Duty on newspapers was abolished in 1855 and excise duty on paper six years later. Telegraph Acts in 1868 and 1870 had further nurtured the growth of the provincial press, weekly circulation figures for which had already reached two and a half million by 1864. The *British and Irish Press Guide for 1874* listed Newcastle upon Tyne as having five dailies and five weeklies. And it was not just the cities. No self-respecting market-town was without at least one weekly. Driffield had three, Trowbridge had two. Disdaining the competition the London-based *Times* assumed the high ground and celebrated an 'age' of 'informed' public opinion. Newspapers, its editor proclaimed, 'constitute one of the great springs of a society so highly civilised and so completely organised as that of Great Britain' (Briggs 1959, 193).

It was also of course a matter of increased literacy levels too; not just more to read, but more people reading. Eighty-seven percent of workhouse children in Norfolk and Suffolk were reported to be functionally literate as early as 1838. There were of course regional variations. Even so the 1871 census suggested the national illiteracy figures had fallen to just nineteen percent for men and twenty-six for women. Education reform had become and centrepiece of progressive 'improvement'. The reason, according to John Forster, after whom the 1870 Education Act would become known, was quite simple. Britain's industrial prosperity' was dependent on the 'speedy provision of elementary education' (Heffer 2013, 413, 439). Between 1863 and 1869, a thousand new schools were opened. And it was not just a matter of educating children. Manchester Free Library opened in 1852. Mechanics Institutes flourished in the north and Midlands. There were 610 in 1860. The 'schoolmaster', as Brougham proudly declared, was 'abroad in the land' (Brantlinger 1977, 21). Dr. Arnold worried that the Institutes spent too little time on the classics, on one occasion informing a room of presumably rather deflated mechanics in Rugby that the prospective neglect of their 'religious' education would lead inexorably to moral deprivation. Huxley, predictably, thought very differently. The basics of arithmetic mattered; the rudiments of 'Syrian geography' did not (Heffer 2013, 609–10).

It was difficult to argue against the virtues of literacy. It was easier to argue against what Melbourne termed the 'vice' of newspaper reading (Mitchell 1997, 22, 25). Back in 1828, WA Mackinnon had written his essay *On the rise, progress, and present state of public opinion* to the same purpose. Only the reinvestment of 'proper religious feeling', Mackinnon warned, could save the English from the coming ravages of democracy (Parry 1993, 27). Carlyle unsurprisingly took the same dim view against the 'tyranny' of 'public opinion' in his *Sign of the Times* (Carlyle 1986, 81, 83–5). So did Peel, bemoaning the 'empire of public opinion' as nothing other than a 'great compound of folly, weakness, prejudice, wrong feeling, right feeling, obstinacy and newspaper paragraphs' (Read 1987, 16; Briggs 1959, 194). Lord Brougham had adopted a more sanguine tone, reconciling himself to the thought that public opinion might be limited to men like himself, the 'intelligence of the country, the glory of the British name' (Parry 1993, 27–8). But few were so readily consoled. Bagehot, as we have already noted, was not, scarcely bothering to hide his disdain for the 'opinion' of the 'bald-headed man at the back of the omnibus' (Bagehot 2001, 30).

As the century drew on the tendency became only too apparent, the 'unstable equilibrium' of public governance and public opinion too easily upset, too many journals, too many journalists, too many people with too many opinions and too many politicians too eager to satiate them (Bagehot 2001, 32–3). 'Vox populi', Bagehot warned, 'will become vox diaboli if worked in that manner'. It did. The particular influence of the *Times* had long caused disquiet. Wellington acerbically alluded to its editors as 'our governors' (Bentley 1996, 97). Its daily sales figures rose from 40,000 to 70,000 between 1851 and 1861, which suggested that around half a million were probably reading each edition. But even these figures paled in comparison with those achieved by the *Daily Mail* when it first hit the stands in 1896. It was immediately selling 400,000 copies. By the turn of the century, sales alone were nearing a million a day. A few years earlier in his 1891 essay *The Soul of Man Under Socialism*, Oscar Wilde had observed:

> In old days men had the rack. Now they have the press. That is an improvement certainly. But still it is very bad, and wrong, and demoralising. Somebody – was it Burke? – called journalism the fourth estate. That was true at the time, no doubt. But at the present moment, it really is the only estate. It has eaten up the other three. The Lords Temporal say nothing, the Lord Spiritual have nothing to say, and the House of Commons has nothing to say and says it. (Himmelfarb 2007, 306)

Bagehot would have appreciated both the argument and the tone. Dicey was rather less of an ironist, but he undoubtedly shared the overriding sentiment; all the wrong people saying too much.

The second improvement, intimately related to the emergence of an increasingly voluble and virile press, was the advance of the railways. Public opinion moved on track. The first politician to appreciate this was Peel. He loved the railway. In 1845, he cut the first sod for the Trent Valley railway, assuring his audience that its construction would further 'promote the moral and social welfare of this country' (Read 1987, 9, 149). The following year, his government supported the passage of 519 railway bills through Parliament. If middle England was looking for a new kind of hero, he surmised, they needed to look no further than George Stephenson. It is easy to imagine what Carlyle thought of that particular recommendation. The growth of the railway was extraordinary. By 1850, there were 6000 miles of track carrying 67 million passengers. By 1875, it had doubled, carrying over 490 million. The *Times* was not impressed, regretting the 'idle debauchery' which railway travel facilitated. The literary world was divided. Arnold and Trollope both rather liked railway travel. Ruskin, however, agreed with the *Times*, whilst Wordsworth spent his declining years penning sonnets bemoaning the egregious advance of track across his Lakeland landscape. Tennyson had aligned a shared anxiety in *Locksley Hall*: 'In the steamship, in the railway, in the thoughts that shake mankind' (Tennyson 1991, 103).

Victoria did not much like shaking either, for which reason the Royal train was forbidden from ever exceeding fifty miles an hour.

It was, however, the more figurative kind of shaking which Dicey chose to address in his *Lectures on Public Opinion*. The *Lectures*, as we have already noted, purported to be historical, adopting a tripartite narrative of nineteenth-century history; Blackstonian or Burkean Toryism from 1800 to 1830; followed by Benthamite 'individualism' from 1825 to 1870; and finally collectivism from 1865 to 1900 (Dicey 1914, 62–9). In truth, the 'history' scarcely masked a visceral account of what can happen when political classes abandon their conservative principles and allow democracy to run riot, pandering to every populist whimsy. Dicey's history insinuated the mutation of Benthamite reformism leading to the horrors of collectivism and the rise of the regulatory state. In a sense, the *Lectures* might be read as an expression of nostalgic regret, not unlike in their very different way Arnold's *Dover Beach* or Tennyson's *Sixty Years After*. The younger Dicey had found much in Bentham to admire. He had been an 'unrepentant Benthamite'. The younger Dicey had also been an ardent admirer of John Stuart Mill, an affinity which might seem at odds with his innately Burkean empathies until it is remembered just how Whiggish Mill's *Considerations on Representative Government* can read (Burrow 1988, 102–6). 'At Oxford', Dicey later testified, 'we swallowed Mill, rather undigested: he was our chief intellectual food' (Cosgrove 1980, 12). As to Bentham, he had literally rewritten English law. The 'history of modern English law', Dicey averred, was quite simply 'the history of a gigantic revolution produced by the ideas of one man' (Cosgrove 1980, 181). Bentham, as readers of the *Lectures* were informed, was a 'genius', the greatest 'reformer' in English legal history, someone who cut through the 'fallacies' of metaphysical jurisprudence (Dicey 1914, 132, 145). In fact, as the *Lectures* made plain, Dicey admired a particular kind of Benthamism, one the 'essential strength' of which resided not in 'transitory' radicalism, but 'in its correspondence with tendencies of English thought and feeling which have exhibited a character of permanence' (Dicey 1914, 174). There was a lot of Burke in the Bentham Dicey preferred. Benthamite 'conservatism', he elsewhere confirmed, was 'marked' by a 'perpetual compromise between the spirit of innovation and the spirit of conservatism, which is the essential character of English legislation and of English public life' (Dicey 1914, 358).

And it was precisely here that Dicey and a generation of like-minded anxious later Victorians found themselves, trapped between the march of improvement and the nostalgia of conservation. And whilst they struggled to reach an accommodation, the modern state simply continued to evolve. Dicey, like indeed Bagehot, blamed Parliament. Too many laws passed by parliamentarians who should have known better. Here again was the darker side of reform. And the chronology was convenient. The 1834 Poor Law, commonly identified as the first significant statutory step towards the fashioning of the later Victorian regulatory state, arrived just two years after the first Reform Act. A year later came the Municipal Corporations Act. By the end of the decade, there was also a Prisons Act and a first Education Act. Amongst the myriad reforms of the 1840s could be counted a series of employment statutes, including the 1842 Mines Act, the 1844 Factory Act and the 1847 Ten Hours Act along with two 1844 enactments intended to better regulate the world of finance, the Bank Charter Act and the Companies Act. The same decade also saw the passage of the 1848 Public Health Act, which was intended to add legal force to the various measures recommended in Edwin Chadwick's *Sanitary Conditions of the Labouring Classes* report, including the establishment of a system of local health boards under the broader jurisdiction of a National Health Board. The following two decades were perhaps quieter. But further reforms continued, including the Police Act in 1856, which established county police forces, and the 1866 Sanitary Act, which again addressed a number Chadwick's recommendations on draining things. Another Chimney Sweepers Regulation Act in 1864, vigorously championed by Lord Shaftesbury, revisited the seemingly intractable subject of who might be asked to go up what, when and why.

By the 1870s, Parliament appeared to have drawn a second breath. Successive Education Acts appeared on the statute book in 1870, 1876 and 1893, by which time primary education was state-regulated and free. Public Health and Licensing Acts appeared in 1872. The reach of the state into matters religious continued with the 1874 Public Worship Regulation Act, followed twenty years later by the passage of the rather more prosaic Fowler's Act which regularised the governance of parish councils in communities of over three hundred persons. A Public Health Act of 1875 sought to regulate food standards, street lighting, markets and the notification of diseases. The great Factory Act of 1878 consolidated a mass of often conflicting factory, health and safety legislation, whilst also refining, and re-funding, the operation of an existing factory inspectorate. The 1888 Local Government Act which established county councils addressed a different aspect of local governance. And so, it went on. The 1871 Royal Commission on Sanitation reached a blunt conclusion. Increased administrative regulation was 'essential', the 'essence' indeed of 'our national vigour' (Best 1979, 59). Jerusalem was being rebuilt statute by statute, council by council, street light by street light.

Mid and later Victorian England, Bagehot concluded in slightly understated terms, evidenced 'a sort of leaning towards bureaucracy' (Bagehot 2001, 132–3). Not everyone was sceptical of course. Gladstone celebrated a 'golden age of useful legislation and administrative improvement' and placed its advancement at the heart of his new Liberalism (Shannon 1999, 329). Dickens too evinced a degree of cautious enthusiasm; his trilogy of 'condition of England' novels written during the 1850s each intimating the need for administrative reform. Dicey, as we have already noted, was an ambivalent admirer of Dickens, acknowledging his sense of humour, but resenting the 'crude satire' of utilitarianism written into *Hard Times* (Dicey 1914, 418–22). Gradgrind was the wrong kind of Benthamite, Dickens in 1854 the wrong kind of reformer. *Bleak House*, which completed its serialisation a year earlier, had invited its readers to contemplate the case for reforming another evidently dysfunctional part of the regulatory state, the legal system (Blake 2009, 8–17). Here, again there had been a range of statutory reforms during the middle and later decades of the nineteenth century, from the establishment of local bankruptcy and country courts in 1844 and 1846 to the establishment of a dedicated Divorce Court in the 1857 Matrimonial Causes Act, and then on to the 1873 and 1875 Judicature Acts. In regard to legal reform, Dicey was again grudgingly reconciled. The 'faults' in legal procedure were 'patent', reformers such as Brougham, Romilly and Peel all 'men of common sense', and 'all at bottom individualists' (Dicey 1914, 168–9). In this rather tempered spirit, Dicey thus approved a succession of Evidence Acts, Common Law Procedure Acts and of course the Judicature Acts. He was positively enthused by the 1857 Divorce Act which had established a distinct Divorce Court; a 'triumph of individualistic liberalism and common justice' (Dicey 1914, 347).

He was not, however, anything like so enthused by the idea of a distinctive branch of administrative law which might be developed to regulate the regulatory state. He had already broached this subject in the first editions of his *Law of the Constitution*. The subject of the twelfth chapter was the French *droit administratif*. Dicey's particular distaste for French public law was something else which he shared with Bagehot.

The English may not have a 'written' constitution, but at least they were not burdened with a demarcated system of public law designed to provide a spurious legitimacy to the exercise of discretionary government, as the French did. For added sustenance, Dicey turned once again to history and more particularly to the prerogative courts of the early seventeenth century. Prerogative courts, he argued, were a species of administrative law, something which was fundamentally 'opposed to those habits of equality before the law which had long been essential characteristics of English institutions'. The English Revolution had rid itself of prerogative courts; the French Revolution had reinvested them. Dicey never relented in his distaste for administrative law and its 'despotic' tendencies; as a consequence of which, it is suggested, generations of English lawyers were turned against its very idea (Cosgrove 1980, 91–100). In 1915, as he was writing the introduction to the eighth edition of the *Law*, he took time out to write another diatribe on the same subject. The title of the article, published in the *Law Quarterly Review*, was 'The Development of Administrative Law in England'. It asked the question as to whether 'a body of administrative law resembling in spirit' the dreaded French *droit administratif* had arisen in England (Dicey 1959, 493–9). The answer was implicit in the title.

There were then closer jurisprudential reasons why Dicey distrusted the regulatory state. But they were driven by deeper political suspicions. Above all, the growth of the state enervated 'individualism' and impinged common law rights. He expressed his appreciation of the familiar tension in a tempering comment on Mill:

> Individuality in its true sense is a source of both greatness and of goodness, and much as we must value all social progress with its accompanying restrictions, we must watch jealously lest these restrictions endanger individuality, and thus destroy that originality which is the very spring of true social progress. (Cosgrove 1980, 12)

His barrister brother Edward reached a more determinative variant of the same conclusion. The 'result of every attempt made hitherto to promote the well-being of mankind by taking the management of their affairs out of their own control has been to degrade, not improve, their condition' (Dicey 1885, 466–7). And plenty of others felt much the same, including the historian Henry Buckle. With 'the exception of certain necessary enactments respecting the preservation of order', readers of his 1857 *History of Civilization in England* were informed, 'nearly everything which has been done has been done amiss' (Buckle 1871, 271; Hibbitts 1994, 10). Salisbury habitually moaned about the 'recklessly extravagant' regulatory bodies which governed his England. He was peculiarly exercised by Boards of Education (Bentley 2001, 98–9). It was the prevalence of municipal libraries which bothered Herbert Spencer, who likened the Victorian regulatory state to the 'tyranny' of 'ancient Peru' in his pointedly entitled *Man Versus the State*, published in 1884 (Gilmour 1993, 174).

And along with the regulatory state came collectivism, and a whole host of similarly hideous spectres, of the Tolpuddle martyrs, the Chartists, suffragettes and ill-dressed Members of Parliament. In 1892, the electors of West Ham South chose the Scottish Labour Party candidate Keir Hardie to be their MP. Eschewing the convention that he should turn up for his first day wearing a black frock coat, silk-hat and wing collar Hardie entered the chamber in a tweed coat, red-tie and deerstalker. Not only was the future of democracy apparently God-less, so too was it unkempt. Socialism was not, Dicey averred, a 'necessary' consequence of democracy. But it was an evident tendency (Dicey 1914, lxiv). And it would be regulated too. The first annual Trades Union Congress had met in 1868, followed in due course by the first employment legislation intended to regulate union activities. The 1871 and 1875 Trade Union Acts legalised peaceful picketing for the first time, whilst also safeguarding the essential features of collective bargaining. In 1882, WH Smith was moved to admit that the country was 'drifting into radical socialism very fast indeed' (Bentley 2001, 153). The year after his election Hardie helped to found an independent Labour Party. We can be pretty sure what Dicey thought of Hardie and his new party. He dreaded socialism and he dreaded socialists, amongst whom he counted William Morris, the 'iniquitous' Herbert Asquith, Winston Churchill and the 'shameless' Lloyd George. And eventually, John Stuart Mill too, Dicey's admiration for whom ran out at precisely the point where he opened the first page of the *Chapters on Socialism*. He was, to revisit the metaphor, 'much shaken' (Dicey 1914, 426–32; Cosgrove 1980, 13).

Professor Dicey's Study

Interestingly, Dicey would later attest that the *Lectures on Public Opinion* were the 'best thing I have ever written and much more mature than the *Law of the Constitution*' (Bingham 2002, 41).

They have not, however, stood the same test of time. In relative terms, the 1905 *Lectures* are forgotten, a history too readily belonging to the past. Conversely, generation after generation of law students would continue to learn their constitutional law courtesy of Dicey's *Lectures Introductory*, precisely because it seemed to withstand the passage of time. It would become the 'oracle' to which politician and professor alike would turn for guidance throughout much of the twentieth century. Between 1885 and 1915, it went through eight editions, each of which reinforced its determinative authority. We will take a closer look at Dicey in 1915 in due course, and the enduring reputation of the 'oracle'. First, however, we must take a closer look at the law of the English constitution, as Dicey perceived it to be.

And the matter of perception is of course critical. Dicey wanted to present an objective account of the fundamental principles of English constitutional law. But what he presented, unavoidably, was Dicey's opinion as to what the fundamental principles of English constitutional law might be. It is different, but also, in the edifying sense, the same. The necessary tension was spotted by Sir Ivor Jennings in 1935. Despite its jurisprudential aspiration, the *Law of the Constitution* should still be read as a politically charged commentary written by a Burkean Whig who 'saw the constitution in 1885 through Whig principles' (Jennings 1935, 125, 128).[5] Elsewhere in a sense, Dicey confessed as much. The 'four writers whom I read with perpetual profit and enjoyment on all constitutional matters', he once remarked, 'are Burke, Paley, Macaulay & Bagehot' (Cosgrove 1980, 69). The very first chapter of the *Law of the Constitution* opens with Burke, a writer of especial historical 'insight' (Dicey 1959, xxv–xxvii, 149). Much later, Dicey would recommend Wordsworth's 'Sonnets on Liberty' precisely because they are informed by the 'teaching of Burke', because they 'appeal to the inherited and the historical virtues handed down to us by men of heroic mould whom it is our duty to follow' (Dicey 1917, 59–70, 133). Burke too set a mould. It shaped Macaulay and Bagehot, and it shaped Dicey.

Paley is though a bit different, for which reason his presence in Dicey's pantheon is peculiarly suggestive. William Paley was a contemporary of Burke, perhaps most famous for publishing a treatise entitled *Natural Theology* in 1802 in which he wrestled with pretty much

[5] In an 'Autobiographical Fragment', Dicey described his father in these terms, admiringly, confirming the 'noblest characteristics of the Whig reformers' (Hibbitts 1994, 3).

the same dilemma which Kingsley engaged in his *Water Babies*. He too was a man of the cloth, later sub-dean of Lincoln Cathedral. But he was also a man of science. Darwin would later express his admiration for *Natural Theology*. Dicey made it compulsory reading for his students when they came to study the precepts of inductive reasoning. If we apply the same technique to Dicey's *Law of the Constitution*, we can induce from his testament to Paley another presence. Paley was a disciple of Jeremy Bentham. So too was John Austin, whose treatise entitled *The Province of Jurisprudence Determined* had been published in the same auspicious year that Parliament passed the first Reform Act. Austin's *Province* is commonly regarded as a founding text of modern legal positivism. Whilst Dicey retained some reservations in regard to Bentham, for reasons we have already noted, he was much less ambiguous in his regard for Austin and his *Province*. It was, he averred, a book of 'rare power' written with an enviable clarity of mind (Dicey 1914, 413). He aspired to the same. Sir Frederick Pollock famously regretted that Dicey seemed unable to get himself 'clear of the damnable heresies of Austin' (Cosgrove 1980, 168).

Or perhaps unwilling. Dicey adhered rigorously to the core precepts of Austinian positivism. Time and again he attested to the pivotal distinction between law and morality. 'Law', he confirmed in a lecture given at the Working Men's College in 1901, 'is concerned with acts, Morality with character' (Cosgrove 1980, 27). And he defined the law itself in terms which were just as familiar, as 'any rule which will be enforced by the courts' (Dicey 1959, 40). The idea that law might be understood as a science was not accepted without demur of course. James Fitzjames Stephen, for example, sought to reinvest the alternative principles of natural law in his *Liberty, Equality, Fraternity*. But the march of science moved against classical jurists such as Stephen in much the same way as it was moving against bishops such as Wilberforce. And Dicey marched with science. Before the positivists appeared on the jurisprudential scene, he famously observed, the English common law had resembling nothing other than 'the most fanciful dreams of *Alice in Wonderland*' (Dicey 1914, 92).

For this reason, as the Preface to the *Study* confirmed, the constitution discovered in the pages which followed would be very different from that found in Bagehot's *Constitution*; which, he supposed, had been not really been about the constitution at all. And, whilst he averred a similar admiration, it would also be very different from that which might be found in Macaulay's *History*. Too much time spent on the past deflects the jurist from a proper contemplation of what has 'become' (Dicey 1959, ii–vi). The reader must at all times

> remember that antiquarianism is not the law, and that the function of a trained lawyer is not to know what the law of England was yesterday, still less what it was centuries ago, or what it ought to be tomorrow, but to know and be able to state what are the principles of law which actually and at the present day exist. (Dicey 1914, 14)

But if Dicey's constitution lacked the nostalgic historicism that could be found in Burke or Macaulay, it did not lack history. Indeed, the opening chapter serves as a kind of historical introduction; its deeper purpose being to present readers with a critical commentary on the 'quaint' constitutional 'language' of the later Hanoverians (Dicey 1914, 2). The chapter which follows, introducing the principle of parliamentary sovereignty, similarly proceeds as a historical narrative, leading the reader back through Blackstone to the defining events of the seventeenth century. Even if the 'trained lawyer' should eschew the 'historical' in their study of the constitution, they must still recognise that the root of sovereignty 'lies deep in the history of the English people' (Dicey 1959, 69).

As with Bagehot's *Constitution*, it is as much a question of style as substance. Most obviously Dicey did not spend long dreaming about romantic revolutions. In his *Lectures on Public Opinion*, he would reaffirm his opinion of the 1688 Revolution as 'glorious' only insofar as it confirmed what a bunch of intelligent 'Whig lawyers' might achieve if left to write a constitutional settlement (Dicey 1914, 82). There are no fleeing princesses in the *Study*, no murderous judges or mendacious monarchs, no heroic princes sailing from afar to save a troubled people. Readers of Macaulay would have missed the romance, readers of Bagehot the irony. But then Dicey was not writing for the kind of men and women who passed their evenings reading Macaulay or Bagehot. In place of historical anecdote, Dicey presented his readers with lots of legal principles. The reason of history is replaced by the less corruptible reason of juridical science. The sense of celebration may as a consequence seem rather muted. But in the end, Dicey's readers were left with the same underlying impression as those who sought reassurance in the rather more fanciful pages of Burke or Macaulay. The English constitution was a very good thing, particularly when compared with the American or the

French, and it was for this reason that nothing was more urgent than maintaining it, as it was.[6]

At the start of his *Law* Dicey suggests that 'two or three guiding principles pervade the modern constitution of England'. A first is parliamentary sovereignty, to which Dicey the Whig paid a customary reverence. Its peculiar significance might be inferred from the preliminary definition of constitutional 'law'; being the 'term' used 'to include all rules which directly or indirectly affect the distribution or the exercise of the sovereign power of the state' (Dicey 1959, 23). The sovereignty of Parliament is therefore the 'dominant characteristic of our political institutions' (Dicey 1959, 39). In terms of constitutional architecture, it is the 'keystone' (Dicey 1959, 70). It is moreover unlimited. The Westminster Parliament is 'an absolutely sovereign legislature', having 'the right to make or unmake any law whatever; and further, that no person or body is recognised by the law of England as having a right to override or set aside the legislation of Parliament' (Dicey 1959, 39–40). There were, Dicey conceded, various political limitations. But there were none that might be properly termed constitutional. The idea that there may be moral margins was dismissed with alacrity. No 'modern judge' would 'listen to a barrister who argued that an Act of Parliament was invalid because it was immoral' (Dicey 1959, 63). The possibility of legal limitations was met with similarly short shrift. Here there were three 'alleged' possibilities, none of which withstood close scrutiny. The notion that Parliament might be limited by international law was quickly despatched. The idea that it might be limited by prerogative was attributed to the prejudices of 'another age'. Finally, there was the supposition that 'one Parliament can make laws which cannot be touched by any subsequent Parliament'. Here, again history had its uses. Dicey's readers were taken

[6]Much of the *Study* is written as an exercise in comparative constitutional law, and the two most commonly compared constitutions are those of America and France. The whole of chapter three develops into an extended critique of federal constitutions. Dicey, predictably, was not a fan, though he did concede that the American constitution, though its differences were 'immense' in terms of institutional configuration, was in 'spirit little else than a gigantic development of the ideas' which underpin the English constitution. In general though, federal government is 'weak' government, tending to an excess of both 'rigidity' and 'legalism' (Dicey 1959, 139, 171–5). A comparative approach was commonly adopted in many nineteenth-century constitutional treatises. Much of Bagehot's *English Constitution* was, of course, comparative.

through a couple of centuries of failed attempts by earlier Parliaments to limit their successors.

In a sense there was nothing particularly new here, as Dicey acknowledged. The same principle, and the same accompanying sentiments, could be extracted from Blackstone's *Commentaries*. It had moreover very recently found ringing endorsement in the renowned 1871 case of *Lee v Bude and Torrington Junction Railway*. 'If an Act of Parliament has been obtained improperly' Willis J opined famously, 'it is for the legislature to correct it by repealing it: but so long as it exists in law, the courts are bound to obey it' (*Lee* 1871, 582). There again, as Dicey conceded, parliamentary sovereignty was ultimately 'no better than a legal fiction', for which reason there were not only effective limitations of both political practice and 'common sense', but also consequential concerns (Dicey 1959, 71). There was of course the classical Whig dilemma in regard to the Bill of Rights. If Parliament could in theory make or unmake any law it chose, then it could unmake the Bill of Rights too. Peel had averted to precisely this issue back in 1833. He would have been 'very sorry to have it proved' that the King was bound by his oath to refuse his 'consent' to any bill which appeared to contravene some law which had been enacted 'in the year 1689' (Gash 1965, 18). Dicey agreed. Whilst he was prepared to countenance the idea of 'fundamental constitutional laws' he was not prepared to countenance the idea that they might be somehow entrenched. As a consequence therefore, whilst the Act of Union for example was evidently more 'important' than the Dentists Act of 1878, 'neither has more claim than the other to be considered a supreme law' (Dicey 1959, 89, 145).

But more pressing perhaps, at least to Dicey, was the sense that Parliament was tending towards the despotic. Bagehot had inferred as much, noting the transition from prerogative to parliamentary government. Dicey simply added a jurisprudential gloss. Interestingly, Dicey sought recourse to *Bradlaugh v Gossett* and Mr Justice Stephen's tortuous explanation as to why a there may be 'no legal remedy for every moral or political wrong' (Dicey 1959, 55–6). Two decades of 'collectivism' took a further toll. In 1885, Dicey had noted the practical effect of parliamentary elections. By the time he arrived at Harvard in 1906 to deliver his lectures on public opinion, it had become only too obvious that parliamentary sovereignty had become 'an instrument well adapted for the establishment of democratic despotism'. It had 'come to mean, in the last resort, the unrestricted power of the wage-earners' (Dicey 1914,

305–6, 310). There was a significant difference between the constitutional principle of parliamentary sovereignty and the political practice. And Victorian constitutional history could be written in terms of their immanent tension.

The second of Dicey's 'guiding' principles was the rule of law, something which was of course again revered in Whig constitutional mythology. Whig clubs still held dinners to celebrate the resolution of Wilkes's case, just as they did the 'glorious' revolution. Dicey attended them. It might have been thought that parliamentary sovereignty and the rule of law would prove to be a rather indigestible mix. But not so. A short chapter was devoted to the 'relation' of the two principles, at the end of which readers were reassured that the rule of law simply reinvested the authority of Parliamentary statute; all part of the pervasive 'spirit of legality' which characterises the English constitution (Dicey 1959, 409, 413–4). The rule of law conceived in this 'spirit' is a rule of the common law, the same body of jurisprudence about which Blackstone wrote and which, as readers of Macaulay's *History* already appreciated, had been restored in 1688 following the tyranny of James and his psychotic Lord Chief Justice. Dicey wrote in this tradition. Although he despaired of the 'hopeless confusion' that pervaded Blackstone's *Commentaries*, Dicey cherished the common law; particularly after a century of mutant Benthamite purgation (Dicey 1959, 7). He made much of those collateral common law principles revered by generations of Whig constitutional historians, such as the 'celebrated writ' of habeas corpus, and associated rights to freedom of discussion and to hold meetings; each of which earned a discreet chapter in the *Study*.[7] Nowhere in his *Law of the Constitution* was Dicey's residual Whiggism more evident than in his veneration for the rule of law.

Dicey liked the rule of law most, however, because he detected in its judges a shared determination to establish a bulwark against collectivism

[7] Being chapters five, six and seven, respectively. In chapter five, Dicey was especially concerned to emphasise the deleterious consequences that might flow from attempts to suspend habeas corpus. In chapter six, he took time to insinuate misgivings regarding the 'forgotten law of blasphemy', whilst also using the opportunity to cast further aspersions in regard to the relative absence of an equivalent right to free expression in French constitutional law. Conversely in chapter seven, it is possible to detect a more conservative caution in Dicey's attempts to legitimate the suppression of public meetings which might otherwise threaten 'the Queen's peace'.

and the reach of the regulatory state. 'Our constitution, in short, is a judge-made constitution, and it bears on its face all the features, good and bad, of judge-made law', and the good far outweighed the bad (Dicey 1959, 196). Dicey liked judges for the reasons he made plain in his *Lectures on Public Opinion*:

> The judges are the heads of the legal profession. They have acquired the intellectual and moral tone of English lawyers. They are advanced men in life. They are for the most part persons of a conservative disposition. They are in no way dependent for their emoluments, dignity or reputation upon the favour of electors, or even of Ministers who represent in the long run the wishes of the electorate. (Dicey 1914, 364)

But Dicey liked judges most of all because there were not politicians, and he liked the rule of law because it lent the expression of their collected prejudices a peculiar sense of legitimacy. The 'success' of the rule of law 'in England is wholly due to and is the most extraordinary sign of, public confidence in the judicial bench' (Dicey 1959, 394; McEldowney 1985, 48). As a consequence, Dicey was just as keen to impress the singular virtue of an 'independent' judiciary. He never subscribed to the Lockean idea of 'separate' powers, but he did like the idea that judges might stop the government from doing certain things, particularly the kinds of things recommended by 'collectivists'. In sum, the rule of law rightly earned the 'admiration' and 'astonishment' of foreign observers, so obviously conducive was it to the pervasive 'legality of English habits and feelings' (Dicey 1959, 184; Allison 2007, 87–8).

Of course, different Whigs admired the rule of law differently. Lord Russell supposed that the rule should reinforce a reformed parliament, advising in 1839 that 'laws must be respected as well as enacted; the minds of men must be engaged to a willing conformity with the new order of the State' (Parry 1993, 3, 6). Dicey had a different perspective. To him, the rule of law meant three things. It first established a basic principle of legality, that 'no man is punishable or can be lawfully made to suffer in body or goods except for a distinct breach of law established in the ordinary legal manner before the ordinary courts of the land' (Dicey 1959, 188). Second, it established an 'idea of legal equality', that 'with us no man is above the law' and that 'every man, whatever be his rank or condition, is subject to the ordinary law of the realm' (Dicey 1959, 193). Third, it confirmed that the constitution was 'judge-made', and we have already noted just how much Dicey approved of this particular tradition. Each principle chimed very obviously with the collected mythologies of Whig constitutionalism, and in large part did so because each appeared to limit government and the exercise of prerogative. The rule of law also meant the:

> absolute supremacy or predominance of regular law as opposed to the influence of arbitrary power, and excludes the existence of arbitrariness, of prerogative, or even of wide discretionary authority on the part of the government. Englishmen are ruled by the law, and by the law alone; a man may with us be punished for a breach of law, but he can be punished for nothing else. (Dicey 1959, 202–3)

It was an assurance born of history, but it was also an observation written in 1885. Prerogative had always been something regarded by right-thinking Whigs with a due measure of suspicion. By 1885, however, it was the 'arbitrary power' of government which had become the greater concern. It was not through a spectre which required any extraordinary exorcism. The common law and the rule of law were perfectly adequate to deal with prospective arbitrariness or unlawful exercise of discretion. At the conclusion of a conspicuously brief chapter eleven on 'The Responsibility of Ministers', Dicey confirmed that 'Behind parliamentary responsibility lies legal liability, and the acts of Ministers no less than the acts of subordinate officials are made subject to the rule of law' (Dicey 1959, 327). The same theme underpinned the following chapter, on the French *droit administratif*, the tenor of which we have already noted. The common law had proved itself capable of keeping the prerogative in check, by and large, and it was perfectly capable of regulating the regulatory state; provided its judges exhibited the same perspicuity. It was of course the reason of history which provided this reassurance, not the reason of legal science.

There was, finally, something else, along with the defining principles of parliamentary sovereignty and the rule of law, and the satellite principle of judicial independence. And it, as much as anything else that might be read in the *Law of the Constitution*, confirmed the Whiggish predilections of its author. Less a matter of principle, more a testament to habit, or what Dicey termed in rather grander tones 'constitutional morality', there were conventions (Dicey 1959, 24, 422). Bagehot, as we noted, was not much taken by conventions. Dicey, however, was. What Bagehot and Disraeli had dismissed as little more than parliamentary 'gossip', Dicey elevated into fundamental 'maxims' of constitutional 'practice' (Dicey 1959, 26–7). And they were certainly consonant, especially so in 1908 when the seventh edition came out. By then, it was apparent that a constitutional crisis was looming, as the Tory dominated Lords threatened to throw out his 'People's budget'. The Cabinet, as we have already noted, was circulated with copies of Dicey's chapter on parliamentary conventions. Meanwhile Lord Chancellor Loreburn sought to remind his more recalcitrant colleagues in the upper chamber of what they could do by 'the letter of the law' and what they should do by convention. Before taking the critical step of voting down the budget once again, Loreburn cautioned:

> They must look even more to custom, usage, convention – call it whatever you please – by which inveterate practice had so modified the hard law itself that we are governed more by custom in this country in great matters than we are even by law. (Le May 1979, 195)

The House was not persuaded. The Finance bill was rejected by 350 votes to 75. As the prospect emerged that the King might have to create a mass of new peers constitutional historians alighted on the obvious parallel, 1832; only this time it was rumoured that Asquith would ask for five hundred, not just sixty or seventy. In the end, the Lords back down, as indeed they had eighty years earlier. The budget passed in 1910. The following year Asquith drove through his Parliament Act.

The resolution of the crisis in 1910, as in 1832, further affirmed the relation of convention and prerogative. Bagehot noted the affinity, and so did Dicey. The 'conventions of the constitution are in short rules intended to regulate the exercise of the whole of the remaining discretionary powers of the Crown, whether these powers are exercised by the Queen herself or by the Ministry' (Dicey 1959, 425). There was again nothing particularly solid here, except for the practice of history. And it was on these terms, accordingly, that Dicey confirmed the compatibility of conventions with the established principles of parliamentary sovereignty and the rule of law. All contribute to the essential 'harmony' that exists in the English constitution between 'the legal and the political sovereign power', whilst further confirming that what really holds everything together is a common 'spirit' of legality (Dicey 1959, 438, 444, 456). Burke could not have put it better.

The Oracle

The first edition of *Lectures Introductory to the Study of the Law of the Constitution* was published by Macmillan and Sons. Dicey chose the same as Darwin. And Macmillan and Sons were just as cautious in regard to the *Law of the Constitution* as they had been with the *Origin of Species.* The first print run was limited to seven hundred, and again it sold out in weeks. Cursed to live in an age of seemingly incessant questioning late Victorian readers developed a craving for books that purported to tell them everything. It famously consumes Mr Casaubon in George Eliot's *Middlemarch.* Dicey's ambition appeared to be rather less, a set of *Lectures Introductory* rather than *The Key to all Mythologies*; though an ironist might suppose that the latter title would have been just as suited. Moreover, Dicey harboured grander designs than his modest, if rather cumbersome, title seemed to first impute.

He had in fact two audiences in mind. Bagehot, as we have noted, had a similarly bifocal aspiration. The first was shared. Like Bagehot Dicey wanted his *Law* to be read by people who mattered. He was gratified to hear that Gladstone was, just a few weeks later, quoting from the first edition in Parliament. Shortly after Hartington was doing the same (Craig 1990, 30). He especially coveted Hartington's approval, having already sent him a copy of his essay *England's Case Against Home Rule* just a few months earlier, along with an effusive note appraising the Marquis as 'the only leader in whose honesty, common-sense, and patriotism, men of the most different parties absolutely confide' (Cosgrove 1980, 138). A few months later he joined Hartington's newly formed Liberal Unionist party. It was a step forward into a fast-receding past. Dicey was a strategic sender of books to people he thought mattered. He had sent Salisbury a copy of the *Law of the Constitution* as soon as it was published. Gladstone received his copy through a friend, addressed to 'the highest authority on constitutional questions'. His concentration caught most especially by Dicey's theory of unfettered parliamentary sovereignty, Gladstone was apparently inspired to re-read his Burke at the same time (Jenkins 1995, 536). Much later, during the constitutional crisis of 1908–1909, it was reported that Asquith's Cabinet was being given printed extracts of his chapters on parliamentary sovereignty and conventions; not, as we shall see, that they appeared to pay proper attention.

The second audience that Dicey had in mind was very different. Where Bagehot also wrote for the informed journal-reading middle classes, Dicey wrote for a rather narrower, if captive, audience of prospectively informed law students. The full title of his *Lectures Introductory to the Study of the Law of the Constitution* is here again suggestive. Students needed to be instructed not romanced. And this was Dicey's job. He was a 'professional' lawyer in the same sense as Buckle and Froude and Gardiner were 'professional' historians. In 1882, he had been appointed to the Vinerian Professorship of Law at Oxford, a position which he would hold until 1909, at which point he transferred to the still-new London School of Economics. Thus whilst he would frequently engage matters of wider public concern, such as indeed Home Rule, his primary audience was academic and his principal subject matter jurisprudential. His treatise on the *Conflict of Laws*, published in 1896, was for example widely acclaimed by international lawyers. As a consequence, the circles in which he moved were different too. He got read by Gladstone, but he did not get invitations to breakfast with him.[8] Evenings were commonly spent at All Souls High Table rather than the dining room at Brook's or the Reform Club. Bagehot he had briefly contemplated a career at the Bar. But he was no more enthused by the idea. So in the end, he settled for the halls of academe, and a career teaching and writing.

The parallels between Bagehot and Dicey are then variously configured. Their professional worlds were different, but their political prejudices close, and of course they were both passionately interested in the condition of England and more especially its constitution. In a sense, it might be ventured that they also shared the characteristic famously identified by GM Young; a peculiar ordinariness. Dicey worried about much the same as Bagehot and in much the same way, and in both he was representative of his age and his class. He kept his faith in much the same way as Bagehot, more out of habit than zeal. And he undertook much the same intellectual journey, flirting momentarily with the more Radical wing of the Gladstone's new Liberal party, before declining into a

[8] By the end of the decade, Dicey had come to loathe Gladstone. When the 'Grand Old Man' spent ten days in residence as an Honorary Fellow at All Souls College in Oxford, Dicey, a Fellow, tried to absent himself, but the Master of the College persuaded him to at least attend the reception. The event was apparently excruciating, for both parties (Cosgrove 1980, 68–9, 147–8).

familiar brand of Burkean Whiggery which he liked to term 'enlightened' but which with each passing year became ever more obviously reactionary. The path was well enough trodden. Rather later, in 1935, George Macaulay Trevelyan would write to his Prime Minister Stanley Baldwin confirming pretty much the same passage, observing by way of explanation that 'Whiggism and Conservatism are not opposed as fundamental principles' (Cannadine 1992, 161).

A few months before his death in 1922 Dicey confessed to a 'terrible moral and political depression which the present circumstances bring upon me'. Of course, the circumstances were very different from those which Bagehot might have imagined. No one, tragically, anticipated the full consequence of war in 1914. It is unsurprising that critics have looked back to Arnold's 'darkling plain' and then forward to those of Ypres and the Somme and then on to TS Eliot's *Wasteland* and wondered the coincidence. War changes writers. The second 'world' war changed Herbert Butterfield as we have already noted. And the first changed Dicey in much the same way. Regretting that he had 'sedulously fought shy of verses and poets' in the past, and motivated by the thought that he might be able to extract some 'lessons for the present war', in 1917 he published an extended essay on *The Statesmanship of Wordsworth*. It was, he confessed, an 'odd piece', which might cause his customary readers some 'perplexity' (Dicey 1917, 1; Cosgrove 1980, 271–2). Here, again the rite of passage is familiar. At various moments, propelled by similar motivations, both Mill and Bagehot made the same journey. And in both cases, they ended up writing essays which were supposed to be about Wordsworth the poet, but which ended up being more about Wordsworth the apostate Tory. Dicey did the same, as the title of his essay suggested, directing his readers towards Wordsworth's political essays rather than his poetry. Engaged in a 'sacred war', England in 1917 could learn much from the later Wordsworth's patriotic fervour, his optimism, his 'judicial habit of mind' and his innately conservative good sense (Dicey 1917, 116–7).

By then Dicey had completed the eighth edition of his *Law of the Constitution*. It would be the last in his lifetime. Nearing eighty he elected to bolt on a new introductory essay rather than edit the existing text. Here, again there is an obvious resonance, in regard to both tone and purpose; with the introduction which Bagehot wrote to the second edition of his *English Constitution*. In both cases, the immediate stimulus was the passage of a particular statute. For Bagehot, it was the 1867

Reform Act. For Dicey, it was the 1911 Parliament Act. The 1911 Act had disturbed the sensitive balance of the two Houses of Parliament. The idea of reforming the second chamber was not new. Back in 1834, the radical *Black Book* had suggested that 'we are still in the course of revolution', insinuating that the next stage would be the abolition of the House of Lords (Gash 1965, 35). In the wake of the third Reform Act, Labouchere had presented proposals in the Commons. When, a few years later, Lord Rosebery conceded that there might indeed be a case for redrawing the boundaries of the Lords' legislative reach, Victoria accused her Prime Minister of talking 'revolutions' and conspired to have him removed from office (Bentley 1996, 277). Dicey felt much the same and suggested much the same solution. He blamed the 1911 Act on democracy and public opinion and the 'iniquitous' Asquith. Exercised by the thought that Asquith was about to gift Home Rule to his nationalist allies in exchange for their support for his Parliament bill, Dicey went to so far as to recommend that the King exercise his prerogative right to remove the Prime Minister and his 'essentially lawless' government (Cosgrove 1980, 234, 241–50).

Asquith and his Act was certainly not the only constitutional matter which troubled the ageing Dicey. A second was very familiar. In 1914, he penned another introduction, this time to the second edition of his *Lectures on Public Opinion*. Barely a decade had passed since the first, but the situation in regard to the rise of 'collectivism' and the regulatory state had only gotten worse. Dicey listed a range of Edwardian statutes; the 1906 Trade Disputes Act, the Education (Provision of Meals) Act, the 1908 Old Age Pensions Act, the 1908 Coal Mines Regulation Act, the 1911 National Insurance Act, the 1913 Trade Union Act, the 1913 Mental Deficiency Act. There could be no better example of 'public opinion' being 'guided far less by the force of argument than by the stress of circumstances'. There had, in effect, been a 'revolution', one that 'is not the more entitled to respect because it is carried through not by violence, but under the specious though delusive appearance of taxation imposed to meet the financial needs of the State' (Dicey 1914, liii, 295–6, 301). The final pages of the introduction were crammed with statistics and charts, all emphasising the 'financial burdens of collectivism' (Dicey 1914, lxxxii–vii). There was, he concluded in terms again reminiscent of Bagehot in 1872, 'something' in 'the present condition of public sentiment to arouse fear' (Dicey 1914, lxiii). And there was of course the same jurisprudential consequence. In 1915, as we have already noted, Dicey felt the need to write a further diatribe against the idea of administrative law.

Both introductions, to the 1914 edition of the *Lectures* and to the 1915 edition of the *Law of the Constitution*, were then expressions of late Victorian anxiety. Both the 1911 Act and the various statutes which continued to shape the regulatory state were, in Dicey's opinion at least, the consequence of a process of reform which had mutated hideously during the past century. And it was not just a matter of statues already enacted. There was, just as much, the fear of statutes which were yet to come. No one really believed in 'finality' any more. But the case against further reform could still be made. In the 1914 introduction, Dicey reaffirmed his concerns:

> The democratic idea that the people, or any large number of the people, ought to have whatever they desire simply because they desire it, and ought to have it quickly, is absolutely fatal to that slow and sure kind of progress which alone has the remotest chance of producing fundamental and beneficial social changes. (Dicey 1914, lxxxvii–iii)

Burke could not have put it better, democracy defined by sentiment rather than suffrage. All that stood between England and revolution in summer 1914, as in spring 1790, was an underlying sense of decency and a 'kindly disposition', together with a visceral preference amongst right-thinking men for Benthamite 'individualism' (Dicey 1914, lxii). War would of course intervene. But Dicey sensed, correctly, that there was still no 'finality' to the issue. A further Reform Act would be enacted in 1918, granting universal suffrage to all men aged twenty-one and women aged thirty. Nearly eight and a half million women found themselves enfranchised as a consequence.

Dicey despaired. He had never been much of a suffragette. He took particular exception to the idea that the constitution might be reformed by a concerted strategy of civil disobedience, of the kind recommended by Christabel Pankhurst in her 1911 *Votes for Women*. 'What is the good of a constitutional policy', she queried, 'to those who have no constitutional weapon?' (Bentley 1996, 335) It was a reasonable question. Within two years Emily Wilding Davidson had fallen under the King's horse at the Epsom Derby in 1913 and captured suffragettes were being force-fed under the provisions of the notorious 'Cat and Mouse Acts'. Dicey despaired and joined the Men's Anti-Suffrage League. It was not simply a matter of crude misogyny; though it was certainly that too. Dicey, like Bagehot, worried that women were too uneducated to vote. Bagehot assumed a more progressive approach, advocating the admission of women to universities in his 1874 essay *The Woman's Degrees*. Disraeli interestingly enough recommended the same. His 'Faery Queen', however, did not. The campaign for 'women's rights', in Queen Victoria's opinion, was a 'mad, wicked, folly' which neglected 'every sense of womanly feeling and propriety' (Strachey 1971, 238). Dicey, and an awful lot of later Victorian men, agreed.

Dicey may have lived on and through the Edwardian period, and the Great War, but his intellectual life remained trapped by the collective anxieties of the later nineteenth century; by reform and its evident lack of 'finality', by the rise of the regulatory state, by the seemingly irresolvable 'question' of Irish Home Rule. The latter issue came to obsess him. Whilst putting the final touches to the draft of the first edition of his *Law of the Constitution* back in 1885, Dicey had felt the need to break off and write a series of articles which culminated in *England's Case Against Home Rule*. He had sent Hartington a copy and a few months later finally broken with Gladstone and joined his new Liberal Unionist party; the final refuge of the despairing and disorientated Whig (Burrow 1988, 129). Dicey was a confirmed Unionist and imperialist. He entirely approved the 1876 Royal Titles Act by which Victoria had become Empress of India. In this, he was certainly not alone. Strachey later supposed that the 1876 Act saved the monarchy (1971, 202). It certainly cheered Victoria who developed a passion for all things Indian, including its servants and its curries. And her subjects seemed to be equally enthused; an entire generation brought up on the novels of Rider Haggard and Rudyard Kipling. Successive Jubilee celebrations assumed a distinctive imperialist tenor; a precedent set by the Thanksgiving Service held at St Paul's for the recovery of Bertie from a bout of typhoid in 1871. Ireland was not encompassed in the 1876 Act; though Victoria had rather fancied the idea of becoming 'Empress of Great Britain, Ireland and India'. But in a visceral sense, it seemed to belong, and the idea that it might be detached from the Union imported serious constitutional concerns. Empires could get bigger, but it was not obvious how they might be made smaller. Dicey supposed that any form of devolved governance would militate against six centuries of jurisprudence; an argument repeatedly deployed by Hartington in parliamentary debate. Home Rule would destroy the 'undisputed supremacy of the law' (Parry 1993, 299).

At times it seemed to be almost too much. Returning to the time of Burke in his 1917 essay on Wordsworth, he felt moved to remind his readers that the spectres of 'Jacobin tyranny' and the 'terrible crimes' of 1790 were vivid still (Dicey 1917). It was not just the Kaiser who had to be defeated. And amidst all this, he kept writing and re-writing his *Law of the Constitution*. It provided Dicey with a constant, and he hoped fervently that it would provide his readers with the same. So long as the fundamental principles of the English constitution were properly understood, and as a consequence preserved, then all would not be lost. It was why the Irish 'question' was so important. And it was of course this larger hope which made Dicey's seminal text so irreducibly Whiggish in its aspiration, and so intensely conservative in its writing. It was written to exactly the same purpose that Burke wrote his *Reflections*, Macaulay his *History* and Bagehot his *Constitution*. It may not have been so obviously historical, but it was written to impress upon its readers just how much they owed to the past.

And, in Dicey's case, this matters especially. For where Burke and Macaulay and Bagehot might themselves be consigned to history, Dicey and his *Law* retain a presence. It is not simply that modern public law syllabuses continue to move around the jurisprudential coordinates that he set; parliamentary sovereignty, the rule of law, conventions. It is also the matter of temper and tone:

> The duty of an English professor of law is to state what are the laws which form part of the constitution, to arrange them in their order, to explain their meaning, and to exhibit where possible their logical connection. (Dicey 1959, 32)

Written for 'trained lawyers' and law students, there was never the need for depictions of Versailles under siege or George III wandering the terraces of Windsor castle (Dicey 1959, 14; McEldowney 1985, 39–40; Allison 2007, 8). The need was for principles, instruction not romance. And Dicey was revered for precisely this reason. He had made the study of jurisprudence important again. In this, his influence was 'remarkable' (Craig 1990, 54–5). On his retirement from the Vinerian Chair his successor, Martin Geldert, paid glowing tribute:

> To a style no less weighty, no less forcible, clearer and more terse than Blackstone's, to a learning no less thorough and detailed, he has added a

> critical insight and analytical power, of which Blackstone could not boast. (Cosgrove 1980, 62)

There could, to the common lawyer at least, be no more pointed comparison. His friend Bryce made exactly the same comparison. Dicey mattered like Blackstone mattered. Harold Laski applauded the 'most considerable figure in English jurisprudence since Maitland' (Cosgrove 1980, 293). The adoration was peculiarly intense in Oxford. He was, FH Lawson later observed, 'one of the glories of the Oxford Law School and of English law in general' (Cosgrove 1980, 63). It is interesting to pause here and speculate on how Bagehot might have reviewed Dicey's *Law of the Constitution*. He would have appreciated the sentiment. But more than likely the Vinerian Professor would have been tarred with the same brush as Macaulay. The problem with Macaulay, Bagehot famously observed, was his 'inexperiencing nature'. He spent too long 'in his study' where 'nothing' really 'happens'; which given the extent of Macaulay's parliamentary career suggests that Bagehot would have been still more dismissive of Dicey's chosen 'profession' (Bagehot 1965, 2.426).

More generally, however, Dicey's *Study* was warmly received by contemporaries (Bingham 2002, 40). It articulated common concerns and aspired, if not to resolve them, at least to contribute a measure of credible reassurance. If all else fails, if Parliament continues to disappoint, and the Church proves unable to offer succour, at least there was the common law and all its associated constitutional 'principles'. This was evidently the supposition shared by the great legal historian William Searle Holdsworth, who succeeded to the Vinerian chair in 1922. As we have already noted Holdsworth devoted most of his intellectual life to the writing of a vast seventeen volume *History of English Law*. Holdsworth's *History* is an intriguing and entirely suggestive composite, betraying its author's Tory prejudices alongside the larger Whiggish aspiration, but written in the emergent tone of the 'professional' historian. In fact, all seventeen volumes were really dedicated to securing the overarching authority of one particular principle in the common law; the rule of law. It was a *History* for a purpose; and it bore all the hallmarks of Diceyan jurisprudence.

For much of the twentieth century Dicey retained an iconic status in legal education, his *Study* a 'classic treatise', a 'living work', serving, it has been suggested, as a 'surrogate written constitution', a book of 'enormous influence' in the recent words of the former Lord Chief Justice, Tom Bingham (Craig 1990, 12–13; Bogdanor 2009, xiii; Jowell and Oliver 2007, v; Jennings 1935, 123–4, 129; Harlow 1985, 75; Bingham 2010, 3). According to AWB Simpson, 'The basic book and the best written book, is Dicey, and it is around Dicey that nearly all lawyers study constitutional law. This has been so for so long now'. The 'oracle spoke, and came to be accepted' (Simpson 1973, 96). Successive generations of 'neo-Diceyan' constitutional lawyers paid obeisance (Cosgrove 1980, 76). At the same time, it was possible to detect a gnawing doubt, certainly by the time that ECS Wade wrote his Introduction to the tenth edition of Dicey's *Study* in 1959. On the one hand, Wade suggested, the importance of resisting the lure of history and instead focussing on the 'present state of the law and practice of the constitution' had never been greater (Dicey 1959, xix). The great merit of Dicey's *Study* is its 'application of the analytic method to constitutional law' (Dicey 1959, cxci). Conversely, or perhaps perversely, consideration of the previous seventy years of English constitutional and political history emphasised the extent to which the 'prestige' of Parliament had fallen (Dicey 1959, xxii–iii). History ironically had proved Dicey right and wrong. The state had continued to grow, as had the associated jurisprudence of judicial review. Lord Greene's seminal judgement in the *Wednesbury* case arrived in 1948. The courts would be sensitive to the distinction between judicial and constitutional review; at least for now. In the meantime, successive Parliament Acts gestured towards a coming age of statutory reinforcement. Wade cited the 1931 Statute of Westminster and the 1949 Parliament Act, together with a series of judicial pronouncements which have subsequently assumed a primary place in modern constitutional law casebooks; *Vauxhall Estates v Liverpool Corporation*, *Ellen Street Estates v Minister of Health*, *British Coal Corporation v King*, *MacCormick v Lord Advocate* (Wade 1959, xxxvii–lxiv, xcii–vi).

The passage of certain 'constitutional' statutes in the final decades of the twentieth century further suggested that history was moving against Dicey. So was opinion. Writing in 1980 Dicey's last substantive biographer Richard Cosgrove regretted the 'neglect' into which his subject had fallen (Cosgrove 1980, xiii). But it was not just neglect. There was also distaste. Critical legal scholars were especially affronted by Dicey's disdain for democracy and socialism. Dicey had not been neglected enough. Ian Loveland attested to the thoroughly 'unfortunate' but still 'enormous influence' that Dicey retained in the law school classroom (Loveland 1996, 29). David Sugarman did for Dicey's *Law* what Kennedy did for Blackstone's *Commentaries*; noting not just the presence of myriad Whig prejudices, but the necessary paradox of their presentation in a text that pretended to eschew history. It was, Sugarman concluded, time to put Dicey in context, to lay bare his 'basic conservatism', to place him squarely within the 'Whig tradition of historical writing' (Sugarman 1983, 102–11). The intimation had already been made. Dicey's *Law*, as Sir Ivor Jennings concluded, was 'impregnated with Whig ideas' and 'Whig principles' (Jennings 1935, 128–9).

Dicey's attitude to history has generated a range of different critical responses. It led Bingham to conclude that Dicey's 'approach' to constitutional law was 'not only anti-intellectual, but plainly misguided' (Bingham 2002, 42). In like terms, John Allison concludes that a constitution which is conceived by 'scientific rationalism' alone, such as that written by Dicey, is blighted by the consequential 'problems' of 'fidelity, ossification and insularity' (Allison 2007, 8–9). Others are kinder. Likening him to the seventeenth-century jurist Sir Edward Coke, Trevor Allan praises Dicey for his role in promoting the transmission of 'common law' constitutional principles (Allan 2001, 13–14, 18–19). Cosgrove, his only modern biographer, argued that Dicey 'the famous lawyer' might be detached from Dicey the 'frustrated politician' (Cosgrove 1980, 299). Bingham flirted with the same dichotomy; before rejecting it. The case is difficult to argue for precisely the reason Jennings identified; Dicey's *Law of the Constitution* is thoroughly 'impregnated' with history and political prejudice (Hibbitts 1994, 30–1; Harlow 1985, 72–3).

Dicey then retains his admirers. But they are fewer, and the detractors have become the louder. The irony is patent. Dicey diminished the place of history in jurisprudence, but history has shown this to be impossible. Much has happened since 1915, more still perhaps since 1885. Indeed much has happened since Cosgrove's biography in 1980. It has not of course happened evenly. History is not so simple, for which reason consequential intellectual movements tend to be less measured too. Thus some bits of Dicey have retained rather greater credibility than others. There is for example a retaining admiration for his determination of constitutional conventions; a 'magnificent contribution to English public law' according to Jennings (Jennings 1935, 130; Leyland 2012, 33–5). It has certainly become apparent that Dicey was more right than either

Disraeli or Bagehot. Conventions are rather more than mere 'gossip'. But as expressions of constitutional 'morality', they remain something less than law. Gentlemen's agreements, as Dicey observed, only work if there are gentlemen. There were fewer in 1885 than Dicey would have liked, fewer still in 1915. There are few more today.

Conversely, it has become very apparent that the sands have shifted dramatically under the principle of parliamentary sovereignty; so much so it has been recently argued that Dicey's constitutional 'analysis' is now 'irrelevant' (Bogdanor 2009, xiii). Dicey, as we have already noted, flirted with the idea that certain statutes might be 'fundamental', and by insinuation import a different constitutional standing. The Act of Settlement has always tempted Whig historians. But he remained unconvinced. By the end of the twentieth century, however, it was evident that some statutes were different. The European Communities Act in 1972, at the very least, 'qualified' the Diceyan principle of continuing sovereignty (Leyland 2012, 52–3). Interestingly only three years earlier Lord Reid had endorsed the Diceyan conception of parliamentary sovereignty in ringing tones in *Madzimbamuto v Lardner-Burke*. No court could hold an 'Act of Parliament invalid' no matter how 'strong' might be the 'moral' or 'political' objection to it (1969, 723). In truth, the more perceptive had already noted the like accession to various instruments of international law imputed the kind of problems writ large by the 1972 Act. Moreover, the turn of the last century witnessed the passage of a range of further 'fundamental' statutes; the Human Rights Act, successive devolution statutes, the Constitutional Reform Act. It is has been recently supposed, with good reason, that Dicey would have retained 'very mixed views' in regard to the Human Rights Act (Bingham 2010, 5, 161–2; Bogdanor 2009, 62–4). Courtrooms have become havens of apostasy; none more so perhaps than those which listened, for year after year, to the internecine judicial squabbling that moved around the vexed European case of *Factortame*; the *Jarndyce v Jarndyce* of its so many, many days. It might be argued, as some do, that Parliament retains the sovereign capacity to review these 'fundamental' statutes (Bingham 2010, 164–8). And in a strict constitutional sense, this may be so. But political sovereignty and constitutional sovereignty are very different things; as Dicey well knew.

It has, most recently, become fashionable to contemplate a 'common law constitutionalism', in which parliamentary sovereignty becomes a judicially approved expression of the common law. Thus Trevor Allen has suggested that 'Legislation obtains its force from the doctrine of parliamentary sovereignty, which is itself a creature of the common law and whose detailed contents and limits are therefore of judicial making. Parliament is sovereign because the judges acknowledge its legal and political supremacy' (Allan 1993, 10). It is a perception which, perhaps unsurprisingly, has evoked enthusiasm in some sections of the judiciary. Thus in *Jackson* Lord Steyn approved a common law principle of parliamentary 'supremacy' which might, in 'exceptional circumstances' authorise courts to review parliamentary legislation which appears to infringe the larger integrity of the rule of law (*Jackson*, para. 102). It is interesting to speculate as to how Dicey might have responded to such juridical wizardry. Never entirely sure of judicial review, it is unlikely he would have relished its apparent evolution into a surrogate principle of constitutional review. There again he retained a stubborn Whiggish faith in the jurisprudential sanctity of the common law, and he might have been reconciled by the idea that judges were deploying the complementary principle of the rule of law in order to restrain the wilder excesses of parliamentary democracy (Craig 1990, 16–17, 53–4).

As for the rule of law, it may have been 'rather an unruly horse' at times, as Jennings famously put it, but as a functioning constitutional principle it has retained a credibility that has become increasingly hard to attribute to 'continuing' parliamentary sovereignty (Jennings 1935, 54–62). As the laudatory Lawson declared: 'You cannot escape Dicey. And what a feather it is in his cap to have coined the phrase "the Rule of Law"' (Cosgrove 1980, 87). Judicial praise has remained conspicuous. At the same time, however, it has been more recently suggested that Dicey's conception of the rule of law, rather being a 'timeless truth', should also be understood as a 'highly contingent historical phenomenon' founded on a range of political 'prejudices'; most obviously perhaps Dicey's zeal for 'individualism' (Hibbitts 1994, 2–3). Moreover, here again history has taken its toll. The presence of the Human Rights Act rather obviously questions the assertion that the rule of law adequately protects the rights and liberties of Englishmen and women (Leyland 2012, 66–8). Moreover, as Jennings inferred, modern society is more complex now, the regulatory state has grown; and so too, despite the denunciation of later Diceyans, has the reach of administrative law (Jennings 1959, 312–4). Vast tracts of undergraduate public law courses are dedicated to the myriad complexities of judicial review procedure.

Dicey's presence remains then rather like that of Carroll's Cheshire cat, gradually receding from view until only a grin remains; except that, as we have already noted, he was not much of an ironist. From one perspective it might indeed seem that the age of Dicey, and the constitution which he did so much to write, is now passing. But we would be wise to be cautious, not least because it can be argued that Dicey's most enduring bequest is not anyway what he taught, but how he taught. History still enjoys a marginal place in modern English constitutional law textbooks, at best an introductory section here or there. There is much within these texts that would have bothered Dicey, chapters exploring the impact of 'fundamental' statutes and shifting conceptions of sovereignty, devolution and the EU, the practice of administrative law. But he would not have been disorientated. The modern constitutional law textbook is still imprinted on the template which he first designed a hundred and thirty years ago. The Victorians liked templates. Their engineers took the idea and the word, from the French 'templet' and built an Industrial Revolution on it. Dicey did the same. He took a constitutional tradition, variously Whig and Burkean, 'great and glorious', and reset it for a generation of 'professional' lawyers. The science of legal practice replaced the romance of national history. And it convinced. Much as we still express our admiration for the bridges built by Telford and Brunel, and travel along the cuttings dug by Stephenson's navvies, so too must we admit the tensile strength of the constitution Dicey described, just as we travel along the intellectual track that he laid.

The metaphor invites a closing irony. The Diceys were a railway family. Thomas Edward Dicey, Albert's father, was Chairman of the mighty Midland Railway until his death in 1858. It had come into existence courtesy of Peel and the 1844 Midland Railway Consolidation Act. A second statute the 1863 Midland Railway Extension Act allowed the company to open a line to Manchester, and also build St Pancras Station and the Midland Grand Hotel. It was designed by Sir Gilbert Scott and opened in 1868, four years before his other masterpiece the Albert Memorial. The Diceys were at the heart of the 'age of progressive improvement'. As well as being Chairman of the Midland Railway, Thomas Edward was also proprietor of the Northampton Mercury. His eldest son Edward James Dicey became a journalist, foreign correspondent for the Daily Telegraph during the Schleswig-Holstein war in 1864 and later editor of the *Empire Review*, a committed imperialist like his younger brother. He dined with Bagehot at the Athenaeum. Newspapers and the railway; together they made the Diceys. And so when Albert Venn Dicey sat down and wrote his *Lectures* unveiling the insidious relation of press, public opinion and reform, it might be supposed that he did so with a due sense of ironic appreciation. He owed his comfortable existence, and his expensive education, to the subscribers of the Northampton Mercury and the shareholders of the Midland Railway.

References

Aldous, R. (2007). *The Lion and the Unicorn: Gladstone v Disraeli*. London: Pimlico.

Allan, T. (1993). *Law, Liberty and Justice*. Oxford: Oxford University Press.

Allan, T. (2001). *Constitutional Justice: A Liberal Theory of the Rule of Law*. Oxford: Oxford University Press.

Allison, J. (2007). *The English Historical Constitution: Continuity, Change and European Effects*. Cambridge: Cambridge University Press.

Arnold, M. (1986). *Matthew Arnold: A Critical Edition of the Major Works*. Oxford: Oxford University Press.

Arnold, M. (1993). *Culture and Anarchy, and Other Writings*. Cambridge: Cambridge University Press.

Arnstein, W. (1962). Gladstone and the Bradlaugh Case. *Victorian Studies, 5*, 303–330.

Arnstein, W. (2003). *Queen Victoria*. Basingstoke: Palgrave.

Bagehot, W. (1965). *The Collected Works of Walter Bagehot* (St. John Stevas, Ed.). London: The Economist.

Bagehot, W. (2001). *The English Constitution*. Cambridge: Cambridge University Press.

Bentley, M. (1996). *Politics Without Democracy 1815–1914*. London: Fontana.

Bentley, M. (2001). *Lord Salisbury's World: Conservative Environments in Late-Victorian Britain*. Cambridge: Cambridge University Press.

Best, G. (1979). *Mid-Victorian Britain 1851–75*. London: Fontana.

Bingham, T. (2002). Dicey Revisited. *Public Law*, pp. 39–51.

Bingham, T. (2010). *The Rule of Law*. London: Allen Lane.

Blake, K. (2009). *Pleasures of Benthamism: Victorian Literature, Utility, Political Economy*. Oxford: Oxford University Press.

Bogdanor, V. (2009). *The New British Constitution*. Oxford: Hart.

Brantlinger, P. (1977). *The Spirit of Reform: British Literature and Politics 1832–1867*. Cambridge, MA: Harvard University Press.

Briggs, A. (1959). *The Age of Improvement*. London: Longmans.

Buckle, H. (1871). *History of Civilization in England*. London: Longman.

Burke, E. (1986). *Reflections on the Revolution in France*. London: Penguin.

Burrow, J. (1988). *Whigs and Liberals: Continuity and Change in English Political Thought.* Oxford: Oxford University Press.
Cannadine, D. (1992). *GM Trevelyan: A Life in History.* London: HarperCollins.
Cannadine, D. (1994). *Aspects of Aristocracy: Grandeur and Decline in Modern Britain.* New Haven: Yale University Press.
Carlyle, T. (1986). *Selected Writings.* Harmondsworth: Penguin.
Craig, P. (1990). *Public Law and Democracy in the United Kingdom and the United States of America.* Oxford: Clarendon Press.
Cosgrove, R. (1980). *The Rule of Law: Albert Venn Dicey, Victorian Jurist.* Chapel Hill: University of North Carolina Press.
Dicey, A. (1914). *Lectures on the Relation Between Law and Public Opinion in England During the Nineteenth Century.* London: Macmillan.
Dicey, A. (1917). *The Statesmanship of Wordsworth.* Oxford: Clarendon Press.
Dicey, A. (1959). *An Introduction to the Study of the Law of the Constitution.* London: Macmillan.
Dicey, E. (1885). The Plea of a Malcontent Liberal. *Fortnightly Review, 44,* 466–467.
Gash, N. (1965). *Reaction and Reconstruction in English Politics 1832–1852.* Oxford: Oxford University Press.
Gilbert, W., & Sullivan, A. (2008). *The Savoy Operas.* London: Penguin.
Gilmour, R. (1993). *The Victorian Period: The Intellectual and Cultural Context of English Literature 1830–1890.* London: Longman.
Harlow, C. (1985). Power from the People? Representation and Constitutional Theory. In P. McAuslan & J. McEldowney (Eds.), *Law, Legitimacy and the Constitution: Essays Marking the Centenary of Dicey's "Law of the Constitution".* London: Sweet & Maxwell.
Hawkins, A. (1989). Parliamentary Government and Victorian Political Parties c.1830–c.1880. *English Historical Review, 104,* 638–669.
Heffer, S. (2013). *High Minds: The Victorians and the Making of Modern Britain.* London: Random House.
Hibbert, C. (2001). *Queen Victoria: A Personal History.* London: HarperCollins.
Hibbitts, B. (1994). The Politics of Principle: Albert Venn Dicey and the Rule of Law. *Anglo-American Law Review, 23,* 1–31.
Himmelfarb, G. (2007). *The Spirit of the Age: Victorian Essays.* New Haven: Yale University Press.
Jenkins, K. (1995). *On 'What Is History?' From Carr and Elton to Rorty and White.* London: Routledge.
Jenkins, R. (1965). *Dilke: A Victorian Tragedy.* London: Macmillan.
Jenkins, T. (1996). *Parliament, Party and Politics in Victorian Britain.* Manchester: Manchester University Press.
Jennings, I. (1935). In Praise of Dicey. *Public Administration, 13,* 123–134.

Jennings, I. (1959). *The Law and the Constitution*. London: London University Press.

Jowell, J., & Oliver, D. (Eds.). (2007). *The Changing Constitution*. Oxford: Oxford University Press.

Kingsley, C. (2013). *The Water Babies*. Oxford: Oxford University Press.

Le May, G. (1979). *The Victorian Constitution: Conventions, Usages and Contingencies*. London: Duckworth.

Levi, P. (1993). *Tennyson*. London: Macmillan.

Leyland, P. (2012). *The Constitution of the United Kingdom: A Contextual Analysis*. Oxford: Hart.

Longford, E. (1998). *Victoria RI*. London: Weidenfield & Nicolson.

Loveland, I. (1996). *Constitutional Law: A Critical Introduction*. London: Butterworths.

McEldowney, J. (1985). Dicey in Historical Perspective. In P. McAuslan & J. McEldowney (Eds.), *Law, Legitimacy and the Constitution: Essays Marking the Centenary of Dicey's "Law of the Constitution"*. London: Sweet & Maxwell.

Mitchell, L. (1997). *Lord Melbourne 1779–1848*. Oxford: Oxford University Press.

Parry, J. (1993). *The Rise and Fall of Liberal Government in Victorian Britain*. New Haven: Yale University Press.

Read, D. (1987). *Peel and the Victorians*. Oxford: Blackwell.

Simpson, A. (1973). Common Law and Legal Theory. In A. Simpson (Ed.), *Oxford Essays in Jurisprudence*. Oxford: Clarendon Press.

Shannon, R. (1999). Peel, Gladstone and Party. *Parliamentary History, 18*, 317–352.

Strachey, L. (1971). *Queen Victoria*. London: Penguin.

Sugarman, D. (1983). The Legal Boundaries of Liberty: Dicey, Liberalism and Legal Science. *Modern Law Review, 46*, 102–111.

Tennyson, A. L. (1991). *Selected Poems*. London: Penguin.

Wade, W. (1959). Introduction to A. Dicey, *An Introduction to the Study of the Law of the Constitution*. London: Macmillan.

Waddams, S. (1992). *Law, Politics and the Church of England: The Career of Stephen Lushington 1782–1873*. Cambridge: Cambridge University Press.

Wilson, A. (1999). *God's Funeral*. London: John Murray.

Wilson, A. (2002). *The Victorians*. London: Hutchinson.

Woodward, L. (1962). *The Age of Reform 1815–1870*. Oxford: Oxford University Press.

Bibliography

Ackroyd, P. (1991). *Charles Dickens*. London: Methuen.
Adams, E. (2011). *Liberal Epic: The Victorian Practice of History from Gibbon to Churchill*. Charlottesville: University of Virginia Press.
Aldous, R. (2007). *The Lion and the Unicorn: Gladstone v Disraeli*. London: Pimlico.
Allan, T. (1993). *Law, Liberty and Justice*. Oxford: Oxford University Press.
Allan, T. (2001). *Constitutional Justice: A Liberal Theory of the Rule of Law*. Oxford: Oxford University Press.
Allison, J. (2007). *The English Historical Constitution: Continuity, Change and European Effects*. Cambridge: Cambridge University Press.
Alter, R. (1968). The Demons of History in Dickens, *Tale. Novel, 2*, 135–142.
Anderson, A. (2007). Trollope's Modernity. *ELH, 74*, 509–534.
Anderson, O. (1967). The Political Uses of History in Mid Nineteenth Century England. *Past and Present, 36*, 87–105.
Arnold, M. (1968). *Essays in Criticism*. Chicago: Chicago University Press.
Arnold, M. (1986). *Matthew Arnold: A Critical Edition of the Major Works*. Oxford: Oxford University Press.
Arnold, M. (1993). *Culture and Anarchy, and Other Writings*. Cambridge: Cambridge University Press.
Arnstein, W. (1962). Gladstone and the Bradlaugh Case. *Victorian Studies, 5*, 303–330.
Arnstein, W. (2003). *Queen Victoria*. Basingstoke: Palgrave.
Bagehot, W. (1965). *The Collected Works of Walter Bagehot* (St. John Stevas, Ed.). London: The Economist.

I. Ward, *Writing the Victorian Constitution*, Palgrave Modern Legal History, https://doi.org/10.1007/978-3-319-96676-2

Bagehot, W. (2001). *The English Constitution.* Cambridge: Cambridge University Press.

Balfour, A. (1928). Introduction to W. Bagehot, *The English Constitution.* Oxford: Oxford University Press.

Barzun, J. (1968). Bagehot as Historian. In St. John Stevas (Ed.), *The Collected Works of Walter Bagehot* (Vol. 3). London: The Economist.

Baudrillard, J. (2002). *The Spirit of Terrorism.* London: Verso.

Baumgarten, M. (1983). Writing the Revolution. *Dickens Studies Annual, 12,* 161–176.

Bentham, J. (1982). *An Introduction to the Principles of Morals and Legislation.* London: Methuen.

Bentham, J. (1998). *A Fragment on Government.* Cambridge: Cambridge University Press.

Bentley, M. (1996). *Politics Without Democracy 1815–1914.* London: Fontana.

Bentley, M. (1999). *Modern Historiography: An Introduction.* London: Routledge.

Bentley, M. (2001). *Lord Salisbury's World: Conservative Environments in Late-Victorian Britain.* Cambridge: Cambridge University Press.

Berger, C. (2003). Partying with the Opposition: Social Politics in *The Prime Minister. Texas Studies in Literature and Language, 45,* 315–336.

Best, G. (1979). *Mid-Victorian Britain 1851–75.* London: Fontana.

Bignall, J. (1984). Dickens and the Catastrophic Continuum of History in *A Tale of Two Cities. English Literary History, 51,* 575–587.

Bingham, T. (2002). Dicey Revisited. *Public Law* 39–51.

Bingham, T. (2010). *The Rule of Law.* London: Allen Lane.

Birrell, A. (1986). Walter Bagehot. In St. John Stevas (Ed.), *Collected Works of Walter Bagehot.* London: The Economist.

Blackstone, W. (1828). *Commentaries on the Laws of England.* London: William Walker.

Blake, K. (2009). *Pleasures of Benthamism: Victorian Literature, Utility, Political Economy.* Oxford: Oxford University Press.

Blakemore, S. (1988). *Burke and the Fall of Language.* Lebanon, NH: University Press of New England.

Bogdanor, V. (2009). *The New British Constitution.* Oxford: Hart.

Bourke, R. (2000). Edmund Burke and Enlightenment Sociability: Justice, Honour and the Principles of Government. *History of Political Thought, 21,* 632–656.

Brantlinger, P. (1977). *The Spirit of Reform: British Literature and Politics 1832–1867.* Cambridge, MA: Harvard University Press.

Briggs, A. (1959). *The Age of Improvement.* London: Longmans.

Briggs, A. (1990). *Victorian People.* London: Penguin.

Bromwich, D. (1995). Wollstonecraft as a Critic of Burke. *Political Theory, 23,* 617–634.

Brown, D. (2010). *Palmerston: A Biography.* New Haven: Yale University Press.

Buchan, A. (1959). *The Spare Chancellor: The Life of Walter Bagehot.* London: Chatto & Windus.

Buckle, H. (1871). *History of Civilization in England.* London: Longman.

Burke, E. (1986). *Reflections on the Revolution in France.* London: Penguin.

Burke, E. (1990). *A Philosophical Enquiry into the Origins Our Ideas of the Sublime and the Beautiful.* Oxford: Oxford University Press.

Burke, E. (1999). *Letters on a Regicide Peace.* Indianapolis: Liberty Fund.

Burrow, J. (1983). Sense and Circumstances: Bagehot and the Nature of Political Understanding. In S. Collini, D. Winch, & J. Burrow (Eds.), *That Noble Science of Politics: A Study in Nineteenth Century Intellectual History.* Cambridge: Cambridge University Press.

Burrow, J. (1988). *Whigs and Liberals: Continuity and Change in English Political Thought.* Oxford: Oxford University Press.

Burrow, J. (2007). *A History of Histories.* London: Penguin.

Butte, G. (1977). Ambivalence and Affirmation in *The Duke's Children. Studies in English Literature, 17,* 709–727.

Butte, G. (1981). Trollope's Duke of Omnium and "The Pain of History": A Study of the Novelist's Politics. *Victorian Studies, 24,* 209–227.

Butterfield, H. (1931). *The Whig Interpretation of History.* London: Bell & Sons.

Butterworth, H. (1944). *The Englishman and His History.* Cambridge: Cambridge University Press.

Byatt, A. (1997). *Unruly Times.* London: Vintage.

Cannadine, D. (1992). *GM Trevelyan: A Life in History.* London: HarperCollins.

Cannadine, D. (1994). *Aspects of Aristocracy: Grandeur and Decline in Modern Britain.* New Haven: Yale University Press.

Cannadine, D. (2003). *In Churchill's Shadow: Confronting the Past in Modern Britain.* Oxford: Oxford University Press.

Cannon, J. (1973). *Parliamentary Reform 1640–1832.* Cambridge: Cambridge University Press.

Carlyle, T. (1986). *Selected Writings.* Harmondsworth: Penguin.

Carr, E. (2001). *What Is History?.* Basingstoke: Palgrave.

Claeys, G. (2000). The *Reflections* Refracted: The Critical Reception of Burke's *Reflections on the Revolution in France* During the Early 1790s. In J. Whale (Ed.), *Edmund Burke's Reflections on the Revolution in France: New Interdisciplinary Essays'.* Manchester: Manchester University Press.

Clark, K. (1962). *The Making of Victorian England.* Cambridge: Harvard University Press.

Clarke, P. (2012). *Mr Churchill's Profession.* London: Bloomsbury.

Coleridge, S. (1969). *Complete Poetical Works.* Oxford: Oxford University Press.

Coleridge, S. (1977). *Biographia Literaria*. London: Dent.

Collini, S., Winch, D., & Burrow, J. (1983). The Governing Science: Things Political and the Intellectual Historian. In S. Collini, D. Winch, & J. Burrow (Eds.), *That Noble Science of Politics: A Study in Nineteenth Century Intellectual History*. Cambridge: Cambridge University Press.

Cosgrove, R. (1980). *The Rule of Law: Albert Venn Dicey, Victorian Jurist*. Chapel Hill: University of North Carolina Press.

Cowles, T. (1937). Malthus, Darwin, and Bagehot: A Study in the Transference of a Concept. *Isis, 26*, 341–348.

Cowling, M. (1967). *1867: Disraeli, Gladstone and Revolution*. Cambridge: Cambridge University Press.

Craig, D. (1983). The Crowd in Dickens. In R. Giddings (Ed.), *The Changing World of Charles Dickens*. New York: Barnes and Noble.

Craig, P. (1990). *Public Law and Democracy in the United Kingdom and the United States of America*. Oxford: Clarendon Press.

Crossman, R. (1963). Introduction to W. Bagehot, *The English Constitution*. London: Fontana.

Danby, J. (1960). *The Simple Wordsworth: Studies in His Poems 1797–1807*. London: Routledge.

Davies, G. (1939). The Treatment of Constitutional History in Macaulay's *History of England*. *Huntington Library Quarterly, 2*, 179–204.

De Bruyn, F. (2004). Edmund Burke, the Political Quixote: Romance, Chivalry, and the Political Imagination. *Eighteenth Century Fiction, 16*, 695–753.

De Tocqueville, A. (1994). *Democracy in America*. London: Fontana.

Dicey, A. (1914). *Lectures on the Relation Between Law and Public Opinion in England During the Nineteenth Century*. London: Macmillan.

Dicey, A. (1917). *The Statesmanship of Wordsworth*. Oxford: Clarendon Press.

Dicey, A. (1959). *An Introduction to the Study of the Law of the Constitution*. London: Macmillan.

Dicey, A. (1986). Walter Bagehot. In St. John Stevas (Ed.), *Collected Works of Walter Bagehot* (Vol. 15). London: The Economist.

Dicey, E. (1885). The Plea of a Malcontent Liberal. *Fortnightly Review, 44*, 466–467.

Dickens, C. (2000). *A Tale of Two Cities*. London: Penguin.

Dickens, C. (2003). *Barnaby Rudge*. London: Penguin.

Dinwiddy, J. (1974). Utility and Natural Law in Burke's Thought: A Reconsideration. *Studies in Burke and His Time, 16*, 105–128.

Dransfield, S. (1998). Reading the Gordon Riots in 1841: Social Violence and Moral Management in *Barnaby Rudge*. *Dickens Studies Annual, 27*, 69–95.

Duff, M. (1986). Walter Bagehot. In St. John Stevas (Ed.), *The Collected Works of Walter Bagehot* (Vol. 15). London: The Economist.

Eagleton, T. (2005). *Holy Terror*. Oxford: Oxford University Press.

Easton, D. (1949). Walter Bagehot and Liberal Realism. *American Political Science Review, 43,* 17–37.

Edwards, O. (1988). *Macaulay.* London: Weidenfeld & Nicolson.

Edwards, O. (2011). Carlyle Versus Macaulay? A Study in History. *Carlyle Studies Annual, 27,* 177–205.

Elton, G. (2002). *The Practice of History.* London: Wiley-Blackwell.

Erskine May. (1861). *The Constitutional History of England Since George III.* London: Longman.

Evans, R. (2000). *In Defence of History.* London: Granta.

Ewing, K. (2000). The Politics of the British Constitution. *Public Law* 405–37.

Fairer, D. (1997). Organizing Verse: Burke's *Reflections* and Eighteenth Century Poetry. *Romanticism, 3,* 1–19.

Fennessy, R. (1963). *Burke, Paine and the Rights of Man.* Dordrecht: Martinus Nihoff.

Ferguson, N. (2003). *Empire: How Britain Made the Modern World.* London: Penguin.

Firth, C. (1929). *Oliver Cromwell and the Rule of the Puritans in England.* London: Putnam.

Firth, C. (1938). *A Commentary on Macaulay's History of England.* London: Macmillan.

Fleishman, A. (1971). *The English Historical Novel: Walter Scott to Virginia Woolf.* Baltimore: Johns Hopkins University Press.

Ford, T. (1970). Bagehot and Mill as Theorists of Comparative Politics. *Comparative Politics, 2,* 309–324.

Foreman, A. (1998). *Georgiana Duchess of Devonshire.* London: HarperCollins.

Forster, J. (1966). *The Life of Charles Dickens.* London: Chapman & Hall.

Freeman, M. (1978). Edmund Burke and the Theory of Revolution. *Political Theory, 6,* 277–297.

Frye, L. (1997) "Great Burke", Thomas Carlyle, and the French Revolution. In L. Crafton (Ed.), *The French Revolution Debate in English Literature and Culture.* London: Greenwood Press.

Furniss, T. (1990). Rhetoric in Revolution: The Role of Language in Paine's Critique of Burke. In K. Hanley & R. Selden (Eds.), *Revolution and English Romanticism.* London: Harvester Wheatsheaf.

Furniss, T. (1993). *Edmund Burke's Aesthetic Ideology: Language, Gender and Political Economy in Revolution.* Cambridge: Cambridge University Press.

Gardiner, J. (2002). *The Victorians: An Age in Retrospect.* London: Hambledon.

Gash, N. (1965). *Reaction and Reconstruction in English Politics 1832–1852.* Oxford: Oxford University Press.

Gash, N. (1986a). *Pillars of Government and Other Essays on State and Society c.1770–1880.* London: Hodder Arnold.

Gash, N. (1986b). *Sir Robert Peel: The Life of Sir Robert Peel After 1830*. London: Faber & Faber.

Gaunt, R. (2010). *Sir Robert Peel: The Life and Legacy*. London: I.B. Tauris.

Gilbert, W., & Sullivan, A. (2008). *The Savoy Operas*. London: Penguin.

Gilley, S. (1983). Macaulay as Historian. *Australian Journal of Politics and History, 29*, 328–343.

Gilmartin, K. (2000). Burke, Popular Opinion, and the Problem of a Counter-Revolutionary Sphere. In J. Whale (Ed.), *Edmund Burke's Reflections on the Revolution in France: New Interdisciplinary Essays*. Manchester: Manchester University Press.

Gilmour, R. (1993). *The Victorian Period: The Intellectual and Cultural Context of English Literature 1830–1890*. London: Longman.

Gladstone, W. (1876, July). Review of Trevelyan's *Life and Letters*. *Quarterly Review*, pp. 14–49.

Glavin, J. (2001). Politics and *Barnaby Rudge*: Surrogation, Restoration and Revival. *Dickens Studies Annual, 30*, 95–112.

Godwin, W. (1985). *An Enquiry Concerning Political Justice*. Harmondsworth: Penguin.

Goldberg, M. (1972). From Bentham to Carlyle: Dickens' Political Development. *Journal of the History of Ideas, 33*, 61–76.

Goldberg, M. (1983). Carlyle, Dickens, and the Revolution in 1848. *Dickens Studies Annual, 12*, 223–232.

Goode, M. (2007). The Man of Feeling: The Erotics of Historicism in *Reflections on the Revolution in France*. *ELH, 74*, 829–857.

Gordon, R. (1981). Historicism in Legal Scholarship. *Yale Law Journal, 90*, 1017–1056.

Gordon, R. (1984). Critical Legal Histories. *Stanford Law Review, 36*, 57–125.

Gordon, R. (1996). The Arrival of Critical Historicism. *Stanford Law Review, 49*, 1023–1029.

Gottshall, J. (1961). Devils Abroad: The Unity and Significance of *Barnaby Rudge*. *Nineteenth Century Fiction, 16*, 133–146.

Haley, W. (1965). Walter Bagehot: A Literary Appreciation. In St. John Stevas (Ed.), *Collected Works of Walter Bagehot*. London: The Economist.

Hall, N. (1991). *Trollope: A Biography*. Oxford: Clarendon Press.

Halperin, J. (1977). *Trollope and Politics*. London: Macmillan.

Hamburger, J. (1976). *Macaulay and the Whig Tradition*. Chicago: University of Chicago Press.

Hampsher-Monk, I. (2005). Edmund Burke's Changing Justification for Intervention. *Historical Journal, 48*, 65–100.

Hanley, B. (2004). The "Greatest Victorian" in the New Century: The Enduring Relevance of Walter Bagehot's Commentary on Literature, Scholarship and Public Life. *Papers on Language and Literature, 40*, 167–199.

Hardy, T. (1974). *The Collected Poems of Thomas Hardy*. London: Macmillan.
Harlow, C. (1985). Power from the People? Representation and Constitutional Theory. In P. McAuslan & J. McEldowney (Eds.), *Law, Legitimacy and the Constitution: Essays Marking the Centenary of Dicey's "Law of the Constitution"*. London: Sweet & Maxwell.
Hawkins, A. (1989). Parliamentary Government and Victorian Political Parties c.1830–c.1880. *English Historical Review, 104*, 638–669.
Hayek, F. (1960). *The Constitution of Liberty*. Chicago: Chicago University Press.
Hearnshaw, F. (1933). *The Social and Political Ideas of Some Representative Thinkers of the Victorian Age*. London: Harrop.
Heffer, S. (1996). *Moral Desperado: A Life of Thomas Carlyle*. London: Phoenix.
Heffer, S. (2013). *High Minds: The Victorians and the Making of Modern Britain*. London: Random House.
Hennessy, P. (1995). *The Hidden Wiring: Unearthing the British Constitution*. London: Gollancz.
Herzog, D. (1991). Puzzling Through Burke. *Political Theory, 19*, 336–363.
Hibbert, C. (1997). *Wellington: A Personal History*. London: HarperCollins.
Hibbert, C. (1998). *George III*. London: Viking.
Hibbert, C. (2001). *Queen Victoria: A Personal History*. London: HarperCollins.
Hibbert, C. (2004). *Disraeli: A Personal History*. London: HarperCollins.
Hibbitts, B. (1994). The Politics of Principle: Albert Venn Dicey and the Rule of Law. *Anglo-American Law Review, 23*, 1–31.
Hill, B. (1974). Fox and Burke: The Whig Party and the Question of Principles 1784–1789. *English Historical Review, 89*, 1–24.
Himmelfarb, G. (2007). *The Spirit of the Age: Victorian Essays*. New Haven: Yale University Press.
Hodson, J. (2007). *Language and Revolution in Burke, Wollstonecraft, Paine and Godwin*. Aldershot: Ashgate.
Holloway, J. (1965). *The Victorian Sage*. New York: Norton.
Homans, M. (1998). *Royal Representations: Queen Victoria and British Culture 1837–1876*. Chicago: University of Chicago Press.
Hoppen, T. (1998). *The Mid-Victorian Generation 1846–1886*. Oxford: Oxford University Press.
Horwitz, M. (1981). The Historical Contingency of the Role of Law. *Yale Law Journal, 90*, 1057–.
House, H. (1942). *Dickens' World*. Oxford: Oxford University Press.
Howsam, L. (2004). Academic Discipline or Literary Genre? The Establishment of Boundaries in Historical Writing. *Victorian Literature and Culture, 32*, 525–545.
Hughes, T. (1986). Spontaneous Order and the Politics of Anthony Trollope. *Nineteenth Century Literature, 41*, 32–48.

Hutcheon, W. (Ed.). (1913). *Whigs and Whiggism: Political Writings by Benjamin Disraeli*. London: John Murray.
Hutchinson, A. (1988). *Dwelling on the Threshold: Critical Essays in Modern Legal Thought*. London: Sweet and Maxwell.
Hutter, A. (1978). Nation and Generation in *A Tale of Two Cities*. *Proceedings of the Modern Language Association, 93*, 448–462.
Jackson, P. (1994). *The Last of the Whigs: A Political Biography of Lord Hartington*. Cranbury, NJ: Associated Presses.
James, R. (1970). *Churchill: A Study in Failure 1900–1939*. New York: World Publishing.
Jann, R. (1980). Democratic Myths in Victorian Medievalism. *Browning Institute Studies, 8*, 129–149.
Jenkins, K. (1995). *On 'What Is History?' From Carr and Elton to Rorty and White*. London: Routledge.
Jenkins, R. (1965). *Dilke: A Victorian Tragedy*. London: Macmillan.
Jenkins, R. (2001). *Churchill*. London: Macmillan.
Jenkins, R. (2005). *Gladstone*. London: Macmillan.
Jenkins, T. (1996). *Parliament, Party and Politics in Victorian Britain*. Manchester: Manchester University Press.
Jennings, I. (1935). In Praise of Dicey. *Public Administration, 13*, 123–134.
Jennings, I. (1959). *The Law and the Constitution*. London: London University Press.
Johnson, N. (1985). Dicey and His Influence on Public Law. *Public Law*: 717–23.
Johnston, K. (1998). *The Hidden Wordsworth: Poet, Lover, Rebel, Spy*. New York: Norton.
Jones, G. (2009). Introduction. In G. Jones (Ed.), *Charles Dickens, A Tale of Two Cities and the French Revolution*. Basingstoke: Palgrave.
Jowell, J., & Oliver, D. (Eds.). (2007). *The Changing Constitution*. Oxford: Oxford University Press.
Kaplan, C. (2007). *Victoriana: Histories, Fictions, Criticism*. Edinburgh: Edinburgh University Press.
Kennedy, D. (1979). The Structure of Blackstone's *Commentaries*. *Buffalo Law Review, 28*, 205–382.
Kilcup, R. (1977). Burke's Historicism. *Journal of Modern History, 49*, 394–410.
Kingsley, C. (2013). *The Water Babies*. Oxford: Oxford University Press.
Knowles, D. (1960). *Lord Macaulay 1800–1859*. Cambridge: Cambridge University Press.
Kramnick, I. (1977). *The Rage of Edmund Burke: Portrait of an Ambivalent Conservative*. New York: Basic Books.
Kucich, J. (1980). The Purity of Violence: *A Tale of Two Cities*. *Dickens Studies Annual, 8*, 119–137.

Kuhn, W. (2006). *The Politics of Pleasure: A Portrait of Benjamin Disraeli.* London: Simon & Schuster.

LaCapra, D. (2000). *Rethinking Intellectual History: Texts, Contexts, Language.* Ithaca: Cornell University Press.

Lacey, N. (2011). The Way We Lived Then: The Legal Profession and the 19th Century Novel. *Sydney Law Review, 3,* 599–621.

Lang, T. (1995). *The Victorians and the Stuart Age.* Cambridge: Cambridge University Press.

Lansbury, C. (1970). *The Reasonable Man: Trollope's Legal Fiction.* Princeton: Princeton University Press.

Lecky, W. (1899). *Democracy and Liberty.* London: Longmans.

Ledger, S. (2009). From the Old Bailey to Revolutionary France: The Trials of Charles Darnay. In C. Jones, J. McDonagh, & J. Mee (Eds.), *Charles Dickens, A Tale of Two Cities and the French Revolution.* London: Palgrave.

Laski, A. (1960). Myths of Character: An Aspect of the Novel. *Nineteenth Century Fiction, 14,* 333–343.

Le May, G. (1979). *The Victorian Constitution: Conventions, Usages and Contingencies.* London: Duckworth.

Levi, P. (1993). *Tennyson.* London: Macmillan.

Levine, G. (1968). *The Boundaries of Fiction: Carlyle, Macaulay, Newman.* Princeton: Princeton University Press.

Leyland, P. (2012). *The Constitution of the United Kingdom: A Contextual Analysis.* Oxford: Hart.

Lock, F. (2000). Rhetoric and Representation in Burke's *Reflections.* In J. Whale (Ed.), *Edmund Burke's Reflections on the Revolution in France: New Interdisciplinary Essays.* Manchester: Manchester University Press.

Longford, E. (1998). *Victoria RI.* London: Weidenfield & Nicolson.

Loveland, I. (1996). *Constitutional Law: A Critical Introduction.* London: Butterworths.

Lukacs, J. (2002). *Churchill: Visionary, Statesman, Historian.* New Haven: Yale University Press.

Macaulay, T. (1825, August). Milton. *Edinburgh Review,* pp. 304–346.

Macaulay, T. (1828, September). Hallam's Constitutional History. *Edinburgh Review,* pp. 96–169.

Macaulay, T. (1829, March). Utilitarian Logic and Politics. *Edinburgh Review,* pp. 159–189.

Macaulay, T. (1832, July). Dumont's *Recollections of Mirabeau. Edinburgh Review,* pp. 552–576.

Macaulay, T. (1841, October). Warren Hastings. *Edinburgh Review,* pp. 160–255.

Macaulay, T. (1969, May 1). William III. *Times Literary Supplement,* pp. 469–470.

Macaulay, T. (1986). *The History of England*. London: Penguin.
Mandler, P. (1990). *Aristocratic Government in the Age of Reform: Whigs and Liberals 1830–1852*. Oxford: Oxford University Press.
Marcus, D. (1976). The Carlylean Vision of *A Tale of Two Cities*. *Studies in the Novel*, 8, 56–68.
Marcus, S. (1985). *Dickens from Pickwick to Dombey*. London: Penguin.
Marr, A. (2007). *A History of Modern Britain*. London: Macmillan.
Marshall, G. (1999). The Analysis of British Political Institutions. In J. Hayward, B. Barry, & A. Brown (Eds.), *The British Study of Politics in the Twentieth Century*. Oxford: Oxford University Press.
Mather, F. (1959). The Government and the Chartists. In A. Briggs (Ed.), *Chartist Studies*. London: Macmillan.
Mayo, R. (1972). The Contemporaneity of the *Lyrical Ballads*. In A. Jones & W. Tydeman (Eds.), *Wordsworth's Lyrical Ballads*. London: Macmillan.
Mayr, E. (1990). When Is Historiography Whiggish? *Journal of the History of Ideas*, *51*, 301–309.
McCalman, I. (1996). Mad Lord George and Madame La Motte: Riot and Sexuality in the Genesis of Burke's *Reflections on the Revolution in France*. *Journal of British Studies*, *35*, 343–367.
McCalman, I. (1999). Controlling the Riots: Dickens, Barnaby Rudge and Romantic Revolution. *History*, *84*, 458–476.
McEldowney, J. (1985). Dicey in Historical Perspective. In P. McAuslan & J. McEldowney (Eds.), *Law, Legitimacy and the Constitution: Essays Marking the Centenary of Dicey's "Law of the Constitution"*. London: Sweet & Maxwell.
McLamore, R. (1993). To Forge a New Language: Burke and Paine. *Prose Studies*, *16*, 179–192.
McMaster, J. (1978). *Trollope's Palliser Novels: Theme and Pattern*. London: Macmillan.
McMaster, R. (1986). *Trollope and the Law*. London: Macmillan.
McNally, D. (2000). Political Economy to the Fore: Burke, Malthus and the Whig Response to Popular Radicalism in the Age of the French Revolution. *History of Political Thought*, *21*, 427–447.
Messenger, R. (2006). The Last of the Whigs: Churchill as Historian. *New Criterion*, *25*, 16–23.
Mettam, R., et al. (1984). What Is History? The Great Debate. *History Today*, *34*(May), 5–16.
Michasiw, K. (1989). *Barnaby Rudge*: The Since of the Fathers. *English Literary History*, *56*, 571–592.
Mitchell, L. (1997). *Lord Melbourne 1779–1848*. Oxford: Oxford University Press.
Morley, J. (1886). *Critical Miscellanies* (Vol. 1). London: Macmillan.

Mosher, M. (1991). The Skeptic's Burke. *Political Theory, 19,* 391–418.
Mowat, R. (1995). *The Victorian Age.* London: Senate.
Newsome, D. (1998). *The Victorian World Picture.* London: Fontana.
O'Brien, C. (1992). *The Great Melody: A Thematic Biography of Edmund Burke.* London: Sinclair Stevenson.
Orwell, G. (1946). *Dickens, Dali and Others: Studies in Popular Culture.* New York: Reynal & Hitchcock.
Orwell, G. (1984). *The Penguin Essays of George Orwell.* London: Penguin.
Paine, T. (1985). *The Rights of Man.* Harmondsworth: Penguin.
Parker, M. (1991). The Institutionalization of a Burkean-Coleridgean Literary Culture. *Studies in English Literature, 31,* 693–713.
Parry, J. (1993). *The Rise and Fall of Liberal Government in Victorian Britain.* New Haven: Yale University Press.
Paulson, S. (1983). *Representations of Revolution.* New Haven: Yale University Press.
Phillips, M. (1989). Macaulay, Scott, and the Literary Challenge to Historiography. *Journal of the History of Ideas, 50,* 117–133.
Plumb, J. (1963). *Men and Places.* London: Cresset.
Pocock, J. (1960). Burke and the Ancient Constitution—A Problem in the History of Ideas. *Historical Journal, 3,* 125–143.
Pocock, J. (1982). The Political Economy of Burke's Analysis of the French Revolution. *Historical Journal, 25,* 331–349.
Pollard, A. (1968). *Trollope's Political Novels.* Hull: University of Hull Press.
Poser, N. (2013). *Lord Mansfield: Justice in the Age of Reason.* Montreal: McGill-Queen's University Press.
Pratt, B. (1983). Carlyle and Dickens: Heroes and Hero-Worshippers. *Dickens Studies Annual, 12,* 233–246.
Price, R. (1991). *Political Writings.* Cambridge: Cambridge University Press.
Prochaska, F. (2010). The View from Albion: Bagehot and the American Constitution. *History Today, 60,* 35–41.
Prochaska, F. (2013). *The Memoirs of Walter Bagehot.* New Haven: Yale University Press.
Read, D. (1987). *Peel and the Victorians.* Oxford: Blackwell.
Rice, T. (1978). *Barnaby Rudge*: A Vade Mecum for the Theme of Domestic Government in Dickens. *Dickens Studies Annual, 7,* 81–102.
Rice, T. (1983). The Politics of *Barnaby Rudge.* In R. Giddings (Ed.), *The Changing World of Charles Dickens.* New York: Barnes & Noble.
Ritchie, D. (1989). Burke's Influence on the Imagination of Walter Bagehot. *The Modern Age, 32,* 324–328.
Roberts, J. (1978). *The French Revolution.* Oxford: Oxford University Press.
Roe, N. (1988). *Wordsworth and Coleridge: The Radical Years.* Oxford: Oxford University Press.

Rorty, R. (1980). *Philosophy and the Mirror of Nature*. Princeton: Princeton University Press.

Rorty, R. (1989). *Contingency, Irony, and Solidarity*. Cambridge: Cambridge University Press.

Rose, K. (2014). *The Literary Churchill: Author, Reader, Actor*. New Haven: Yale University Press.

Royle, E. (1996). *Chartism*. London: Longman.

Royle, E. (2000). *Revolutionary Britannia? Reflections on the Threat of Revolution in Britain 1789–1848*. Manchester: Manchester University Press.

Sanders, A. (1978). *The Victorian Historical Novel 1840–1880*. London: Macmillan.

Schmidt, P. (2002). The Dilemma of a Free People: Justice Robert Jackson, Walter Bagehot, and the Creation of a Conservative Jurisprudence. *Law and History Review, 20,* 517–539.

Sellars, W., & Yeatman, R. (1993). *1066 and All That: A Memorable History of England*. Stroud: Sutton.

Shannon, R. (1999). Peel, Gladstone and Party. *Parliamentary History, 18,* 317–352.

Simpson, A. (1973). Common Law and Legal Theory. In A. Simpson (Ed.), *Oxford Essays in Jurisprudence*. Oxford: Clarendon Press.

Smalley, D. (1969). *Trollope: The Critical Heritage*. London: Routledge.

Smith, E. (1990). *Lord Grey 1764–1845*. Oxford: Oxford University Press.

Smith, E. (1999). *George IV*. New Haven: Yale University Press.

Smith, P. (2001). Introduction to W. Bagehot, *The English Constitution*. Cambridge: Cambridge University Press.

Speare, M. (1924). *The Political Novel: Its Development in England and in America*. Oxford: Oxford University Press.

Spence, G. (1975). Dickens as Historical Novelist. *The Dickensian, 71,* 21–29.

Spring, D. (1983). Walter Bagehot and Deference. *American History Review, 81,* 524–531.

Stanlis, P. (1992). Burke, Rousseau and the French Revolution. In S. Blakemore (Ed.), *Burke and the French Revolution: Bicentennial Essays*. Athens: University of Georgia Press.

St. John Stevas, N. (1959). *Walter Bagehot*. London: Eyre & Spottiswoode.

St. John Stevas, N. (1987). *The Omnipresence of Walter Bagehot*. Oxford: Oxford University Press.

Stephan, F. (1860, January 7). Lord Macaulay. *Saturday Review*, p. 9.

Strachey, L. (1931). *Portraits in Miniature and Other Essays*. London: Chatto and Windus.

Strachey, L. (1971). *Queen Victoria*. London: Penguin.

Strauss, L. (1953). *Natural Right and Natural History*. Chicago: Chicago University Press.

Sugarman, D. (1983). The Legal Boundaries of Liberty: Dicey, Liberalism and Legal Science. *Modern Law Review, 46,* 102–111.

Sullivan, R. (2009). *Macaulay: The Tragedy of Power.* Cambridge, MA: Harvard University Press.

Swann, K. (1977). Martha's Name or the Scandal of "The Thorn". In Y. Prins & M. Schreiber (Eds.), *Dwelling in Possibility: Women Poets and Critics of Poetry.* Ithaca: Cornell University Press.

Syrett, K. (2011). *The Foundations of Public Law: Principles and Problems of Power in the British Constitution.* London: Palgrave.

Taylor, A. (1976). *Essays in English History.* Harmondsworth: Pelican.

Tennyson, A. L. (1991). *Selected Poems.* London: Penguin.

Thompson, E. (1991). *The Making of the English Working Class.* Harmondsworth: Penguin.

Timko, M. (1983). Splendid Impressions and Picturesque Means: Dickens, Carlyle and the French Revolution. *Dickens Studies Annual, 12,* 177–195.

Tombs, R. (2014). *The English and Their History.* New York: Alfred Knopf.

Tosh, J. (1984). *The Pursuit of History: Aims, Methods and New Directions in the Study of Modern History.* London: Longman.

Trevelyan, G. (1939). *The English Revolution 1688–1689.* London: Henry Holt.

Trevor-Roper, H. (1957). *Historical Essays.* London: Macmillan.

Trilling, L. (1949). *Matthew Arnold.* London: George Allen & Unwin.

Trollope, A. (1978). *Ralph the Heir.* New York: Dover.

Trollope, A. (1995). *The Duke's Children.* London: Penguin.

Trollope, A. (1996). *An Autobiography.* London: Penguin.

Vanden Bossche, C. (1983). Prophetic Closure and Disclosing Narrative: *The French Revolution* and *A Tale of Two Cities. Dickens Studies Annual,* 12, 209–221.

Vile, M. (1967). *Constitutionalism and the Separation of Powers.* Oxford: Clarendon Press.

Waddams, S. (1992). *Law, Politics and the Church of England: The Career of Stephen Lushington 1782–1873.* Cambridge: Cambridge University Press.

Wade, W. (1959). Introduction to A. Dicey, *An Introduction to the Study of the Law of the Constitution.* London: Macmillan.

Ward, I. (2005). A Man of Feelings: William Godwin's Romantic Embrace. *Law and Literature, 17,* 21–46.

Weber, R. (1967). Singer and Seer: Macaulay on the Historian as Poet. *Papers on Language and Literature, 3,* 210–219.

Weeks, R. (1989). Disraeli as Political Egoist: A Literary and Historical Investigation. *Journal of British Studies, 28,* 387–410.

Weintraub, S. (1993). *Disraeli: A Biography.* London: Hamish Hamilton.

Weston, J. (1961). Edmund Burke's View of History. *Review of Politics, 23,* 203–229.

Wheare, K. (1974). Lecture on a Master Mind: Walter Bagehot. *Proceedings of the British Academy, 62*, 173–197.

White, H. (1978). *Tropics of Discourse: Essays in Cultural Criticism*. Baltimore: Johns Hopkins University Press.

White, J. (1984). *When Words Lose Their Meaning: Constitutions and Reconstitutions of Language, Character and Community*. Chicago: Chicago University Press.

Williams, R. (1965). *The Long Revolution*. London: Pelican.

Wilson, A. (1999). *God's Funeral*. London: John Murray.

Wilson, A. (2002). *The Victorians*. London: Hutchinson.

Wilson W. (1986). A Literary Politician. In St. John Stevas (Ed.) *The Collected Works of Walter Bagehot* (Vol. 15). London: The Economist.

Wood, M. (2010). *The Story of England*. London: Penguin.

Wood, N. (1964). The Aesthetic Dimension of Burke's Political Thought. *Journal of British Studies, 4*, 41–64.

Woodward, L. (1962). *The Age of Reform 1815–1870*. Oxford: Oxford University Press.

Worden, B. (2001). *Roundhead Reputations: The English Civil Wars and the Passions of Posterity*. London: Penguin.

Wordsworth, W. (1935). *The Complete Poetical Works*. Oxford: Oxford University Press.

Young, G. (1986). The Greatest Victorian. In St. John Stevas (Ed.), *The Collected Works of Walter Bagehot* (Vol. 15). London: The Economist.

Cases

Lee v Bude and Torrington Junction Railway co. [1871] LR 6 CP 576.

R (Jackson) v Attorney General [2005] UKHL 56 [2006] 1 AC 262.

Index

A
Acton, John Dalberg-Acton, Lord, 4, 93, 117
Act of Settlement 1701, 85
Addison, Joseph, 83
Affirmation Act, 1888, 151
Albert Memorial, the, 108, 190
Albert, Prince, 51, 89, 93, 105, 107, 124, 133
Alfred, King, 51
Allan, Trevor, 187
Amberley, Katharine Russell, Lady, 104
Annual Register, 45
Arbuthnot, Mrs Harriet, 71, 139
Arnold, Matthew
  Dover Beach, 154, 164
Arnold, Thomas, 48
Ashley, Maurice, 6
Asquith, Herbert Henry, 168
Athenaeum Club, 190
Attwood, Thomas, 64, 70
Austin, John
  The Province of Jurisprudence Determined, 170

B
Bacon, Sir Francis, 82
Bagehot, Walter
  The Advantages and Disadvantages of Becoming a Member of Parliament, 147
  The Character of Sir Robert Peel, 126
  The English Constitution, 119, 122
  The First Edinburgh Reviewers, 118
  Lombard Street, 117
  Physics and Politics, 119, 133
  Tennyson and Browning or Pure, Ornate and Grotesque Art in English Poetry, 117
  The Woman's Degrees, 183
Baldwin, Stanley, 180
Balfour, Arthur James, 14, 136, 152, 160

I. Ward, *Writing the Victorian Constitution*, Palgrave Modern Legal History, https://doi.org/10.1007/978-3-319-96676-2

Bank Charter Act 1844, 165
Barzun, Jacques, 138
Benson, Edward Frederick, 15
Bentham, Jeremy, 19, 82, 170
Bentley, Michael, 7, 19
Berlioz, Hector, 66
Besant, Annie, 147
Best, Geoffrey, 14
Bill of Rights 1689, 36
Bingham, Tom, Lord Chief Justice, 186
Birrell, Augustine, 138
Black Book, 181
Blackstone, Sir William
Commentaries on the Laws of England, 19
Blackwood's Magazine, 53
Blakemore, Steven, 47
Blenheim Palace, 15
Bogdanor, Vernon, 17
Braddon, Mary Elizabeth, 21, 122
Bradlaugh, Charles, 112, 147
Bradlaugh v Gossett, 173
Braxfield, Robert McQueen, Lord Justice Clerk, 18
Briggs, Asa, 16, 103
Bright, John, 113
British Coal Corporation v King, 186
British and Irish Press Guide, 161
Brook's Club, 179
Brougham, Henry Peter, Lord, 103, 115, 166
Browning, Robert, 117
Buchan, Alistair, 105, 117, 125–128, 137, 139
Buckingham Palace, 1, 72, 108
Buckingham, Richard Chandos Grenville, 3rd Duke of, 72
Buckle, Henry
History of Civilization in England, 8, 168
Bulwer, Sir Henry, 112
Burke, Edmund
Appeal from the New to the Old Whigs, 46
Letters on a Regicide Peace, 46
Letter to a Noble Lord, 57
A Philosophical Enquiry, 32
Reflections on the Revolution in France, 13, 28, 152
Burney, Fanny, 42
Burrow, John, 6, 49, 92, 137
Butterfield, Herbert
The Whig Interpretation of History, 8

C

Cairns, Hugh McCalmant, Lord Chancellor, 19
Cambridge University, 15
Cannadine, David, 5, 9
Canning, George, 47
Carlton Club, 115
Carlyle, Thomas
Chartism, 49, 63, 155
History of the French Revolution, 49, 81
Letters and Speeches of Oliver Cromwell, 51
Shooting Niagara: And After?, 115
Sign of the Times, 14, 68
Carr, Edward Hallett
What is History?, 6
Carroll, Lewis
Alice in Wonderland, 170
The Hunting of the Snark, 12
Catherine, Queen of Russia, 42
'Cat and Mouse' Act 1913, 182
Chadwick, Edwin
Sanitary Conditions of the Labour Classes, 165
Chamberlain, Joseph, 158
Chandler, James
England in 1819, 11

Chaplin, Henry, 150
Charlemont, James Montagu Caulfeild, 3rd Earl of, 28
Charles I, King, 31
Chesterton, Gilbert Keith, 155
Chimney Sweepers Regulation Act 1864, 165
Churchill, Lord Randolph, 151
Churchill, Sir Winston
History of the English Speaking Peoples, 6, 47
Clarendon, George Villiers, 4th Earl of, 99, 107
Clarke v Bradlaugh, 150
Clark, Kitson
The Making of Victorian England, 137
Coal Mines Regulation Act 1908, 181
Cobbett, William
Rural Rides, 74
Cobden, Richard, 77
Coke, Sir Edward, Lord Chief Justice, 187
Coke, Thomas, 2nd Earl of Leicester, 74
Coleridge, John, Lord Chief Justice, 151
Coleridge, Samuel Taylor
The Ancient Mariner, 25
Biographia Literaria, 46
Constitution of Church and State, 155
A Lay Sermon, 46
Collingwood, Robin George, 5
Collins, Wilkie, 21
Companies Act 1844, 165
Constitutional Reform Act 2005, 188
Corrupt Practices Act, 1883, 158
Corry, Montagu, 112
Cox, Homersham, 132
Critical Review, 42
Croker, John Wilson, 75
Cromwell, Oliver, 51, 85
Crossman, Richard, 133, 137
Cross, Richard, 151

D
Darwin, Charles
Origin of the Species by Means of Natural Selection, 153
The Descent of Man, and Selection in Relation to Sex, 153
Davidson, Emily Wilding, 182
Declaration of Indulgence, 87
Dentists Act 1878, 173
Derby, Edward Smith-Stanley, 14th Earl of, 115
Despatch, The, 73
Dicey, Albert Venn
Conflict of Laws, 179
The Development of Administrative Law in England, 167
England's Case Against Home Rule, 178, 183
An Introduction to the Study of the Law of the Constitution, 13
Lectures on Public Opinion, 157, 164, 168, 173, 175, 181
The Statesmanship of Wordsworth, 180
Dicey, Edward James, 190
Dicey, Thomas Edward, 190
Dickens, Charles
Barnaby Rudge, 55–57
Hard Times, 55
Oliver Twist, 68
A Tale of Two Cities, 55, 57
Dilke, Sir Charles, 109
Disraeli, Benjamin
Coningsby, 54, 74
Sybil, 54
Vindication of the English Constitution, 52

Dryden, John, 83
Duff, Sir Mountstuart Grant, 136
Durham, John Lambton, 1st Earl of, 131

E

Easton, David, 136
Economist, The, 116, 127
Edinburgh Review, The, 15, 81
Education Acts 1839, 1876 & 1893, 165
Education Act 1870 (also known as Forster's Act), 161
Education (Provision of Meals) Act 1906, 181
Edward VII, King (also Prince Bertie), 15
Elgar, Edward
  Pomp and Circumstance March, No.1, 15
Eliot, George
  Middlemarch, 104, 178
Eliot, Thomas Stearns
  The Wasteland, 180
Ellen Street Estates v Minister of Health, 186
Elton, Sir Geoffrey, 9
Empire Review, 190
Engels, Friedrich, 64
European Communities Act 1972, 188
Evans, Richard, 11, 21
Evidence Amendment Acts, 1869 & 1870, 148
Examiner, The, 14

F

Factortame cases, 188
Factory Acts 1844 & 1878, 165
Ferguson, Adam
  Essay on the History of Civil Society, 31
Ferguson, Niall, 7
Feuerbach, Ludwig Andreas, 153
Figes, Orlando, 11
Filmer, Sir Robert, 40, 48
Firth, Sir Charles Harding
  Commentary on Macaulay's History of England, 92
Fitzherbert, Maria, 70
Fitzwilliam, William Fitzwilliam, 4th Earl, 42
Forster, John, 55
Fortnightly Review, 116
Foucault, Michel, 17
Fowler's Act 1894, 165
Fox, Charles James, 27, 43, 78
Fraser's Magazine, 156
Freeman, Edward, 77
Froude, John Antony, 50
Furniss, Tom, 47

G

Gandhi, Mohandas, 150
Gardiner, John, 48, 139
Gardiner, Samuel Rawson
  History of the Commonwealth and Protectorate, 8
  History of England from the Accession of James I to the Outbreak of the Civil War, 8
  History of the Great Civil War, 8
Gaskell, Elizabeth
  North and South, 68
Geldert, Martin, 184
George III, King, 39, 42, 122
George IV, King, 70, 74, 89
Gibbon, Edward, 42
Gilbert, Sir William Schwenk
  His Excellency, 150
  The Mikado, 152

Gladstone, William Ewart
The Declining Efficiency of Parliament, 113
The State and its Relations with the Church, 94
Godwin, William
Caleb Williams, 43
An Enquiry Concerning Political Justice, 43
Gordon, Lord George, 56
Gordon, Robert, 20
Goulburn, Henry, 71
Grant, James
Recollections of the House of Commons, 79
Great Exhibition of the Works of Industry of All Nations, 105
Greene, Lord, Master of the Rolls, 186
Grenville, Lord William, 42
Greville, Charles, 1
Grey, Charles Grey, 2nd Earl
Parliamentary Government Considered with Reference to Reform of Parliament, 131

H
Haggard, Rider, 183
Halifax, Charles Montagu, 1st Earl of, 88
Hallam, Henry
Constitutional History of England, 81, 124
Hamburger, Joseph, 92
Hanley, Brian, 117
Harcourt, William Vernon, 160
Hardie, Keir, 168
Hartington, Spencer Compton Cavendish, Marquis of, 159
Harvard University, 161
Hayek, Friedrich, 92
Hazlitt, William, 14
Heffer, Simon, 16, 137
Hennessy, Peter, 137
Hicks-Beech, Michael, 101
Himmelfarb, Gertrude, 14, 16
Holdsworth, William Searle
History of English Law, 8, 185
Holt, John, Lord Chief Justice, 18
Hood, Edwin Paxton, 68
Hooker, Richard, 48
Human Rights Act 1988, 188
Hume, David
History of England, 31
Hutchinson, Allan, 20
Hutton, Richard Holt, 117
Huxley, Thomas Henry, 154
Hyde Park, 111

I
Inglis, Sir Robert, 71

J
Jackson, William, 1st Baron Allerton, 152
James II, King, 86
James, Henry, 68
Jeffreys, George Jeffreys, Lord Chief Justice, 85
Jenkins, Keith, 9
Jenkins, Roy, 15
Jenner, William, 107
Jennings, Sir Ivor, 169, 187
Johnson, Samuel, 40, 56
Jones, Ernest, 66
Judicature Acts 1873 & 1875, 166

K
Kennedy, Duncan, 20
Keynes, John Maynard, 137

King James Bible, Authorized Version of, 156
Kingsley, Charles
The Water Babies, 154, 170
Kipling, Rudyard, 183
Knowles, David, 91
Knowlton, Charles
The Fruits of Philosophy, or the Private Companion of Young Married People, 147

L
Labouchere, Henry, 147
LaCapra, Dominic, 10
Laski, Harold Joseph, 185
Lawson, F.H., 185
Leader, The, 56
Lecky, William Edward Hartpole, 107
Lee v Bude and Torrington Junction Railway, 173
Leopold, King of the Belgians, 109
Licensing Act 1872, 165
Lisle, Alice, 87
Lloyd George, David, 168
Local Government Act 1888, 165
Locke, John, 28, 40
London Chronicle, 42
London Corresponding Society, 63
London School of Economics, 179
Lord Cranborne, 114
Loreburn, Robert Reid, 1st Earl & Lord Chancellor, 177
Loughborough, Alexander Wedderburn, Lord & Lord Chancellor, 42
Louis XVI, King, 64
Loveland, Ian, 186
Lowe, Robert, 114
Lyell, Sir Charles
Principles of Geology, 153

M
Macaulay, Lord Thomas Babington
Essay on William III, 88
History of England, 78
Lays of Rome, 83
MacCormick v Lord Advocate, 186
Mackinnon, William Alexander
On the rise, progress, and present state of public opinion, 162
Mackintosh, James
Vindicae Gallicae, 42
Madzimbamuto v Lardner-Burke, 188
Magna Carta, 19, 53, 118
Malthus, Thomas
An Essay on the Principles of Population, 67
Manchester Free Trade Hall, 53, 136, 159
Manchester Mercury, 63
Manners, Lord John, 112
Marie Antoinette, Queen, 29, 32, 34, 35, 88
Marlborough, John Churchill, 1st Duke of, 6
Marr, A.
History of Modern Britain, 7
Martineau, Harriet
The Positive Philosophy of Auguste Comte, 153
Marx, Karl
The Communist Manifesto, 67
Mary Stuart, Queen, 88
Matrimonial Causes Act 1857, 166
Mayhew, Henry
London Labour and the London Poor, 68
May, Sir Thomas Erskine
Constitutional History of England, 131
Melbourne, William Lamb, 2nd Viscount, 52

Mental Deficiency Act 1913, 181
Midland Railway Consolidation Act 1844, 190
Midland Railway Extension Act 1863, 190
Midlothian campaign, 159
Mill, James
  Essay on Government, 94
Mill, John Stuart
  Chapters on Socialism, 168
  Considerations on Representative Government, 164
Milton, John, 28, 84
Mines Act 1842, 165
Monthly Review, 42
Moore, George Edward
  Principia Ethica, 153
Mordaunt v Mordaunt, 123
Morley, John, 94, 133, 160
Morning Chronicle, 73
Morris, William, 168
Municipal Corporations Act 1835, 165

N
Namier, Lewis, 9, 21
Napier, Sir Charles, 67
Napoleon III, Emperor of France, 65
National Insurance Act 1911, 181
National Reformer, The, 147
Nelson, Horatio Lord, 51
Nettleton, John Sutton, 151
Newcastle, Henry Pelham, 6th Duke of, 72, 78
Newman, Cardinal John Henry
  Tracts for the Times, 154
Normanby, George Phipps, Lord, 78
Northampton Mercury, 190
Northern Star, 65

O
O'Brien, Conor Cruise, 47
O'Connor, Feargus, 64, 66
O'Kane, Timothy Joseph, 99
Old Age Pensions Act 1908, 181
Orwell, George
  The Lion and the Unicorn, 15
Osborne House, 66
Overend Gurney, Bank of, 116
Owen, Robert, 68
Oxford University, 154

P
Paine, Tom
  The Rights of Man, 45
Paley, William
  Natural Theology, 169
Palmer, Roundell, 114
Palmerston, Henry John Temple, Viscount, 99
Pankhurst, Christabel
  Votes for Women, 182
Parliament Act 1911, 181
Parliamentary Oaths Act 1866, 148
Paxton, Joseph, 105
Pease, Joseph, 149
Peel, Sir Robert, 71, 127, 134, 156, 162, 163, 173, 190
Peter, Hugh, 31
Plumb, John Harold, 6, 92, 94, 95
Police Act 1856, 165
Pollock, Sir Frederick, 170
Ponsonby, Sir Henry, 110
Poor Law 1834, 165
Poor Man's Guardian, 72
Portland, William Bentinck, 4th Duke of, 26
Price, Richard

A Discourse on the Love of Our Country, 27
Priestley, Joseph, 27
Prisons Act 1839, 165
Prochaska, Frank
Memoirs of Walter Bagehot, 138
Public Health Acts 1848, 1872 & 1875, 165
Public Worship Regulation Act 1874, 165
Punch, 66, 111, 113, 115

Q
Quarterly Review, The, 129

R
Ranke, Leopold von, 8
Redistribution Act, 1885, 158
Reform Act, 1832, 52, 69, 74, 79, 101, 106, 157
Reform Club, 179
Representation of the People Act 1867, 115
Representation of the People Act 1884, 158, 159
Representation of the People Act 1918, 182
Ridley, Sir Matthew, 115
Robinson, Henry Crabbe, 69
Rolle, John, 1st Baron, 2
Roman Catholic Relief Act, 70
Romilly, Samuel, 118, 166
Rorty, Richard
Contingency, Irony, and Solidarity, 10
Rosebery, Archibald Primrose, 5th Earl of, 51, 128, 181
Rothschild, Lionel de, 149
Royal Commission on Sanitation 1871, 165
Royal Titles Act 1876, 183
Ruskin, John, 3, 105, 163
Russell, William, Lord
Essay on the History of the English Government and Constitution, 121

S
Salisbury, Robert Gascoyne-Cecil, 3rd Marquis of, 93. *See also* Lord Cranborne
Samuel, Raphael, 4
Sanitary Act 1866, 165
Schama, Simon, 11
Scott, Sir Gilbert, 190
Scott, Sir Walter, 70, 83
Seditious Meeting Act, 26
Seeley, John Robert, 8
Sellar, Walter
1066 and All That, 17
Shaftesbury, Anthony Ashley-Cooper 7th Earl of, 165
Shakespeare, William, 117
Shaw, George Bernard, 150
Shelley, Percy Bysshe, 70
Sheridan, Richard Brinsley, 43
Sidney, Algernon, 28, 40, 86
Simpson, Alfred William Brian (AWB), 186
Smiles, Samuel
Self-Help, 51
Smith, Adam
Theory of Moral Sentiments, 120
Smith, Henry Walton, 151, 168
Smith, Sydney, 118
Solomons, David, 149
Spencer, Herbert
Man Versus State, 168
Stanley, Edward Stanley, Lord (later 15th Earl of Derby), 52, 111, 113, 157

Stephen, James Fitzjames
Liberty, Equality, Fraternity, 36, 170
Stephen, Leslie, 125
Sterne, Laurence
The Adventures of Tristram Shandy, 83
St John Stevas, Norman, 1st Lord St John, 138
St Paul's Cathedral, 183
Stockmar, Christian Friedrich, Baron, 133
Strachey, Lytton
Eminent Victorians, 15
Stubbs, William, 6
Sugarman, David, 187
Sullivan, Arthur Seymour. *See* Gilbert, Sir William Schwenk
Sullivan, Richard, 92
Swift, Jonathan, 83

T
Tamworth Manifesto, 75, 76
Taylor, Alan, 92
Taylor, Cooke, 40
Telegraph Acts, 1868 & 1870, 161
Ten Hours Act 1847, 165
Tennyson, Alfred Lord
Locksley Hall, 153, 163
Locksley Hall Sixty Years After, 106, 153
In Memoriam, 153
Test Acts, 27
Thackeray, William Makepeace, 50, 103, 142
Thelwall, John, 26, 63
Times, The, 27, 28, 70, 108, 109, 150, 155, 163
Tocqueville, Alexis de
Democracy in America, 12
Tomahawk Magazine, 109
Tombs, Robert
The English and Their History, 7
Tosh, John, 47
Trade Disputes Act 1906, 181
Trade Union Acts 1871, 1875 & 1913, 168
Trevelyan, George Macaulay, 5, 93, 180
Trevelyan, Sir George Otto
What Does She Do With It?, 110
Trevor-Roper, Hugh, 92
Trollope, Antony
Autobiography, 102–104, 139, 140
Barchester Towers, 139
The Duke's Children, 140, 142
Ralph the Heir, 103

U
University College, London, 104

V
Vauxhall Estates v Liverpool Corporation, 186
Versailles, Palace of, 30
Victoria, Queen, 13, 49, 69, 104, 148, 183

W
Wade, Emlyn Capel Stewart, 186
Wallington, 110
Walpole, Horace, 57
Walpole, Spencer, 111
Waterloo, battle of, 65, 71
Waugh, Evelyn, 15
Weber, Ronald, 91
Wellington, Arthur Wellesley, 1st Duke of, 65, 71, 73, 127, 139, 162
Westminster Abbey, 1, 14, 110
Westminster Review, 73

Wheare, Sir Kenneth, 137
White, Hayden, 9, 11, 20
White, James Boyd, 47
Wilberforce, Samuel, Bishop of
Oxford, 154, 170
Wilde, Oscar
The Soul of Man Under Socialism,
163
Willey, Basil, 15
William III, King, 2, 83, 88, 91, 118
William IV, King, 1, 70, 74, 125
Williams, Raymond, 91
Wilson, Woodrow, 136
Windsor castle, 39, 184
Wodehouse, Edmund, 160
Wolff, Sir Henry Drummond, 149
Wollstonecraft, Mary
Vindication of the Rights of Women, 43
Wood, Ellen, 122
Wood, Michael
The Story of England, 11
Wordsworth, Christopher, Bishop of
Lincoln, 155
Wordsworth, Dorothy, 39, 122
Wordsworth, William
Lyrical Ballads, 25, 26
Prelude, 26
Sonnets on Liberty, 169
Working Men's College, 170

Y

Yeatman, Justin. *See* Sellar, Walter
Young, George Malcolm
Victorian England-Portrait of an Age, 136

The manufacturer's authorised representative in the EU is Springer Nature Customer Service Centre GmbH, Europaplatz 3, 69115 Heidelberg, Germany. If you have any concerns regarding our products, please contact ProductSafety@springernature.com

Printed and bound by CPI Group (UK) Ltd, Croydon, CR0 4YY
30/09/2026
02225653-0003